YOU MUST PLAY TO WIN!

Praise for
You Must Play to Win!

You Must Play to Win!: A Coach's Journey from the Pit to the Pinnacle touches more than your philosophies as a coach. It has touched the core of humanity.

— Dorothy "Dot" Richardson, M.D.
Director and Medical Director, National Training Center

[*You Must Play to Win!*] is the best book I have read in a long time. It reminded me of why I became a coach in the first place, and it motivated me to think about how someone can live a life filled with life and still remain in touch with why she became a coach in the first place.

— Dan Hughes, former Head Coach, WNBA, now
General Manager of the San Antonio Silver Stars

[*You Must Play to Win!*] is a must-read for male and female coaches of all sports and levels of competition. I also highly recommend it to athletes, parents, athletic personnel, and outdoorsmen. In fact, I believe that just about anyone would enjoy reading this book, and would benefit from it.

— Sharon Drysdale,
Head Coach, Northwestern University Softball

[*You Must Play to Win!*] is a true story of adversity in which priorities are kept in order. You will learn that it is not about winning but cherishing the moments along the way.

— Sylvia Hatchell,
Head Coach, University of North Carolina Women's Basketball

You Must Play to Win!

A *Coach's Journey from the Pit to the Pinnacle*

by

Donna J. Newberry

with the assistance of

Jane Varley

Foreword by

Dorothy "Dot" Richardson, M.D.

The McDonald & Woodward Publishing Company
Granville, Ohio

The McDonald & Woodward Publishing Company
Granville, Ohio
www.mwpubco.com

You Must Play to Win!
A Coach's Journey from the Pit to the Pinnacle

First printing January 2011

Library of Congress Cataloging-in-Publication Data

Newberry, Donna J.

You must play to win! : a coach's journey from the pit to the pinnacle / by Donna J. Newberry ; with the assistance of Jane Varley ; foreword by Dorothy "Dot" Richardson, M.D.

  p. cm.

Includes index.

  ISBN 978-1-935778-15-8 (pbk. : alk. paper) — ISBN 978-1-935778-16-5 (hardcover : alk. paper)

  1. Newberry, Donna J. 2. Coaches (Athletics)—United States—Biography. 3. Women coaches (Athletics)—United States—Biography. 4. Sports for women—Coaching—United States.   5. Coaching (Athletics)—Anecdotes. 6. Muskingum College—Sports—History. I. Varley, Jane. II. Title.

  GV697.N49N49 2011

  796.092—dc22

  [B]

2010052795

Contents

Foreword

My prognosis has caused me to prioritize my time and to assess whether the activities where I choose to spend my time are worthwhile. I have tried to stay free of the "poor me" mentality, and I am endeavoring to be the proper example to my players. I have aspirations that this book will allow some of my legacy to live on in a way that will inspire young coaches towards perseverance, hard work, and dedication to the coaching profession.

Donna J. Newberry
You Must Play to Win!

Donna Newberry grew up in northern West Virginia and, during the late 1960s and early 1970s, against great odds and amidst minimal opportunities for women, matured as a college student, female athlete, educator, and coach determined to establish herself in sport. In 1974, upon graduating from Ohio University with a Master's degree in Physical Education, Donna accepted a teaching and coaching position at nearby Muskingum College in New Concord, Ohio. At the time, she looked at this job as one that would allow her to get some experience which, in turn, would qualify her to move on to another position as opportunity emerged. Thirty-six years later, right up to the time of her death on November 10, 2010, she was still on the faculty of the Athletics department at Muskingum, by this time a university, and owned a nationally recognized record of advocacy and accomplishment in women's collegiate sport – especially in coaching.

Donna's journey as teacher and coach got underway in 1974 during her first term at Muskingum, when she quickly came to recognize many of the practical challenges she was going to have to deal with just to meet – let alone excel at – her new responsibilities. Although the list of challenges was long and some were significant, perhaps none better symbolized the hurdles that lay before her, or her determination to deal with them, than did "The Pit," an old undersized and ill-kept gym to which the Muskingum women's basketball team had been relegated. Antiquated as it was, "The Pit" nonetheless became a developing ground which helped inspire and give voice to the passion and perseverance that came to characterize Coach Donna Newberry! She handled "The Pit" and all of its challenges and, with the successes that ensued, reached the "Pinnacle" of her career, not only by winning a National Championship in softball but also by demonstrating success at building and maintaining what were clearly quality programs in the sports in which she coached and by winning the state, regional, and national recognition of her peers year after year after year! Surely, Donna Newberry's hugely successful coaching career both epitomizes and helped make possible the dramatic social and institutional transformation of women's collegiate athletics that took place during the last third of the twentieth century!

～

In May, 2010, knowing that her breast cancer had metastasized and that she had only a short time to live, Donna committed herself to writing a book that she hoped and believed could provide a useful perspective on the profession of coaching. Central to the book would be her efforts to describe and demonstrate her philosophy of coaching and the context of that coaching in the broader scheme of working with college student-athletes to prepare them for meaningful and satisfying lives beyond their formal higher education. Also important, however, would be reflections on various personal goals, journeys, and milestones, both within and beyond coaching – a sampler of routine, planned, serendipitous, joyous, tragic, and otherwise meaningful processes and events – which made up noteworthy parts of her own life.

Donna's goal for the book has been accomplished! *You Must Play to Win!* touches not only her philosophies as a coach, but more. It touches the core of humanity. Each of us born to share the gifts that God has given us to impact the lives of other people in positive and meaningful ways is truly living a life of purpose and worth. Donna has done this plus even more. Through her example and efforts, she has brought many to Christ! Donna's life is an inspiration in itself as she faced challenges head-on both on and off the court and playing field. She identified injustice and took upon herself the responsibility and fortitude to stand up and fight against it. As a result, she has opened many doors for others. Many athletes and coaches can now walk through those doors and experience less of the battle because she not only cared enough to want to make a difference – she did something about it and made a difference! Donna always believed that actions speak louder than words. Thank you, Donna, for taking action and paving the way!

In reading *You Must Play to Win!,* one can see Donna growing through the years. One sees a young girl filled with excitement and ambition becoming a woman filled with energy, commitment, aspirations and LIFE! God has used her life to impact so many others, from athletes to other coaches and even individuals she never met. One can see why she was a success. She defined "success" as not being at least one point or run ahead of an opponent, but instead by the ability to learn, to improve, and to recognize the life lessons provided through sport and use them to shape oneself into becoming a better human being.

~

Donna, thank you for your life, for your life's work, and for teaching all of us to truly live with passion, dedication, and the commitment to pursue excellence. One of your players once wrote:

> *I never knew another woman like you who carried herself with a confidence that wasn't cocky, but genuine; a woman that commanded and earned respect based on her knowledge and actions; someone who held true to her faith, and showed the love of Christ in her actions, words, and commitment to teaching. You constantly challenged us on the field and in the classroom to be better. I am a different and better person for being in your program.*

You can see by this quote and others that you fulfilled so many of your goals. You said that, "I wanted to build character in my players, I wanted to build citizenship and an understanding of what it was like to be a contributing member of a larger community, and I wanted to increase their work ethic and perseverance." Then, after that you added, "But combined with all of that, I wanted to win a National Championship."

And you did that too!

Donna, you write:

I had always wanted a female role model who could inspire me to greatness, but more importantly who could teach me toughness and perseverance. I wanted someone who would show me that if you don't give up anything is possible.

You found that role model in Anna Biffelt, the Koyukon Indian from Alaska. Let me tell you, many girls and women have found that role model in YOU! Although you wondered if you should have spent your last moments writing this book, we are so glad that you did because you have shared with us moments that will last! We make a living by what we get, but we make a life by what we give! Donna – Coach – thank you so much for giving of yourself to others! Thank you for your LIFE! May God Keep You In His Tender Loving Care.

With You Always, Dot.

Dorothy "Dot" Richardson, M.D.
Two-time Olympic Gold Medalist in softball
NCAA softball Player of the Decade, 1980s
Director/Medical Director, National Training Center

Preface

Life is what happens to you while you are making other plans.

John Lennon

May, 2010.

I am sitting in the loft of my log cabin listening to the rain on the roof and wondering how to go about writing a book, or even if I should attempt such an endeavor. Trying to chronicle some of my coaching experiences and putting on paper some of my coaching philosophies is an idea that has periodically appealed to me, but today it seems different. Today I am actually doing it, rather than just thinking about it.

About nine months ago, I was diagnosed with breast cancer for the third time. The first two times left me with hope, but this time it appears terminal. Although I don't know how long I will live, it seems clear that the end is in sight. When the finality of life sets in, it seems to cause an evaluation of everything that you choose to do. Maybe that's because deciding to do one thing means that there is something else that we will not have time to do. I have debated whether I should invest all this time in writing a book. Is there a more worthwhile way to be spending my time? What if I don't live long enough to finish it? What if I write it and then no one wants to read it? I guess there is no way to know if it is the right thing to do. I should just start writing and let the book take me wherever it goes.

~

Approximately fourteen years ago I accidentally discovered a lump in my breast while taking a shower the night before my softball team was to leave for Florida for its annual spring trip. My first reaction had been one of a bit of panic, but being in my early forties, I was not ready to face the idea of cutting my life short. The first thing that I did when I got back home from Florida was to get an appointment to see a doctor. Within a week I was engulfed in a flurry of activity that seemed surreal. I went from a perfectly healthy middle-aged woman who worked out five days a week to a befuddled patient who was being swept from physician to physician to see what needed to be done to keep me alive.

The initial news was optimistic. It was probably just a benign cyst that was nothing to worry about, but to be safe I probably should get a mammogram. Several weeks after the test was completed and the results were in, I got a phone call from my doctor asking me to stop by and go over the results. Because we had a couple hours before we were leaving for another softball game, I convinced them to fit me in that morning, hoping to get the meeting over with so that I could coach with a clear mind.

The meeting did not go as I had it mapped out in my mind. The lump that I had found was a benign cyst. The breast that I was so concerned about appeared healthy. However, the other breast did show signs of cancer. The good news was that it was discovered very early. As a matter of fact, I was told that for cancer of this size to be a palpable lump, it would need to grow for another two years. I could not have detected it much earlier. The bad news was that it was cancer, and now I needed to make some decisions about how to treat it.

It was agonizing over the next few weeks as I met with additional doctors and sought advice from family and friends. The doctors advised me that although cancer was just showing up on one side, the healthy side was what they called "pre-cancerous" and it would be a matter of "when" rather than "if" cancer would occur on that side as well. I got all my options, ranging from a lumpectomy to a bilateral mastectomy.

Ultimately, I decided to do what would allow me to have the best chance of survival. The cosmetic issues were the least of my concerns. The best chance for long-term survival seemed to be for me to have a bilateral mastectomy. If I removed both breasts, doctors gave me a 95 percent chance that I would be totally cancer-free and never have to worry about it again. I have never been one to make gray decisions. Everything is black and white to me, and once I make a decision, I fully invest in it and prepare to live with the consequences and the rewards. Anything short of that in the decision-making process would make it difficult for me, or anyone, to make a living coaching.

The surgery was performed as soon as softball season was over. By the end of June, I was back to running a couple of miles a day and playing golf. Although it took a while to get over my self-consciousness, within a year I felt totally healthy and planned to live cancer-free the rest of my life.

About twelve years later, I happened to notice a small lump on my chest. Because of where it was located, I thought it was old scar tissue that had broken loose, but I decided that I had better have it checked just in case. It was not scar tissue. The 5 percent chance of the cancer's returning had become a reality and it was now entirely possible, if not likely, that the cancer had metastasized. The old nightmares started to return.

Another surgery to remove the lump proved that it was cancerous. I held onto the hope that it had not moved to other parts of my body. After some thirty consecutive days of radiation on my chest, on the last day of treatment they found a new lump outside the radiation field. The doctors did not know if this was also cancer that the radiation did not kill, or if this was simply a lump. They scheduled me for yet another surgery to get this lump removed.

One of the things that frustrates me about medicine is the amount of time that one must wait between finding a problem and then fixing it. When I am coaching, if I cannot diagnose a problem that the team is having on the floor or on the field with my naked eye, I can plug in my video machine, and by morning I can have it diagnosed. Before we play our next game, I can have it fixed. If I had to wait days or weeks to identify the problem, our season would be over before anything got done. The challenge of immediately identifying and repairing problems is part of what I enjoy about this profession. I have very little tolerance for anything that violates the code dictated by this sense of urgency.

After many days of waiting again for lab results, I got the call to check in with my doctor. The news I received was devastating. The report said that the new lump was cancer growing, and the only way to treat it would be with chemotherapy. My body was already badly worn down, but I braced myself to begin the needed additional treatments. I began to notify my family and friends of this new development, and I had a meeting with my team to break the news to them as well.

About a week after this most recent diagnosis, I received another phone call from my surgeon to tell me that he needed to see me. When I went to the office I was prepared for more bad news. Instead, when I went in, I was told that the doctor had made a mistake. Somehow, he had read the wrong lab report. They had misread my results, and instead of having more cancer, I was cancer-free!

It was hard to separate anger from relief. Although I questioned how such a mistake could be made, I was so ecstatic that I readily celebrated the news. PET scans and CAT scans followed the diagnosis and proved that what I had been told was true. There was not only no new cancer, but I was cancer-free. An extra trip to the James Cancer Center in Columbus confirmed all the test results.

I lived what I assumed was a cancer-free life for the next two years. When I began having severe pain near my shoulder (somewhere between my vertebrae and scapula), I decided to have it checked out. I was sure it was from swinging too many golf clubs, racquetball racquets, and softball bats. However, it was not caused from any of those things. It was caused from cancer that had now metastasized into my bones, liver, and other body parts.

It was this most recent diagnosis that has brought me to where I am now. I have been on chemotherapy for nearly nine months. Coaching through this past softball season has been difficult at best, as I battle lack of appetite, energy drain, and just the overall mental stress of dealing with a terminal diagnosis. My prognosis has caused me to prioritize my time and to assess whether the activities where I choose to spend my time are worthwhile. I have tried to stay free of the "poor me" mentality, and I am endeavoring to be the proper example to my players.

I have aspirations that this book will allow some part of my legacy to live on in a way that will inspire coaches, especially young coaches, towards perseverance, hard work, and dedication to the coaching profession.

Acknowledgments

As I did not begin to write this book until the later stages of my breast cancer, I am deeply indebted to my family for sacrificing their own time and energy to help me maintain my household and working environment. Their willingness to cook, clean, do laundry, and care for my every need went way beyond the boundaries of love.

To my sisters Diane, Debbie, and Dale, and my sister-in-law Jean, I offer many thanks for taking their vacation and personal time and using it to care for my needs, which enabled me to continue working on the book. To my brother, Dave, I offer thanks for all the trips that he made to my house to complete those household chores that needed a man to get them done. Never did I hear anyone complain.

Above all, thanks to my mom, Juanita, who unselfishly has given me the best care possible for over a year. Without her constant presence, strength, and, most of all, love, this book would never have been completed. She always placed my needs above hers, and without her I would have had neither the motivation nor the opportunity to finish this book. She is the strongest example of a Christian woman that I have seen, and I am so fortunate to have had her around me during this process.

To my trusted colleague, Jane Varley, I owe a huge thank you. She graciously invested her time in my project and has given me wonderful advice, critiques, guidance, and, most of all, encouragement. Jane became a person I leaned on heavily to guide me through the process of writing this book. She unselfishly embraced my dream of becoming a coach-turned-writer, shared her expertise with me, and brought to fruition a project that was extremely important to me. She has been a true friend and professional.

Thank you to my readers Jane Sherman, Diane Wooten, Jean Newberry, Ron Vessels, and Donna Edsall, who helped to review the book and move it towards the final draft. The time spent in order to give me input was very much appreciated. Also, I owe a thank you to Aaron Spragg for his ongoing help in graphic design. My colleague, Bil Kerrigan, helped enormously with locating, selecting, and writing captions for the photographs that appear in this book, and I am grateful for his interest and generous support. Tom Caudill, Sports Information Director of Muskingum University, and David W. Newberry and the Newberry family graciously permitted use of the photographs that appear in this book.

Finally, I am grateful to the administration at Muskingum University. Our president, Anne Steele, supported the project and encouraged me as I finished the book by providing additional incentive and inspiration.

YOU MUST PLAY TO WIN!

Chapter 1

The Early Years

Growing up is never easy. You hold on to things that were. You wonder what's to come.

Anonymous

If you were a female athlete, going through high school and college in the late 1960s and early 1970s was probably not the best time to be growing up. There was limited opportunity to compete at any level, and if you did compete, you were certainly labeled as a "tomboy" and, more than likely, you carried the stereotype of being a lesbian. Unless you were a "women's libber," you competed as hard as you could at every opportunity, but did not rock the boat. For the most part you accepted the role of cheerleader and recreational athlete. Attempting to be anything more serious than that categorized you as a radical woman who was unwilling to accept societal norms. Although I disagreed with the norms when it came to sports and gender, I was not yet prepared to fight for the opportunities that I so desperately wanted.

I was one of the best athletes in the neighborhood, all males included. We were fortunate to have a big yard, so it was often at our house that the pick-up games of touch football, softball, or basketball would originate. It was my house, so of course I was allowed to play if I wanted to. I got significant gratification from being chosen for a team before some of my male friends whom I perceived to be pretty good athletes. I was small but could certainly hold my own in just about any sport.

I remember the envy I felt when I would see the neighborhood boys put on their cool uniforms and leave in the early evenings to go to their Little League baseball games. It enraged me when I knew that I could field, throw, and hit better than most of them, yet I did not have

3

an opportunity to compete in an organized league. It never occurred to me that this concept was something that could and should be fought for in a court of law.

I was fortunate to have siblings that provided competition anytime the neighborhood gang was not around. Growing up with three sisters and only one brother, I was glad that my brother tolerated me hanging around him. Although he was four years older than I was, he never seemed to mind my trying to be the brother that he never had. Dave was more of an outdoorsman than he was an athlete, although he could definitely hold his own in the neighborhood pick-up games. His presence at a game gave my participation credibility if the game included some of the older neighborhood boys. If there was no one else around to play with, he was always a willing opponent in a game of Horse, Flies and Grounders, or Indian Ball. If we were stuck inside, he was my best opponent in ping pong or shooting pool.

If Dave allowed me to go on one of his outdoor excursions, it was always a special time. Sometimes the activities would be things like building a tree cabin, checking his trap lines, going blackberry picking, or shooting our BB guns. More often than not, it involved something with hunting or fishing. My favorite time of the year would be when frog season was in and Dave allowed me to go frog gigging with him. There is nothing like the sound of a bullfrog croaking on a dark night and then your flashlight suddenly discovering its eyes staring at you between cattails. I was never promoted to be the one who actually gigged the frog, but rather I was the one who held the flashlight on the frog while Dave gigged it. I would then carry it in an old pillowcase until we got enough for a mess of frog legs. He gave me more than one piggyback ride through the marsh since he owned a pair of hip waders and all I owned was a pair of rubber boots that I wore to school on rainy days.

Dave also was the one who taught me, even though it was an unintentional lesson, that jobs should not be defined by gender. Any boy worthy of manhood, it seemed, eventually had a paper route. My brother tackled a very large route that had many customers and a large geographic area to cover. There was no way that he could deliver all of those papers after school and be done at a reasonable hour. Being the entrepreneur that he was, he asked me if I would be interested in working for him. He would subdivide the route and pay me a penny per house each day for delivering that section. He gave me a small part of the route that was nearest to our home, and I delivered to about thirty houses per day. Over the course of the week I would make $2.10. That doesn't sound like much money now, but then it was a huge supplement to an allowance of 50 cents per week. The only day that I really disliked delivering the papers was Sunday. That day it was a morning instead of an evening paper, and the huge edition made it very heavy to carry. I would have to get up before daylight in order to get the paper to my customers on time.

It was unheard of to have a girl working a paper route. I took great pride in being a girl doing a boy's job. I quickly learned that just because society said young boys should be paperboys and young girls should be babysitters, there was no reason that I could not perform as well as or better than a boy. I went to great lengths to make sure I did it right. I wanted to give my customers no reason to complain that a girl could not do the job. If I missed the front porch on my throw from my bike, I would get off the bike and hand deliver it to their front step. If it was raining, it did not matter if I got wet. All that mattered was keeping their papers dry. The grimy paper sack that I proudly wore slung over my shoulder was my badge of honor that stated I could do anything I made up my mind to do. I felt like I had to do it better than the boys so my gender would not become an issue. When my brother would get angry with me about something, his trump card would be saying to me that he was going to tell his boss that a girl was delivering some of their papers, and I would be fired. In hindsight, I am sure neither of those things would have happened, but at the time, it was enough of a threat that it kept me in line.

Just like paper delivery then, coaching now is one of those professions where females are walking in male territory. I believe that you not only have to do it as well as a man, you have to do it better than a man if you don't want to be accused of being a female who is out of her element. Although this is slowly changing, it is still an annoying challenge to prove that coaching prowess should not be defined by gender.

5

Dave was not the only sibling teaching me early lessons in achievement. My sister Diane, two years my senior, was also a willing competitor during my childhood. Although she was not as good an athlete as I was, she could hold her own and was always up for a challenge. There were countless hours of competition that included just about any game where we could keep score. Our horseshoe pits were dust bowls by the end of summer. We kept a running score of who could hit the most Wiffle balls out of 100, left-handed.

I am sure the neighbors thought we were crazy when we taught ourselves how to play tennis by playing in the road. The most fundamental ground rule was that you had to give the other person plenty of warning if a car was coming behind her. It made for a pretty narrow court, but the road was paved and fairly level by our house. If you used the curb for out-of-bounds and the cracks in the road for a net, all you needed to do was to check a tennis book out of the library and educate yourself on the rules and the basics of forehand, backhand, and the serve. Thanks to my sister, I became a pretty fair tennis player.

I had two younger sisters as well, but probably because of age, they were not as involved in my competitive games as were my two older siblings. I was fortunate to have parents who did not discourage me from being and doing what I wanted to do. It would have been very easy for them to try to turn their "tomboy" daughter into a young lady, but to their credit, they supported me in whatever I chose to do.

My dad was a small wiry man who was a pretty good athlete, but his first love was the outdoors and hunting and fishing. Throughout his life, he usually had his own business, which ranged from a sporting goods store, to a used car lot, to an auction house, and in addition to that, he drove a school bus. He enjoyed watching sports, and as my career evolved he was proud to watch me coach. He was a quiet, church-going man who seldom raised his voice and who got along with just about everyone. He loved music, especially bluegrass, and I am sure that my musical ability with singing and the stringed instruments came through him. Dad died in 2003.

My mom is a very intelligent woman who never had the opportunity to go to college as she was married and started a family shortly after she graduated from high school. I imagine that she could have been just about anything that she wanted to be professionally if she had been able to continue her education. Instead, she juggled her time between a variety of jobs ranging from a retail clerk, to a short order cook, to an accountant, and raising a family of five children. She is an extraordinarily strong woman, and I am grateful for the strength of mind and will that I inherited from her.

With my family background and passion for sports, it would have been wonderful to have had the opportunities for competition that young women have today. However, the highest level of competition that I could find as I entered high school was our GAA (Girl's Athletic Association) play days. There were a few of these held each year. The host school would invite surrounding schools to send their representatives, and it would be an all-day event competing in basketball, volleyball, dodgeball, etc. You could accumulate individual points throughout the day by your performance in the various sports, and individual champions would be crowned at the end of the day. It seems like an almost childish level of competition when I think about it now, but at the time it was one of the most exciting days of the year for me.

My last couple of years in high school, we did manage to have a girls' basketball team that competed interscholastically. We had to have bake sales to buy gas for the cars, and we had to have mothers sew numbers on our "gym suits" so that we would have a uniform. It was thought to be far too taxing on a girl to run the full length of the court in a basketball game, so we played with six people on a team with two stationary forwards who stayed on the offensive end, two stationary guards who stayed on the defensive end, and two rovers who were allowed to cross half court. This style of basketball drove me crazy, but at least I always got to be the rover, so it took some of the sting out of it.

~

The closest thing that I had to a female coaching role model was my high school physical education teacher. It did not occur to me that in the future, the coaching opportunities for females would mushroom with the advent of Title IX. To think that coaching would be an avenue for a female to earn a living was a fairy tale. I tried to think of a way that I could forever stay involved in sport, so I was convinced from junior high age on that I wanted to be a physical education teacher. Unlike many children who announce career aspirations early in life, I never wavered from my original goal. I was determined that being a physical education teacher was a career that I would embrace for life.

When I entered Glenville State College in Glenville, West Virginia, in the fall of 1969, I immediately declared myself as an education major with my focus on health and physical education. A number of people tried to dissuade me from pursuing this major. I was an excellent student, and I felt that the options were unlimited regarding my major. Partly to appease those who said that I could never get a job teaching physical education because the market was so flooded, and partly to appease my own conscience in the event they were actually right, I did choose math as a minor, knowing I could easily find a job teaching math.

In the early seventies, if you chose to live as a single independent woman after college, you had better have a Plan B in place in the event that Plan A did not work out. I was confident enough in myself to instinctively know that I would make Plan A work. I believed that there is always room for another physical education teacher if you are good at what you do. I knew that I would be a very good teacher and never lose my passion for sport, competition, or fitness. However, I was also pragmatic enough to know that a second option was not a bad thing, especially if while pursuing the second option I did not compromise my desire to achieve my first option. I graduated with certification to teach either math or physical education.

The confidence that I have in myself has served me well in making my career choice and excelling within my field. There is a fine line between confidence and arrogance. To be a good coach, both you and your athletes must have confidence. Confidence in yourself is the easy part. You know whether you are working as hard as you can work. You know if you are completely prepared. You know if you have invested the necessary time and effort that enable you and almost entitle you to win. There is a quiet assurance about a confident

8

person. You don't need to announce it. The way you carry yourself allows your confidence to promote your success without your ever becoming overbearing and assuming.

It is more difficult when you try to assess whether those who play for you are confident. They can disguise their confidence to make you think they have it, but when it comes down to "crunch time" and the mask has to be taken off at the peak of competition, you might find a weakling who really does not believe in herself. Too many times, athletes reveal to you only what they think you want to see. Pretending to be something that you are not will defeat you both on and off the field. Anytime there is a difference between the perception of who an athlete is and the reality of who an athlete is, you can be sure that the true identity will eventually be revealed, and the outcome will not necessarily be what you had expected.

Arrogance crosses a line beyond confidence. Belief in yourself and what you are able to accomplish is confidence. Going out of your way to publicly announce your credentials and trying to make sure that people see who and what you are even if they are not interested in your perceived capabilities is arrogance. Trash talking is a primitive form of arrogance. I sometimes think athletes are trying to convince themselves more than their opponents when they have to talk about what they are about to do. Arrogance moves from a quiet pride in what you are capable of doing to an overbearing dialogue and swagger about what you intend to do. Arrogance is a sure step towards self-destruction for either a coach or an athlete.

~

When I was in college, it was thrilling to find out that Glenville actually had teams for women in bowling and in women's basketball even though they were only in their early stages of development. Of course, I readily jumped onto both teams and could hardly wait to get started. Basketball was the first season, and I longed for the day that we would have our first practice. Some of my enthusiasm started to wane when I began to understand that there was no real funding, facilities, coaches, or support system for women's basketball. The opportunity to play was nothing more than a token effort put forth by the college to create an image of providing competition for women, but it lacked any degree of administrative support. There was neither a financial nor a philosophical commitment.

Because there were several physical education majors who were salivating to compete, we refused to let the team die. We rounded up volunteer coaches. We accepted practice times in the gym that allowed us floor time after men's basketball, intramurals, and wrestling were over. Anything scheduled in the gym took priority over our practice time. There were many times when we drove to a local grade school in the evening so that we could have a practice. We did some of our own fundraising so that there would be some funds to help with transportation.

On a brighter note, the rules changed during my freshman year in college. Six-person basketball was now a thing of the past in the state of West Virginia. No longer would there be stationary players who could not cross half court. The same rules that the men played by were adopted for the women. Amazingly, in spite of the fears of the people who had written the rules for six-player basketball, designed to protect us from hurting ourselves, no one died from playing full court.

The male athletes were not thrilled with the idea of a women's basketball team. Even though it did not alter their practices, funding, spectator support, or campus image, there was something about having a female team as a counterpart that rubbed them the wrong way. One evening we were going to practice from 6:00 to 8:00, immediately following their 3:30 to 6:00 afternoon practice. This was a rare luxury for us. No one else was scheduled to use the gym that evening, so this early time was a reprieve from the graveyard shift when we normally practiced because intramurals or other activities pre-empted us. We were standing in the lobby at about 5:50, waiting for their practice to end and watching through the doors as they ran a couple of their final drills. Their practice ran a few minutes long, but we were patient as we waited and watched. Because we had no money for equipment, the men had to share their practice balls with us (this was at a time when basketballs for both sexes were the same size), and they apparently did not appreciate our imposing on the use of their equipment. A ball rack that held twelve basketballs, six on the top row and six on the bottom row, sat by the door where we stood. When they finally finished their practice and began to exit the gym, each player spat on his ball before he slammed it down on the rack, then glared at us as he headed for the sanctuary of the varsity locker room. I began running my warm-up laps that practice with tears in my eyes.

The bowling team was better organized, primarily because we were able to share the men's team coach, and gaining access to the lanes on campus was never an issue. I don't know if we were better funded because the coach also happened to be the athletic director or if it was for other reasons, but at that time I appreciated, without ever questioning, anything that we received as athletes.

As I reflect back on my athletic college experience, I see the challenges and disappointments. We played few games and had to face a great deal of adversity to even be allowed to practice. At a time when I could have greatly benefited from a coaching role model and gained much knowledge about a sport that I would coach for over a quarter of a century, I was almost alone and simply thrilled to be allowed to play a few games. It is only in hindsight that I recognize how much I missed in both information and experience. I am envious of the young athletes today who have so many opportunities just waiting to be seized.

On the negative side, I believe there is a loss of appreciation for the opportunities created for female athletes because the opportunities are now so abundant. On the positive side, the difference that these opportunities have made in the lives of female athletes is immeasurable.

Chapter 2

My First Job

Many people think that if they were just in some other place, or had some other job, they would be happy. Well, that is doubtful. So get as much happiness out of what you are doing as you can and don't put off being happy until some future date.

Dale Carnegie

I do not know if you would refer to my getting my first job at Muskingum College in New Concord, Ohio, as luck, fate, coincidence, or even Divine Providence. All I know is that I did not give it much thought prior to applying for the job, and it took me less than thirty seconds to accept when I was offered the job.

I was offered a graduate assistantship at Ohio University immediately after I graduated from Glenville in 1972. Rather than look for a teaching job, I decided that I would accept the Ohio University offer and get my Master's degree. To fulfill my end of the contract, I taught in their Physical Education department some activity courses that ranged from gymnastics, to squash, to tennis. I also helped coach the softball team and quickly discovered that this was my favorite part of the job.

In early December of 1973, my academic advisor casually asked me if I had seen the job advertisement on the career board for Muskingum College. They were looking for a female physical education instructor and a coach for their field hockey, basketball, and softball teams. My advisor thought the job description was made for me. Muskingum was a small, quiet campus nestled in the hills of southeastern Ohio, with an enrollment of around one thousand students and a reputation for excellent academic programs, especially as related to teacher education. They were looking for someone who had some versatility and who did not mind working hard. When I told her that I had not looked at it, she encouraged me to give it some thought.

A few days later, I read the advertisement and jotted down the basic information in case I decided to further explore it. The deadline for resumes and letters of interest was December 31. It was the day after Christmas and I was at home for the holiday break when I suddenly remembered that if I was going to check into the job, the deadline was quickly approaching. I hastily got my resume together, wrote a letter, and on December 28 I mailed my information to Muskingum.

It was not too far into January when I received a phone call requesting an interview. I eagerly accepted. I had never really interviewed for a job prior to this and certainly did not know what to expect at a college level interview. Things must have gone well, as I received a call in February from the athletic director, offering me the job. The fact that the job paid $8,000 a year was in no way a deterrent. It was my life's dream to be a physical education teacher. Being allowed to coach as part of my job exceeded any expectation that I had of the perfect job.

I was soon to learn that there were plenty of problems and issues that would come along with the job, but at my young age I had neither the experience nor the wisdom to explore any of these before accepting the position. There are times when naïveté is a blessing. Had I fully explored what lay ahead of me I might have turned down the offer, or at the very least, I would have accepted it with less enthusiasm. At any rate, I did not perceive this to be a lifetime decision, so at a minimum, I would get some badly needed experience and expand my resume to make myself more marketable. I figured that Muskingum would be a good starting place, and I could stay a few years then move on to better things. Never did I dream that my first job interview would also be my last, and thirty-six years into the job, I would still love it like the day I began.

My first hint of some of the challenges that I would face came in late February of 1974 when I decided that I would drive from Ohio University in Athens to New Concord on a Tuesday evening and watch the Muskingum women's team play a scheduled basketball game. Since I would inherit the team the following year, it seemed logical to check out the caliber of play and get a better sense of my player personnel for the next year. When I found the basketball court in John Glenn Gym, I was a bit surprised to see men's intramurals being played with no sign of a women's basketball game. I inquired with a student about the game, and he quickly answered that I would probably find the game being played in the "women's gym," located two levels below the men's gym. He also politely made sure that I understood that the basketball court I was presently seeing was for use exclusively by the men.

New Concord was the hometown of John Glenn, who had grown up in a neighborhood near campus and attended the college before going off to the military. Shortly after he made his historic orbit around the earth in 1962, the college gymnasium, built in 1935 and standing on the northern edge of the campus quad, was named after him. The basketball court, fairly small and somewhat dark by most standards, looked like the hometown gym in the movie *Hoosiers*. It had a lot of character and housed many memories of hard-fought ball games, but it was neither aesthetically pleasing nor modern when you compared it to most athletic facilities. In time, Muskingum would build its Recreation Center to showcase its athletic programs, but back in 1974 the "Rec Center" was not yet a reality.

If the men's basketball arena in John Glenn Gym was less than adequate, then the "women's gym" was horrible. The community of Muskingum referred to this gym as "The Pit." It had a court about half the size of a regulation gym with drab yellow brick walls, less than adequate lighting, no out-of-bounds space, and wooden backboards with ugly hand smudges on them. The floor had floorboards that were cracked, chipped, or rippled. This made dribbling a little more of a challenge than it should have been, as occasionally the ball hit dead spots or uneven floorboards that gave an unpredictable bounce. Along one side of the court were windows protected by hinged black iron cages that, with very little imagination, gave you the feeling of being in prison. Each end of the court had well-used mats hanging limply from hooks on the wall, leaking bits of stuffing from their rips. There were a couple of storage closet doors that I would later come to know by the scars from arrows gone astray during archery classes.

The gym had no scoreboard, so plastic flip cards had to be used on the sideline. There was no clock, so time was kept on a stopwatch, and the timer periodically announced how much time was left and then counted down the seconds toward the end of the half. What few spectators there were stood pinned against the sideline with their backs to the wall, trying to keep their feet out of bounds. More than once during the game, the lights went out in the gym. I was told that it was due to the ceiling being shaken with all of the activity upstairs, combined with a short in the wiring.

I was a little discouraged driving home that February night. Somehow I had had the perception that my first job would bring circumstances different than those I had found at Glenville. I thought things would be in place to allow women to compete at an equitable level. Surely, I thought, if they were going to pay me to coach, the tools and facilities would be provided to enable me to do the job. I was still very excited about the level of play and athleticism that I saw that night, but the reality of what I was about to tackle resonated with me as I drove. It would have taken much more than this to discourage me, and perhaps it was good that I got a peephole view of the battles that would need to be fought over the next several years. However, the rose-colored glasses had been removed, and I was slightly more prepared to begin the next leg of my journey.

My job at Muskingum began in the fall of 1974. At the age of twenty-two, I was a full-fledged member of the faculty. I had little in common with the rest of the faculty. All but a handful were male, and the median age had to be well above forty. I was hired during a tumultuous time for the institution. The budgetary problems that would eventually lead to a declaration of exigency were growing, and more faculty members were being let go than were being hired. Tenure could not protect you at a time of financial exigency. Salaries were frozen, so I would live for more than a year with my annual salary of $8,000.

Finding a suitable place to live on my salary was challenging. I was relieved to find that the bottom half of an old house where one of the other female physical education instructors lived was empty and available for rent. For $50 a month I could rent the first floor of the make-shift duplex. What made it even better was that it was right across the street from the administration building of the college, so I not only had cheap rent, but I could save on transportation costs by walking to work. There was plenty of painting and fixing that needed to be done, but this would be my home for the next couple of years.

Fortunately, I was pretty low maintenance when it came to furniture and décor, and my mom and I spent the summer visiting garage sales and trying to piece together enough furnishings to fill the space and give me a place to sleep, eat, and sit. I did not have the money for a television, and I did not really have time to watch it anyway, but looking back I cannot imagine living now for a year without access to television. I was determined that I would not use a credit card and go into debt to furnish an apartment. I had learned to live frugally and those lessons would serve me well as I began to establish my own household and career.

My living room was furnished with the miscellaneous pieces of furniture that I had purchased at garage sales. The couch was the type that you could unfold and make into a bed, so at least I had an extra bed for guests. Thanks to my mom's handiwork, I had matching upholstery on the secondhand couch and chair, and it actually looked pretty good after I refinished the exposed wood on the arms and legs. My other piece of living room furniture was a beanbag chair that matched the color of my couch and chair.

My bedroom contained a used dresser and a bed that I bought from a mobile home that was selling its furniture. The fact that the box springs were full size and the mattress was ¾ size really didn't bother me, but it made it a little awkward to fit the sheets neatly on the bed. About the only thing new that I had in my apartment was an eight-track tape player and speakers that I had gotten for graduation. The bathroom was barely big enough for the essentials of a tub, sink, and toilet, and the pink flamingo color of all the fixtures was something that I had to learn to tolerate. After painting a couple of walls and getting things arranged the way I wanted, the apartment finally became a home to me and provided me with both a safe and convenient place to live.

As I reflect on my own gradual progression in establishing a household, it makes me shudder to watch how inept many of my athletes have been in regard to handling their finances. I have observed this as a problem with youth throughout my career, but as our society has become more affluent, it seems to get progressively worse.

During their college career, students commonly charge clothing, gifts, furniture, and countless other items that are wanted but not really needed. They graduate with more debt on their credit cards than I ever had in a lifetime. They have grown up in an age where "buy now and pay later" is commonplace. Self-deprivation is not in their vocabulary, and sadly I am not even referring to depriving oneself of something that is needed. Many young folks seem unable to postpone satisfying even their whimsical wants as well.

Perhaps if I had grown up around more affluence, I would have demanded a higher standard of living for myself, or equated possessions with success. However, what I had never seemed to be as important to me as what I did with what I had. I was raised believing that hard work and doing the job right the first time is what earned me the credibility to move up to the next level. It never seemed appropriate to borrow in order to satisfy my wants. I was nearly forty years old before I ever got my first credit card, and the only reason I got it then was so I could get a rental car at the airport. They refused to take cash. Ever since that time, the only time I have used the card is for convenience, but never for credit.

I have discovered that a credit card mentality has made it difficult to coach new generations of young athletes. So many things seem to be given to them on credit. There is always immediate gratification, and the concern for paying is postponed until later. Too many young athletes carry that same mentality about their playing time. They expect coaches to give them playing time, and they will pay for that playing time later.

How many times have I heard, "Coach, if you will just let me play, I will show you what I can do. I guarantee you, you won't be sorry." There seems to be a lack of understanding that payments need to be made in installments during practice now in order to eventually purchase their playing time later. The payments actually need to precede

of the product. They want playing time now, and in
payment prior to their playing time. They make pay-
ctice habits that are beyond reproach, with a work ethic
ie level at which they need to work to win a game, and
with good decision-making in practice. To be paid in full, they need
to show me the ability to blend execution with intelligence and intensity, unquestioning loyalty, and off-season habits that allow your body
to go through practices with 100 percent efficiency.

When an athlete has made enough payments, then we will start
to discuss playing time. The goal that a player has for being a starter
or for getting lots of playing time is often realistic; however, it is her
timetable for achieving that goal that is usually unrealistic. It does
not help matters when parents are always readily available to cosign
a loan. Some parents are more than willing to vouch for the athletic
validity of their son or daughter, and they are not shy about telling
you that loaning their offspring some playing time would be a wise
investment that will definitely pay off in the future. It is a difficult
task to teach young players that they may have to wait on what they
want. They are not accustomed to waiting and they are not used to
delayed gratification. Earning her playing time is one of many lessons
that must be learned for an athlete to have a chance to play for me.

～

The work load in my first year at Muskingum College was pretty
overwhelming. Just the teaching load alone would have been a full
plate. I taught numerous courses as part of our physical education
majors program in addition to teaching some activity courses outside
the major. I was teaching jogging, bowling, gymnastics, badminton,
weight lifting, and tennis as activity courses. In the majors program, I
was teaching First Aid, Adapted Physical Education, Foundations of
Athletic Skill, Officiating Basketball, Officiating Softball, and Coaching Methods of Team Sports. The amount of preparation that I had to do
to stay ahead of my students in all of these classes was overwhelming.

On top of that, I was the head coach of four sports with no assistant coaches (Figure 1). Coaching field hockey, basketball, and softball was all part of the original job description. Because the woman

who was supposed to coach volleyball disliked coaching, did not know much about volleyball and did not want to learn, and was being coerced into coaching this year, I agreed to take the volleyball team as well. I did not want to see players subjected to passivity and ignorance in coaching, and I was desperate to see the women's program blossom.

Coaching both volleyball and hockey was especially challenging because they were played during the same season. I had to schedule one practice in the afternoon and the other in the evening in order to practice both teams. Game days had to be staggered so that I did not have two games in one day.

It would have been a blessing to have had a mentor or role model to lean on. Although there were three other women who taught in the Physical Education department, they were not much help to me as they had little interest in the athletic program. One specialized in modern dance, one specialized in synchronized swimming and did coach both the women's swim team and the women's tennis team,

Figure 1. First-year coach Donna Newberry's first field hockey team, one of the teams in the four sports she coached during the 1974–1975 academic year.

and the third was a specialist in elementary physical education and was especially into folk dance and related activities. Although each of these women was very competent and passionate about what she was doing, they were of little help to me in the world of team sports. If I was going to make progress on my goals, I needed to figure it out for myself.

I did not think much about equal opportunity and gender equity during my first year or two. I was too busy just trying to survive. I was trying to establish some degree of credibility for the women's sports. I did not want the men to look at us with a patronizing attitude. I wanted them to respect our passion and work ethic, and to look at us as fellow athletes with goals and desires similar to their own. Somehow, I thought, once we were taken seriously, all the other pieces of the puzzle would fall into place. We would certainly be given equal practice space and times, budgets would become more equitable, and the men's and the women's divisions would emerge arm-in-arm as a stronger and unified department.

However, the only visible change that was made my first year was my attempt to get our basketball games moved out of The Pit and onto the main basketball court in John Glenn Gymnasium. A bad taste had been lingering in my mouth ever since the previous February when I drove to campus to watch my first basketball game. It seemed like it would be a simple request. Surely, I thought, no one had ever asked to play the women's games upstairs because if they had, certainly they could not have been refused. Trying to play an intercollegiate game in The Pit was ludicrous.

I felt if games were going to be played upstairs, then practices needed to be in John Glenn Gym as well. To practice on a floor that was about half the size of the competition court would be counterproductive. How could you practice in one facility, yet play in the other and have any success? The response to my request was an indication of some of the difficult problems that lay ahead.

Ed Sherman was the athletic director, a well-respected man who eventually became one of the best-known coaches in National Collegiate Athletic Association (NCAA) Division III football and a member of the College Football Hall of Fame. He was becoming legendary for his success and hard-nosed coaching techniques. I would develop tremendous respect for Coach Sherman, all of his coaching success, and everything that he did for Muskingum. However, when I started working at the college, I found him to be very old school, and his background did not lend itself to any empathy for women's athletics. He tolerated us, but beyond that, obtaining just about anything that was needed for women's athletics required a real struggle.

Because Coach Sherman was the one in charge, nearly everything that I requested became a battle. Had I arrived when the institution was in better shape financially, maybe things would have been a little easier. Now, I can say that I do not really blame Coach Sherman for all the difficulties. He was as much a victim of society and its mores as I was.

My request to move women's basketball to the "men's gym" did not endear me to the men's basketball coach or to any of the other male coaches. If today I wanted time in the gym, what would I be asking for tomorrow? I took my request to be allowed to practice and play games in John Glenn Gym to every administrative level short of the president. After multiple denials and much stress, I was finally granted permission to use the gym if it did not interfere with any other campus activity. It was not the resolution that I had hoped for, but it was better than total refusal.

I felt like I was back at Glenville State as our practice times ranged from evening to late night. Once the men's basketball team was done, intramurals was done, wrestling did not have a match, and no other activity cropped up, we were free to practice. The men did make a couple of concessions to accommodate a few of our home games in order to avoid changing the date, but mostly, we worked around their schedule.

Today, it is disappointing when I hear some of the young coaches who are just now entering the realm of college coaching complain about how much they have to do. If they are asked to coach more than one sport, it seems they are being pushed beyond their limits. If they are asked to teach, it seems like teaching often takes a back seat to their coaching. I will admit that coaching one sport now takes a good deal more time than it used to because of recruiting demands and the commitment required for the non-traditional season. However, coaches need to learn how to divide their time among different responsibilities so that they give each the attention needed to achieve excellence, yet not slight one area just because they are less knowledgeable or less passionate about that particular area. The ability to multi-task seems to be a source of pride in young people until it is required as part of their job, and then it becomes a source of irritation.

I dislike hearing coaches refer to their "main sport" or their "secondary sport." We need to tackle every job we undertake with passion and determination. I knew very little about field hockey when I began. However, in much the same way I learned to play tennis with my sister when I was young, I read books, observed other coaches, and studied the game until I felt confident. I doubt that you could find one of my former hockey players who would not attest to the fact that for the twelve years that I coached hockey, I coached with passion and confidence. I do not know how we can expect our athletes to be good student-athletes if we do not expect ourselves to be good teacher-coaches. It is inexcusable to enter a classroom unprepared or to present the material in an uninterested manner. More often than not, we use the excuse that we had to prepare for a game or practice and therefore the teaching got put on the back burner.

Excelling at your passion is easy compared to excelling at something that we view with less enthusiasm. To excel all of the time should be the goal for every coach.

Coaching four sports today at the collegiate level would be impossible. I will be the first to admit that the length of the regular season, the advent of non-traditional seasons, the recruiting demands, and the expectations for winning are much different today. However, I also know that there were still many demands that accompanied being a head coach, and in the days when I had no assistant coaches, I performed many duties that my assistant does for me now as well. I coached from before school started until the day school ended. I had no time off in between seasons, and in most cases, the seasons overlapped. I despise seeing any coach who does not try to excel at every component of the job. To do anything less than our best does a disservice to the young people we are trying to serve.

Chapter 3

The Title IX Battle

You may have to fight a battle more than once to win it.
Margaret Thatcher

In order for the reader to fully understand the battle that I undertook in the 1970s for Title IX compliance, it is important to have a common understanding of Title IX and its implications for women's athletics.

Title IX is an extension of the Civil Rights Act, which was passed in 1964 and outlawed discrimination based on race, color, religion, sex, or national origin. Different features of the Civil Rights Act are represented when you study some of the different components of this law. For example, Title I barred unequal application of voter registration requirements, Title II outlawed discrimination in hotels, motels, restaurants, theatres, and other public accommodations, Title III encouraged desegregation of the public schools, etc.

Title IX of the Civil Rights Act was not added until 1972. Title IX states, "No person in the U.S. shall, on the basis of sex, be excluded from participation in, be denied the benefits thereof, or be subjected to discrimination under any educational program or activity receiving federal financial assistance." Although this legislation was not initially controversial, people began to realize that one of the areas where this legislation should apply was in the field of athletics.

During a time when boys outnumbered girls 13:1 in high school sports and when girls received one cent and boys received ninety-nine cents of every dollar spent on sports, over ten thousand complaints were received by the Office of Civil Rights. People were beginning to realize that there was clearly something wrong when you analyzed how lopsided the opportunities and funding were for athletics based on gender. The Office of Civil Rights then published legal clarification in 1975 and gave high schools one year to comply with the law (1976) and gave colleges and universities three years to comply (1978) relative to their sports programs.

I arrived at Muskingum in 1974, and I cannot remember the words "Title IX" ever being uttered during my first three years. I was too busy trying to establish the program to worry about fighting a legal battle that I knew little about. I remained confident that if I could establish the credibility of the women's athletic program and show what hard work and dedication could do, then the college would acknowledge those efforts and do what was needed to help equalize the opportunities for the male and female athletes.

However, by the beginning of my fourth year, my frustration had started to build from the lack of progress (Figure 2). The women sadly lacked in facilities, equipment, practice opportunities, and budgets. I had also been appointed women's athletic director, so now I had an official administrative obligation to try to correct some of the wrongs. In the spring of 1978, I was required to submit an itemized women's budget for the '78-'79 school year. The budget reflected a conservative increase of slightly less than $2,000. However, because our budget was so small to start with, $2,000 still reflected an increase of nearly 20 percent. The Athletics department in total (men and women combined) had been told that increases could not exceed 6 percent for the next year. If the men did not get an increase, the implications for their programs would be that they would have to cut back on the quality of shoes that they purchased for their teams or cut out the expense of pre-game meals. It was standard practice on game day that a male team in football, basketball, or baseball would have a pre-game meal consisting of steak, baked potato, salad, hot rolls, and jello. In contrast, if the women did not get an increase, we were talking about not even having enough money to play all the games on our schedule. Games would need to be canceled.

I insisted that the women's program could be improved tremendously and still be far from where it should be. Coach Sherman stood firm in his belief that if the only way the women had to get money was for the men to cut back, the women would remain where they were. He insisted that the women's program should not reflect growth

Figure 2. Coach Newberry in her office, 1978.

if the men's program was at a standstill. Because we were at opposite ends of the continuum and getting nowhere, I decided that I needed to go to other administrators.

I sought the help of Jan Stults, a woman on campus who had recently been appointed as the Title IX coordinator for the college. I had several meetings with her, followed by several meetings with her and the Dean of the College. These meetings finally culminated in a meeting arranged by the Dean that included all of the male and female coaches, me, Coach Sherman, the Dean, the college Treasurer, and the President of the college. This was to be an open discussion, and I was assured that if I was not satisfied with the results that came from the meeting, then the Dean would pursue it further.

By mid-June, it was apparent that nothing had resulted from the meeting except perhaps a few less-than-friendly feelings that were generated between the men's and women's athletics programs. I then decided to meet with the Affirmative Action Committee. Prior to this, I did not even know that an Affirmative Action Committee existed on our campus, but I had been advised that this was the next step in trying to get my voice heard. I prepared an extensive document that outlined the steps that I had already taken and explained some of the areas of non-compliance. Following is the introduction to the document and some of its content.

Introduction: *During the past three years there have been several changes that have given the women a better opportunity to participate in the realm of athletics than they had been given previously. Although there have been some positive changes, the women still believe there are many areas that are discriminatory in both physical education and athletics.*

To justify this discrimination, the argument has long been perpetuated that the women here do not show enough interest in athletics to justify demanding a more equal opportunity in that area. There is not a lack of interest, but rather a lack of opportunity that has necessitated fewer number of women participants. With no junior varsity programs, a minimal number of coaches, less than desirable practice or playing areas, and the personal expense to each athlete (since our budget does not provide them with all necessities), it is surprising that we can attract as many women as we do. Given a more equal opportunity to explore their athletic interests, the women's participation should increase even more markedly in the future. It must be remembered that institutions are required to satisfy the interest and abilities of women to the same degree as they satisfy the interests and abilities of men, by providing competitive opportunities which address the interests and abilities of each sex equally.

Because the female coaches and athletes are presently dissatisfied with their athletic opportunity as compared to the opportunities for the men, it has become necessary to list those areas where we feel there is non-compliance with Title IX.

Areas of Non-Compliance: (This will not include everything that was in the Title IX document that I originally submitted, but it will highlight some of the more obvious areas.)

Work Load

Second semester during basketball season, the work load for our men's coach was:

Teaching assignment – 1 hour course Lifetime Sports
Coaching assignment – Head Coach of Men's Varsity
    Basketball (also had one full time assistant coach)
Second semester during basketball season, the work load for me was:

Teaching assignment –

1 hour course	Bowling
1 hour course	Track and Field
1 hour course	Gymnastics
1 hour course	Foundations of Athletic Skill
2 hour course	Officiating Basketball
2 hour course	Officiating Softball
3 hour course	Coaching Methods of Team Sports

Coaching Assignment –
    Head Coach of Women's Varsity Basketball (no
        asst. coach)
    Head Coach of Women's Softball (no asst. coach)
    Administrative Assignment – Women's Athletic Director

Locker Room

The men have one physical education locker room, two varsity locker rooms, and a third area that can be used as a locker room if it is needed.

The women have only one locker room that is shared by physical education classes and all varsity teams (both home and visitors).

Training Room

The training room is located in the men's locker room. The female athletes, therefore, have no access to the trainer or to the training room.

27

Equipment and Supplies

The men's budget allows for equipment purchases, buys shoes for the team, buys practice uniforms, purchases audio visual equipment, etc.

The women's budget allows only for the purchase of basic equipment needed to play the game, such as game balls. No women's team has practice clothes. Basketball and volleyball share the same game uniforms and they are worn for both home and away games. Softball has worn cut off blue jeans and tee shirts for a uniform.

Playing Areas

All men's teams have regulation courts or fields that they use for competition.

Field hockey is played in a non-regulation field that is seven yards too narrow. The softball team has to use the hockey field for their games as well. The goal cages from hockey have to be used as the backstop. The infield is entirely grass with strap down bases, and right field is so short that you have to make the bank in right field a ground rule double.

Volleyball is allowed to use the competition court in John Glenn gym for matches only if they will put down the lines each time and then remove them. If men's basketball wants to use the court for practice, basketball practice will take precedence over an intercollegiate match.

Practice Times

The main problem with practice time is with women's volleyball and basketball. Volleyball is forced to practice in the Pit so that men's basketball can use John Glenn gym for preseason workouts and open gym. During basketball season, men have prime practice time of 3:00 pm to 6:00 pm daily. The women's practice time is 6:00–8:00 pm daily. If either intramurals or a wrestling match is scheduled, the women's practice time moves to 9:30 pm–11:30 pm.

Game Schedule

Women are not given enough money in their budget to allow them to play a full number of games. This is particularly true in volleyball, basketball, and softball.

Volleyball – Volleyball plays 15 matches and needs a minimum of 20–25 matches.

Basketball – Basketball plays 14 games and needs a minimum of 18 games. Men's basketball plays 22 varsity games. (This number excludes all of their tournament games.) In addition, they play 15 junior varsity games.

Softball – Softball plays 13 games each season. Baseball plays 23 games each season.

Opportunity to Receive Coaching

Women coaches have a heavier teaching load during their season than the men do, as was illustrated earlier in the comparison between me and the men's basketball coach. The women have no assistant coaches and no junior varsity teams. Male athletes have a better opportunity to receive quality coaching simply because there are more male coaches employed and each coach is permitted to spend more time coaching during their season.

I also believe, although I cannot access the information to prove it, that the male coaches have a substantially higher salary than the female coaches. When new coaches are hired in, the female coaches are always hired with an entry level salary, which limits our viable pool of candidates to those with little or no experience. The men seem to be able to replace their positions with candidates who are as qualified, or perhaps more qualified, than the coach who vacated the position. As a result, I believe our male athletes are subject to a higher and more competent level of coaching than our female athletes.

With my Title IX documentation in place, there began another period of waiting to see if other things would be done. With the leverage of July 21, 1978, being the deadline for colleges and universities to be in compliance with Title IX, my naïve belief that the institution would surely change when they had all the inequities pointed out to them, and the determination that there were better things ahead for female athletes, I felt confident that many of the issues would soon be resolved. However, as the deadline for compliance approached and I was officially informed that the women's budget would be held to a 6 percent increase the next year, it became apparent that nothing positive was happening. My despair finally drove me to submit the following letter to the Dean.

> *According to Ed Sherman, the women have been given the budget for next year that I have termed all along as professionally unacceptable. I have been waiting to hear from you as to whether or not this is definitely the way things stand. I realize the college is in a great deal of financial difficulty and I am more than willing to keep our budget at a minimum as long as there is not a double standard enforced for men and women in budgets. At this point, the double standard exists not only in budgets but in many other areas as well.*
>
> *I would like for you to let me know immediately if you plan to do anything else about budgets in particular and other areas in general. The areas of noncompliance that I listed in the document that you received a few weeks ago are to be dealt with by July 21, 1978. If nothing else is going to be done, I feel obligated to begin the process of filing a grievance. I feel that I have done everything else that I can do to remedy the situation.*

The deadline came and went. Some small increases in our budget above the 6-percent mandate were approved, but I dug my heels in by starting the official grievance process. The last thing I wanted was to be involved in a lawsuit. However, the changes I saw in our conditions were not the changes that I wanted. The primary change that I noticed was increased animosity between male and female athletes and male and female coaches. It might have been easier if Muskingum had been on financially stable ground, but with many restrictions in play, there was simply no extra money available with which to increase budgets or improve facilities. It seemed that the only place to get money for the women's program was to trim it from the men's program. For us to have more, it meant that the men would have less. Sadly, the men's budgets could have been substantially trimmed and they would have still far exceeded anything that we were used to, but belt tightening was not something that the men were interested in doing.

By the time 1980 rolled around, the college still had not made many legitimate efforts to comply with Title IX mandates. The deadline for compliance had come and gone two years before, and it seemed that no one was interested in hearing my arguments or taking the steps needed to get the institution in compliance. Sadly, it was not just Muskingum that was in this situation. The same problems could be seen nationwide at nearly every institution of higher learning. Even in large universities, where finances were not such a difficult problem, the inequities existed.

When you are dealing with difficult problems, you always reach a point where you have to evaluate if it would be better to stop fighting the battle and move on. By this time, I had established enough credibility that I could have probably gotten another job at the college level if I decided to change jobs. Perhaps staying here and challenging the system longer was nonproductive. Would it not be easier to go somewhere else and start over again? At what point does perseverance become stupidity?

While I was wrestling with the wisdom of continuing what seemed like a losing battle at the professional level, I observed athletes trying to answer similar concerns at a personal athletic level. Although I was still relatively young, I had already hardened myself enough that it took a great deal of adversity to discourage me. I struggled to understand how quickly athletes became discouraged and chose to give up on the dream that they had once pursued. In many cases, it did not take much to discourage them.

Sometimes it was an injury that sidelined athletes for a period of time and forced them to miss practices or games. Sometimes it was contentious teammates who did not always mesh well with the athlete's personality or temperament. Sometimes it was a coach who withheld playing time or demanded more discipline than the athlete was willing to display. Perhaps it was a coach who had a different strategic approach to the game than what the athlete was accustomed to playing. If I were to encompass all the "reasons" for quitting that I have heard over the past thirty-six years, the list would be endless. Although the reasons that are given for quitting a sport have changed slightly over the years, the problem remains that often athletes don't

31

recognize what they are letting go of, and by the time they realize that it might have been better to "hang in there," it is too late to reverse the decision. More often than not, their lack of perseverance becomes stupidity.

It has been sad for me to see how quickly some athletes abandon their sport because they have not learned to deal with adversity. I will admit that there are a few times when dropping out of a sport is the best thing for an athlete to do, but those occasions are rare. My measuring stick for how long I should endure adversity has a good deal to do with how many people will be negatively impacted if I give up. If the issue affects no one but yourself, then you can more readily take the easy road. However, your decision cannot be made in a vacuum when the welfare of others is involved. In a team sport, the decision of one player to quit impacts the entire team. It can be devastating to morale, it hurts depth and versatility, and it calls into question the credibility of team goals and aspirations. The loss of one member of the body will impact the entire body.

When I considered how devastating it would be for the female athletes if I were to leave Muskingum during the Title IX battles, the decision to stay was easy. Although the college could have hired in a competent female replacement who had the background and resolve to continue the fight, in my heart I knew it would be another entry level hire and our program would be set back at least six years. Also, I loved Muskingum. In spite of the setbacks and stagnant state of the program, I remained grateful for the opportunity that had been given to me when I was hired and the faith that the college had placed in me as an unproven professional. I had made friends in the community and church, and, while leaving would have solved some problems, it would have created many more.

Something needed to happen to bring things to a head. In 1980 I started my sixth year at Muskingum and as a result, it was the year I was being reviewed for tenure. Maybe I would not be the one to decide to leave. Maybe the administration would decide that for me. I had rocked the boat enough that there were probably plenty of people who would have liked to see me leave. After six years, you were either granted tenure, which provided job security, or you were given a terminal contract.

Shortly after school started that year, Donna Rios, the president of Women Athletes at Muskingum (WAM) came by my office to visit. Donna was an outstanding field hockey player from New York who was passionate about women's athletics and a bit outspoken, so I considered her to be the perfect person to be in charge of WAM. WAM was a student-initiated organization that had been functioning for a couple of years to try to support some of my Title IX efforts. The group did not endear itself to the male athletes and had already created some animosities on campus. Donna said that she had an idea that she would like to propose to me that she thought would help the cause. WAM wanted to organize a campus-wide debate between me and Ed Sherman to give us an avenue to explain the athletic-related gender issues to the students and to defend or challenge the current Athletics department policies.

I readily agreed to the debate, thinking that it would be a good way to clarify confusion about the issues and to open the eyes of those who had shown little interest in the issues in the past. Ed Sherman, however, refused to debate. I was not really surprised by that since public speaking was not his forte, and he really had nothing to gain by debating. However, he did agree that our men's basketball coach, who was now the assistant athletic director, could replace him in the debate if he was willing to do so. Coach Jim Burson was an excellent public speaker, and he quickly agreed to debate on behalf of the men.

There was a great deal of campus publicity leading up to the debate. My preparation was easy since I had previously worked on documenting the problems and had presented most of these same concerns to the administration. By this time, I was also pretty well versed on Title IX, its interpretations, and its implications. The one area of my preparation, however, that really lacked was getting actual budget numbers for each sport so that I could present some black and white figures. Even though I was the women's athletic director, I was still subject to the men's athletic director. These were not parallel positions.

As a result, I knew all of the women's budget numbers, but none of the men's numbers. Male salaries and budgets for the men's teams were definitely off limits to me.

As they say, "Desperate times call for desperate measures." I needed to get the budget numbers. The night before the debate, I talked to the long-time secretary for the men's department. Even though she had served the men for nearly thirty years, she was very sensitive to our problem and was empathetic to our cause. When I emphasized to her how critical it was to my presentation to be able to present some black and white numbers, she agreed to meet me late that night at the office. Because she had the keys to Coach Sherman's office and to his file cabinet, she was confident that she could help me get the information that I needed.

I am not proud of doing something that was secretive and no doubt illegal. Had I not tried everything I knew to do prior to this, I probably would not have had the resolve to go through with it. I did not know exactly what the numbers would say, but I was confident that they would prove beyond doubt that the inequities between the men and the women were staggering. I appeased my conscience by reminding myself that these numbers should not be kept secret in the first place. I believed you would not try to hide something unless there was something to hide. If I was not willing to step up and do what it took to open everyone's eyes to Title IX, then I no longer deserved to be the Women's Athletic Director. It was a true ethical dilemma as I was trying to weigh seeking justice against violating professional privacy.

There was a feeling of apprehension in my stomach the day of the debate. Much of the discussion around campus throughout the day centered on the upcoming confrontation that evening. I walked over to the student center during the course of the day in order to get a better feel for the set up. The top of the student center was the chosen location for the debate, and all the furniture had been removed to make room for students. Even the chairs had been removed so that the audience would either stand or sit on the floor and seating capacity would not be an issue. When I saw the temporarily erected debate platform, the reality of what I was about to do descended upon me.

That night when I walked in, the student center was packed. A long carpet had been unrolled to create an aisle that approached the platform and that also effectively separated the sexes. On one side were all the female athletes, their roommates, and their friends. On the other side were the male athletes and their contingents. A surprising number of faculty members were present. Neither side was very congenial. The air was thick with animosities that had been building for several years. I felt like a general who was ready to lead her troops into a war of words. I did not feel overmatched, but I knew the opponent was formidable. I was not only fighting against the inequities of the current situation, but I was challenging beliefs that had been ingrained for generations about the roles of male vs. female and the sanctity of the male domain of athletics.

Perhaps it was fitting that the moderator of the debate was the campus minister. I do not believe anyone questioned his objectivity, his integrity, or his resolve for a peaceful resolution. The early stages of the debate brought about pretty predictable points. Coach Burson emphasized how many athletes the men's programs recruited and brought to the campus, the number of spectators who attended their events, and the caliber of athletes that they produced. He highlighted all the positives that men's athletics brought to the campus.

I, on the other hand, tried to delineate all the inequities that existed that could be clearly evident to any member of the student body, ranging from practice times, to locker room space, to lack of adequate playing fields and equipment. I insisted that the quality and commitment level of our women athletes had already improved, but until some changes were made to address some of the inequities, further improvements could not realistically be expected.

As the debate wore on, I sensed that the men were closing their ears to any argument that I presented. I was anxious for the debate to be opened to questions. I was pretty confident that one of the questions would be about disparities in budgets. Much as I expected, as soon as the floor opened for questions, one of the first questions to be asked was about budget. I had withheld my newly discovered numbers, thinking it would have more impact if the information was requested by a student rather than just offered up by me. I was especially glad when it was a male, rather than a female, that asked the question.

I decided that it would not be wise to give out actual budget numbers, but the information that I did present was striking. When I was able to show that the money in the men's basketball budget alone was more than all of money combined in the budgets of our six women's sports, people suddenly were listening. Male coaches and administrators were looking at each other, wondering where this information came from. I am sure it was the first time any of them realized how inequitable the budgets actually were. Females were nodding as if to say, "We told you so."

As I left the debate that night, I didn't feel that there was clearly a winner or a loser. The issues remained hot topics on our campus for months to follow. Shortly after the debate, a satirical cartoon appeared in the *Black & Magenta*, our campus newspaper. It showed me dressed in a witch's costume (this was around Halloween time), knocking on the Athletic Director's door, extending a trick or treat bag with dollar signs on it.

I do believe that the debate brought to the forefront all of the issues that I had been challenging for the past several years. Afterwards, I saw changes being implemented. Women were given more consideration in practice times. Competition facilities began to improve. Budgets were not equalized, but in small increments, the women's budgets continued to increase. Women's basketball and volleyball were granted part-time assistant coaches. It would still take another fifteen years or so before some of the inequities were rectified, but progress, even if it was slow, made the process tolerable.

It also helped that the college had climbed out of its financial crisis and was on much more stable footing. The tight reins that had been holding all budgets in check were gradually loosened, so it made it a little less threatening when women requested either budget increases or things that cost money. As the pressure of money relaxed slightly, so did the animosities between the men and women on staff as well as the grudges held between male and female athletes.

Ed Sherman retired, and as Jim Burson became the Athletic Director, there were still many issues to be resolved but gradual progress continued. The Recreation Center was being built, which nearly tripled our athletic space, so sharing facilities, having adequate locker room space, and having comparable practice times and space became less of an issue. I also believe that as the men saw the success of our women's basketball, softball, and volleyball teams, they began to respect what the female athletes and coaches were capable of accomplishing.

Coach Burson and I established a good working relationship, and to this day I believe that we have built a mutual respect for the other's accomplishments that has superseded the friction created by other battles that had to be fought. Jim was gaining a national reputation as a basketball coach, known for his execution of the Princeton Offense, and eventually serving as President of the National Association of Basketball Coaches and being inducted into the Ohio Basketball Hall of Fame.

Eventually Coach Burson went back to just coaching basketball and Al Christopher, head football coach, was appointed as our men's Athletic Director. It was Al who was able to totally salve the wounds that I had opened throughout the years of fighting for our women. He was a true gentleman who always had an open ear for my concerns and questions. I enjoyed talking with him and getting the insights he had gleaned after many years of coaching. I believe that it was Al who finally rebuilt the bridges between the men and the women. He is now retired, and I continue to value his friendship, his wisdom, and his support.

In the process of coaching teams and teaching classes today, it is surprising to discover how many of our young female athletes have no sense of the history that brought them to the point where they are now. Many female athletes today feel no sense of appreciation for their athletic opportunities, but rather take them for granted as if these opportunities always existed. Some young women are so accustomed to the opportunities to receive coaching and compete that they fail to recognize the battles that were fought to get them there. As more time elapses since Title IX was implemented, it seems there are fewer athletes who know or even care about how all of their opportunities evolved. I now make it a point in my Coaching Team Sports class or in my Sport Ethics class to incorporate some of our campus history in context of the national picture to help them understand that good things don't come easy.

To hear female athletes complain about having to practice, rather than appreciating the fact that they have a coach and a place to practice, tears at my heart. I sometimes hear them complain about the style of their uniform or the brand of shoe that their team wears, rather than appreciating that money has been allotted to purchase those things for them. I hear them complain when a game day coincidentally interferes with their social plans, rather than appreciating the fact that they have an opportunity to play a game. We need to insure that each generation of athlete does not lose sight of how far things have come and the work that it took to achieve that progress.

It is equally frustrating to see us as female coaches falling into the same pitfalls that were previously a source of condemnation from us towards our male counterparts. In some instances, we have become guilty of doing the very things that we criticized in the male athletic model. Have we put so much emphasis on winning that we have taken the fun out of the sport? Do we demand so much of the athletes' time in the preseason and off season that we force them to specialize rather than become well-rounded athletes? Do we spend so much time year-round developing the athlete that she becomes burnt out at an early age? Have we lost our sense of sportsmanship and/or even resorted to cheating if that is what we thought it took to win? Do we have our athletes playing so many contests that it stymies the development of their academic, social, and spiritual lives?

I am proud of the inroads that were made on our campus pertaining to women's athletics. I also acknowledge that with the progress comes a responsibility that it be handled with wisdom. Uncensored sport can be a dangerous thing and can produce problems that are worse than sport being inaccessible. It is up to each of us as coaches to constantly re-evaluate the demands and expectations of our program so that athletes are treated with fairness and compassion. We must find the balance between striving for athletes to excel and an overemphasis that places too much importance on competing, which should be a pleasurable and rewarding experience.

Chapter 4

Climbing Mountains

It is not the mountain we conquer, but ourselves.
Edmund Hillary

The 1980s at Muskingum brought steady progress, both with the Title IX issues and with my personal growth as a coach and teacher. Because I had no mentor or role model in the women's department, I tried to observe, and to some extent mimic, what I saw the male coaches do. Particularly in the sport of basketball, I gained much from observing Coach Burson's practice sessions. Because his team and my team always had to stagger our practice times, I often spent an hour or two each day observing his practices. He was an outstanding coach, and I was not too proud to borrow drills, strategies, or ideas that I saw his team implement. I had experienced many differences of opinion with Coach Burson, and we had several Title IX confrontations, but he was willing to help when it came to basketball, and I believe that I was gradually earning his respect as he appreciated my work ethic and as my teams established themselves as winners. The barriers that Title IX had erected and the animosities that had been created were gradually dissipating.

As I reflect on the athletes that I coached during my first ten years at Muskingum, I often wonder how they would fare if they were to compete against some of my athletes from my last ten years at Muskingum. I doubt that my teams from my first ten years would be able to defeat many of my teams from the later years. This is not due to their being inferior athletes as much as it is probably due to the fact that they did not have access to the same level of coaching and competition before arriving at Muskingum. They had gone through high school in an era when coaching was still very limited for girls and they had simply not been exposed to high levels of competition or coaching.

Jane was one of my first athletes at Muskingum. She was a senior the year that I arrived, and she was slightly less than a year younger than I was. She represents the tremendous hunger that those early athletes had for a competitive opportunity and to have someone push them. She played both basketball and softball. When I arrived at Muskingum, I inherited a slow pitch softball program. My experience with softball was with fastpitch, as I had spent every summer playing high level ASA major league fastpitch softball. I insisted that if I was going to coach softball, then it would have to be switched to fastpitch.

I already had it in my mind that the best player that I had would be converted into a pitcher before we got to the season, and I quickly identified Jane as my best softball player (Figure 3). I talked to her that fall and told her what I wanted to do. In spite of the fact that she was a senior and would only be able to pitch for a year, she readily agreed. Once I showed her the mechanics, she spent countless hours in the Pit throwing against the wall and developing her pitching skills. Never once did I hear her complain. I have not had many players since then who have shown her level of dedication.

My early athletes were more versatile than my later ones. I think of Cindy who, throughout her career at Muskingum, lettered in four sports (field hockey, basketball, softball, and volleyball). She was outstanding in each of those sports and never seemed to tire as she moved from season to season. Today, it is difficult to find a player who will play more than one sport. Part of this is because the timeline for playing has expanded so much that it encompasses the non-traditional season as well as the regular season, and it is partly due to coaches who discourage athletes from diversifying for fear that it will detract from their own sport. However, it is also due to athletes now who do not want to invest all of their time playing a sport. There are so many other things to do and to distract them that often athletics does not hold the highest priority in their lives.

The athletes in my earlier days complained very little. Any progress that was made towards improving the playing facility, or uniform, or equipment was deeply appreciated. They were so grateful to have a regular practice time and an opportunity to compete that it

Figure 3. Coach Newberry with her first softball team in the spring of 1975. Pitcher and team captain Jane Tedrick is standing, second from right.

was hard to look on the dark side of things. They seldom questioned anything that I said. Maybe this is because they had not grown up with having their own hitting coach or pitching coach or personal trainer. For many of them, the first real coaching they ever received was under my tutelage. It was nice to have my word accepted at face value and to have neither player nor parents questioning what I said.

Those players did not hesitate to approach me with their problems. However, the problems then were more about boyfriends, or getting along with their parents, or questions about their spirituality. It seems the problems lately that I have been confronted with are much different. Current problems deal with things like pregnancy and abortions, drug and alcohol problems, and sexual orientation. If you stay in coaching long enough, you will probably deal with about every kind of problem that you can think of, and I do believe that the types of problems that I have dealt with have changed through the years.

I have great respect for those early athletes. They worked hard and embraced the joy of competition. They were not spoiled by having a lot of "things." It did not matter that they did not wear the nicest uniforms or have the latest gear. As long as they had a place to play and an opponent, things were good. They had great respect for me and took steps towards establishing Muskingum as an institution that would excel in women's athletics.

As I look back at those athletes, I don't know how many of them would survive in our world of collegiate athletics today. Today requires much more specialization to excel. Athletes are forced at an early age to choose their "sport of choice" and to focus maybe not just on the sport, but even on a specific position within the sport. Competition has become much more businesslike and has increased in intensity. More time is required in the off-season. Emphasis is placed on weight training, which was almost unheard of for women when I first started coaching. I am not saying that these things are bad, I just don't know if this is what the athletes from an earlier era wanted. There were many good athletes from that era who were probably more interested in participating and simply enjoying the competitive experience than in working year-round to give themselves a chance to win a championship. Perhaps it is something that they would have grown into, but it would have been unfamiliar territory for them.

I can think of a few athletes like Jana from my earlier days, and feel confident that they would have never burnt out or resented whatever you asked them to do. Jana was an incredibly skilled basketball player who loved every moment of competition and could not get enough of the world of athletics. She even agreed to play field hockey for me, although that sport was totally out of her element, just so she could experience another season of competition. She would have probably been an All-American if she had been born ten years later. The greater the challenge and the more she was asked to sacrifice to achieve a goal, the better she liked it.

The majority of the athletes that I saw at that time, however, were more like Amy. Amy was a very good athlete, but she was also carefree and fun-loving and wanted to get enjoyment out of all of her experiences. Had Amy gone through my program at a later time when pre-season, off-season, and in-season demands left very little time for personal life, she might have resented the time demands and perceived that the work was overriding the fun. I do not know if she would have chosen to play all four years and make the sacrifices necessary, or if she would have decided that it was too high a price to pay. It is difficult to speculate how the athletes from my first ten years would have responded if they suddenly had been asked to function with the circumstances of an athlete from a couple of decades later.

There have been positives and negatives with each generation of players. I am grateful that my career has spanned a long enough timeline for me to see and experience both ends of the spectrum.

As I approached the end of my first decade of coaching, most of my success was coming in basketball. By 1983, we had our first twenty-win season, going 23 - 6. We followed it the next year with a 25 - 4 record. I was gaining confidence as a coach, and I was gradually becoming more demanding. As the wins increased, my expectations continued to mushroom. Every year, our activity in the preseason and off season increased. As I pushed my athletes more and more, I was gradually getting away from remembering what it was like to be an athlete and identifying with what it was like to be an established coach. Ten years had passed since I was hired at Muskingum, and I began to think that it would make me a better coach if I could renew my feelings of what it was like to be an athlete. I needed to remind myself what it was like to be pushed. I needed to remember the mental toughness that was needed to fight through physical fatigue and the discipline that was required to get my body in shape not only to survive, but to excel.

〜

In the summer of 1983, I read an article about a program called "Outward Bound." The program had been established as a result of a study conducted during World War II that examined which soldiers most effectively survived the war experience. They quickly discovered that survival had less to do with physical size and strength, and more to do with mental toughness and quiet confidence. Outward Bound was established to mimic some of the Marine basic training techniques that were designed to build mental toughness and self-confidence. It was thought that if these training techniques were useful in war time, then it would be a positive thing to offer a similar experience to civilians during peace time. Thus, Outward Bound was born, and it expanded to be a nationwide program.

The article informed me that the typical Outward Bound adventure lasts for twenty-three days, and participants can choose experiences ranging from dog sledding in Alaska, to sailing off the coast of Maine, to hiking through the canyons in Utah, to kayaking in the Everglades. The common component, regardless of the trip that you choose, is the concept of "experiential learning." Basic instructions are given with each activity, but much of the learning comes from doing. You are taught the essentials, but the quality of the learning will hinge on how much each participant is willing to attempt. Although you are given the information that you need to stay safe, there is an element of risk depending upon how motivated you are to achieve self-established goals. The instructors will allow you to learn by making mistakes. If you make a mistake, there are consequences that are suffered as a result of the mistake. If you make good decisions and execute what you have been taught, you enjoy the innate reward of a feeling of progress and accomplishment.

Learning about Outward Bound came at a perfect time for me and what I thought I needed in my professional life. This program would push me both physically and mentally, and I strongly felt that it would be what I was looking for to restore in me the feeling of being the athlete rather than the coach. After exploring several options, I decided that I would apply to participate in a survival backpacking trip in the Colorado Rockies. The program was nearly a year away, but as soon as I was accepted, they sent me a conditioning program so that I could begin the task of getting in shape for the trip.

As was true with many of my summer adventures, I was not exactly sure what I would gain, but I felt confident that each new experience would enrich my background, make me more capable of understanding other people, and expand my understanding of the world around me. At times I chose to write in a journal, and such was the case with Outward Bound. I will share some of the experience as I recorded it in my journal as well as sharing the lessons that I believe it taught me relative to athletics and coaching.

The trip occurred in the summer of 1984. I really had no idea what to expect. All I knew was that I had followed the conditioning program that they recommended, plus I had done some extra on my own, unlike athletes who ignored their summer conditioning program and came back to school unprepared. My journal began on the flight to Denver.

> *The flight was full with about 400 people on board. It was quite coincidental that a woman sitting just in front of me heard me say that I was going to Denver for Outward Bound and she immediately turned and excitedly said that was her destination also. I spent a good deal of the flight talking to Sue as we both joked about the upcoming trip, discussed our apprehensions and compared what we packed to bring. Sue is a high school science teacher from Michigan. Maybe it is fortunate that she is the first one I've met, as she certainly set my mind at ease concerning my ability to do this in comparison to her qualifications. She is older than I am and stopped smoking just for the purpose of surviving this trip. Never succeeding at running more than two miles non-stop (and that at an 11 min./mile pace), my three mile jogs in 25 minutes suddenly sounded pretty good. She is not very athletic looking and is very concerned about whether she will be able to keep up.*
>
> *When I checked into the motel in Denver that was to be our rendezvous point for all the people on the trip, I met some other people from the group. Sue II (since I don't know last names I have to differentiate between her and the initial Sue that I met) is a marathon runner. She runs about eight miles per day, and once again I am having doubts about my three mile jaunts.*

My first lesson learned was about the value and wisdom of comparing ourselves with other people. The fact that the first Sue I met might be less prepared than I was, or the fact that I might not be able to keep up with Sue II, would have very little to do with my ability to survive the mountain. The only thing that really mattered was whether I was as prepared as I could be.

This idea about preparation relates to coaching. Athletes have a tendency to compare themselves to other athletes on the team when they are confronted about their performance. For example, if I say to an athlete, "You can do better than shooting 60 percent from the foul line, often the first response that I get is something like, "But Susie only shoots 50 percent and she is a starter." We have a tendency to compare ourselves to the worst person we can find in order to make ourselves feel better, or on the other end we might beat ourselves up by comparing ourselves to the best person on the team. All that should matter is whether we are doing the best that we are capable of doing. Measuring ourselves against lesser or greater athletes is counterproductive and gives us either a false sense of security and accomplishment, or gives us an unfounded feeling of accomplishment.

There were twenty-eight people in our Outward Bound group. The first morning we were divided into four groups of seven. It seemed that each patrol was based on perceived ability and conditioning, and if that was the case, I was in the top patrol. Following is a profile of those with whom I would spend the next couple of weeks:

Pat – age 34. Pat is an elementary physical education teacher from northern California. His wife Patty is also on the trip but they put her in another patrol, so she will not see Pat again until the adventure has ended. Pat is a cool guy. He is funny, always keeping the group laughing. He loves to sing while walking. He always wants to know if the groceries are ready when we get into camp. He is also very sensitive and feeling. Some of the insightful things he has said have almost brought tears to my eyes. He's tall and lean at 6' 3" and we call him Spider Man for his appearance and his climbing ability. I really enjoy talking to him.

Dick – age 42. Dick is a teacher and ice hockey and football coach from Boston. He is the oldest member of our patrol. He thought he was shaky at first, but he turned out to be the strongest member of our group. He came to Outward Bound to test his strength and to work out some personal problems. He is not afraid to admit his fears. He was petrified of rock climbing, but did it in style. I'll never forget the look on his face when he made it to the top on a difficult climb. Later, when his knees were cut so badly that he should have been at the hospital, he was running the marathon. He and Pat became like brothers. His favorite expression was, "I am one hurtin' unit!"

Sue – age 32. Sue is a speech therapist from Albuquerque. She is a marathon runner with fiery red hair. She gets excited any time we have a chance to learn something new. I will later recount a story about her fall while we were climbing, and it seems a miracle that she survived. Her example gave me strength to continue when I struggled with my own motivation.

Jenny – age 32. Jenny has spent the past five years in Saudi Arabia as a journalist. Jenny's got real determination and her mental strength is outstanding. She is cool in a crisis. I felt that I could trust her with my life. We had some great conversations under the stars. Jenny takes everything in stride and made me a great walking partner.

Renee – age 31. Renee is a math teacher from Boulder, Colorado, and she is the most timid and fearful member of our patrol. She has to muster up courage every time we do a stream crossing or climb or do anything that requires balance. She shows courage and is able to keep up with all of us during the land hiking. It is too bad that not more people have the desire to prove and conquer their fears like Renee does.

Marietta – age 32. Marietta is a social worker from Binghamton, New York. She is very outspoken, witty, and personable. She is petite, but tough as nails both mentally and physically. She is not tolerant of anyone who cannot keep up. I heard her several times call some of the women who were in the other patrols "wimpy broads." She is a real go getter. I would take her on my team any time.

I had done some backpacking prior to this, so I did not consider myself a novice. I had backpacked a portion of the Appalachian Trail and also in the mountains in Sweden. However, I was very apprehensive when the shuttle bus came to the motel the next morning to pick us up.

About seven hours later when we arrived at base camp, it was hectic as equipment was issued and checked off. I kept thinking about how heavy it would be to carry my pack as I watched my pile of supplies grow. Group dynamics were already in play as we were told that the group would not resupply for the next nine days, so we needed to decide what food should be carried. There were some uncomfortable discussions as we tried to achieve a balance between what we absolutely needed to survive and what we thought we should carry to make the trip more bearable. We blocked out cheese, measured out oats, flour, granola, oil, etc., until finally deciding we were ready. We also had to carry pots and pans, cooking stoves, climbing ropes, sleeping bags, tarps, etc. Anything we did not want to carry, we would have to leave behind.

The next thing I knew, our patrol was told to load equipment into an old van and they would drive us to our starting destination. I was shocked the first time I tried to lift my pack. It had to weigh at least 50 pounds (even though I knew that you were supposed to carry only one third of your body weight, and for me that would mean I should carry about 40 pounds). The weight was uncomfortable and almost unbearable. We spent most of day two hiking through the valleys and slowly gained elevation. We constantly worked on map reading and went over some elementary first aid information. The thing that I remember most about this day was how heavy and uncomfortable the pack seemed and the number of rest stops we made to take them off. As we hiked, each individual fought their own physical pain. I kept wondering if the other people in the group hurt as much as I did. It rained that night and none of us got much sleep due to getting wet and being apprehensive.

I was surprised at the amount of strength that I gained from being part of a group. By the third day, I had an uninterrupted ring of bruises around my waist where the cinch strap rested from the pack, and deep bruises on each shoulder where the shoulder straps pulled on my torso. If I had been doing this alone, I might have already given up. However, there was a strange sense of comfort that could be derived from knowing that others had to be suffering as much as or more than I was. As long as they could do it, then I could do it. As a coach, I knew what this meant; team sports definitely enabled you to dig deep for the good of the team and kept you encouraged when the demands seemed unreasonable.

In the terrain we entered, we could cover about one mile per hour, and then we needed to factor in another hour for each one-thousand-feet of elevation gained. It was slow and tedious walking. In many cases, you needed to balance your weight as you stepped boulder to boulder. Any time that you had to cross a gorge or crevice, it was frightening. It often involved making your way across a downed log or tree that might be spanning a crevice or crossing a stream madly rushing several hundred feet below your position. This would be difficult to do in tennis shoes and no backpack. To do it with the weight of the pack throwing off your center of gravity gave you no room for error and put your heart in your throat until each person was safely on the other side.

The ability to read a compass and topographical map was critical in this type of terrain. Time was spent daily in teaching us how to study the map, figuring out where we were, and then figuring out the best way to carry on the next leg of the journey. That may sound simple enough, but once you got into the Rockies, each peak and valley tended to look the same. It was very easy to misidentify your location and get headed in the wrong direction.

The beginning of day four was not kind to us because Ben, our Outward Bound patrol leader, proclaimed us ready to find our own way. He told us our destination and said that it would be reachable by noon. We were told to figure out exactly where we were, calculate the best route to get to our destination, and meet him there around noon. I was not sure where he went, but at that point, he disappeared. Our experiential learning was now in full gear as he clearly had no intention of helping us or bailing us out if we made a mistake.

There were four of us who huddled around the topo map, took readings, did some calculations, and finally laid out a route. Even though we encouraged the other three to help us, they shrunk into the background and insisted that we should go ahead since we could probably do a better job than they would. It was annoying that they were unwilling to engage in the process. As we started out, the four of us who established the route were the first four in the hiking line. It was clear that the followers wanted to do nothing more than follow. They wanted no part of the responsibility of leading.

About an hour into the walk, it became painfully clear that we were headed in the wrong direction. A couple of landmarks that we should have already seen were nowhere to be found. We had no other choice but to backtrack and get ourselves back into familiar territory. And who were the first to criticize? It was the followers who immediately chirped up with that endearing comment of, "I knew this wasn't right! I knew that we were going in the wrong direction."

It cost us two hours of time and a great deal of energy to correct the mistake. However, the lesson I learned has since stayed with me. It is usually not too hard to identify the leaders. This identification becomes critical when establishing team captains. Those who lurk in the background are often those who are most apt to stir up trouble. A famous general once said, "There is no greater sin than to remain neutral at a time of great moral crisis." You must have an adequate number of people on your team who will step up, show leadership, and accept the ramifications of their decisions to have any hope of being successful.

We were now behind schedule, but we reached our destination by mid-afternoon. We were at an elevation of about ten thousand feet, and I was in misery with breathing the thin air. Our plan was that since we had now reached the snowfields (even though it was mid-July, there was still plenty of snow), we would spend the rest of the day going through what Ben called "Snow School." We would learn the techniques needed to climb and traverse in the snow, and then the next day we were planning on putting these skills to use as we would attempt to cross Heckler's Pass.

Much of our time that afternoon was spent in learning a technique called "self-arrest." Although Ben taught us how to traverse and dig in when crossing steep and snowy slopes, self-arrest becomes the last resort that you use if you fall and start to slide down the slope. In order to self-arrest, you must get yourself into a position where you are on all fours with a firm grip on your ice axe. The ice axe is pointed on both ends and has a leather strap around the handle. Ben spent a good deal of time explaining that deciding to loop the strap around your wrist would make it less likely that you would drop it if you fell, but more likely that you might impale yourself on a flailing ice axe. If you chose to leave your wrist free of the strap, you might lose your ice axe in a fall, but you were less likely to suffer puncture wounds if the ice axe were out of control. Each person needed to make his or her own decision.

To practice self-arrest, Ben took us to a plateau about halfway up a very steep, icy, snowy slope. He had you face him, with your back to the slope. The slope flattened out at the bottom so there were no real consequences if you could not stop. He would push us off so that we started upside down and backwards. We were to get flipped over on all-fours, get our feet headed downhill, dig in our toes, and rake the ice axe from our right shoulder to our left hip as we slid, to eventually get stopped. This is tricky enough without a pack, but with a heavy cumbersome backpack strapped to your back, it was quite a challenge. We did it over and over again to the point that everyone was exhausted. I picked up the skill pretty easily, and I was fairly efficient at it after several practice runs.

I became progressively frustrated as fatigue set in along with the cold, the wet, and hunger. I suggested to Ben that maybe we should call it a day. Everyone was tired and hungry and we had probably practiced enough. He smiled at me when he said, "Watch Renee come down the slope this time." As she came down the slope, she was completely out of control, she could not get flipped over, and she landed in a heap at our feet.

Ben said, "Donna, how was that?"

I quickly replied, "It was terrible."

"If she is above you tomorrow in the climbing line," Ben said, "and she falls and cannot self-arrest, do you realize that she is going to take you down the mountain with her?"

I said, "Maybe we should continue practicing for a while."

Suddenly it brought to mind all of those drills at Muskingum that we repeated over and over again in practice. The good players could execute, but there was always the one or two who didn't get it. The better players would get so frustrated with the repetitions and

51

quickly tire of repeating something that they already knew how to do. What a lesson it was to realize that it is your weakest player who will get you beat. It only takes one person not knowing where to be or what to do to change the outcome of a game. The old cliché of "a chain is only as strong as its weakest link," certainly rang true. I made sure that every member of our patrol was proficient at self-arrest before we called it a day.

It was beginning to get dark by the time we set up camp. Everything was snow-covered and we were above the tree line, so there was no way to build a fire. We set up a couple of cook stoves to heat up some soup. We then used our ice picks to level out enough of a snow platform so that we could string a tarp and have a flat area to lay out our sleeping bags. With this type of backpacking, it is much too heavy to add the weight of carrying a tent, so the most covering that you had was a tarp. Each person had a piece of quarter-inch thick foam about the length and width of the body to give him or her a little insulation from the snow. We zipped all of our sleeping bags together to make one big bag in an attempt to retain our body heat. It was extremely cold that night and most of us just dozed off and on. We were all looking forward to the daylight that would bring a little of the sun's warmth. We were also nervous about the prospects of trying to cross Heckler's Pass the next day.

It started at 5 o'clock the next morning when Ben once again left us. He trusted us to find our way to a smaller pass where he would meet us and help us get over. I guess this was a warm up to Heckler's Pass. Gruffy, the coordinator for the entire Colorado Outward Bound school, had joined our patrol the night before, knowing that we would need her help the next day. She went with Ben, and we were left on our own.

It took about two hours of grueling climbing, but we made it to the first pass. The pass was steeper on the side where we would have to go down than it was on the side where we had climbed to the top. It was so steep that we could not cross it with packs on our backs. We rigged up a system with ropes in order to lower our packs to Ben. Each of us then had to climb down a steep rock face while roped to Gruffy. After getting down the rocks, we put our packs back on and used glissading techniques to slide about three hundred more yards to where the slope leveled out. Glissading involved rolling onto your back with your knees tucked to your chest, and using your backpack a little like a sled. As you held onto the shoulder straps, you just let the steepness of the slope take you down. This was a somewhat scary and difficult descent, as you could control neither speed nor direction very well, but if you relaxed, it leaned more towards being fun and exhilarating.

At this point it was about noon. We munched on some cheese, crackers, peanut butter, and honey. Ben and Gruffy left the group again and said they would see us at the base of Heckler's Pass. We would camp tonight on the other side of the pass.

Determined, we looked at the map and picked our route. The route was almost all snow, difficult and steep. I fell once during a traverse and had to use self-arrest to stop. It was incredibly fatiguing simply to make our way to the pass. Gruffy and Ben were waiting for us at the base of the mountain. It was now about 6:00 P.M. and we had already been hiking and climbing for thirteen hours.

At the time, none of us realized that neither Ben nor Gruffy would be the ones to stop us if we were in over our heads. We also did not know it at the time, but we were the first group of Outward Bound students who had ever attempted crossing this pass. Maybe if Gruffy and Ben had fully understood the difficulty of getting the group across the pass, they might have stopped us anyway. However, part of expe-riential learning is recognizing your limitations and making good de-cisions about when to continue and when to stop. At this point, part of the patrol was crying out of stress and fatigue and fear. I was having my own problems, as my eyes had gotten sunburned over the past couple of days with the glare from the snow. Even though I was wear-ing sunglasses, Ben said too many rays were entering from the side of the glasses. I could barely see. He made some blinders out of tape to put on the sides, and I wore them from that point on.

We had quite a group confrontation in the meadow. Some group members said that we should refuse to continue to go any farther. We were exhausted, it was late, and the pass looked insurmountable. I did not share my opinion with the group. I was afraid that my eye problems clouded my judgment, and I did not want to be the one to slow the group down. If I had it to do over again, I would have been more adamant about exercising some caution, but in the heat of the moment, I was willing to abide by the group's decision.

When Gruffy and Ben started walking towards the base of the pass, we all followed. Why? I don't know. Determination seemed to possess all of us. I will turn back to my journal for a description of the ascent.

> *By perhaps 7:30, we were ready to go up the steepest part of the pass. It was starting to rain and snow and the wind chilled me to the bone. We paused long enough to dig in and get our rain gear out of our packs. I was really fighting the altitude. I felt myself panic inside, but our patrol made the commitment that we could make it. I had no idea where my strength would come from – I just knew I would have to find a way.*
>
> *The next hour was more agony, both mental and physical, than I have ever endured. The pack was cutting into my shoulders. My legs had reached a point of not feeling the pain. It seems they were moving automatically. Gruffy was leading and kicking steps in the snow, then there was Jenny, and then there was me. I did not take my eyes off Jenny's feet the whole way up. I was afraid to look down because it reminded me of the consequences of falling. I would not look up because I didn't want to know how much farther we had to go. No one spoke. The whole ascent I was a robot and every step demanded my full concentration with all my effort geared towards mustering the strength for my next step.*

I have recalled this experience many times as I coached in some big games. Whether I was playing for a conference championship, a regional championship, or a national championship, the lesson I learned remained with me. You must take one step at a time. You can get overwhelmed if you are focusing on how much farther you have to go to reach the top. If you allow yourself to focus on how costly a mistake could be, it is so difficult to keep going. On this climb, I was literally taking one step at a time, but figuratively, in many coaching situations, this lesson has served me well. The bigger the game and the higher the stakes, the more important it is to not let yourself look ahead or behind.

We reached the top about 8:30 and the whole group embraced. It was not exhilaration we felt, it was relief. The wind was howling at the top and it was getting dark, so it did not take long to figure out that we had to keep moving. I felt sick when I looked over the edge and saw the distance and terrain that we would have to descend before we could stop.

We started down slowly and painfully. My mind was exhausted, and I kept thinking about them telling us that most accidents occurred on the descent, not on the ascent. My body was so tired that I did not think I would have the strength to self-arrest even if I fell.

The likelihood of falling on the descent is an interesting coaching phenomenon. Most climbing falls occur on the descent because climbers tend to relax on the way down, thinking the worst is over. You tend to let down your guard because the hardest part of the climb is now behind you. Similarly, I have witnessed many ball games lost because teams have started to relax when they have a comfortable lead. As they come down the home stretch of a ball game, they forget the effort that it took to get them to that point, and as a result they feel it is ok to give less than their best effort. The same effort is needed to close a ball game as it took to open the game – anything less than that is probably not going to be good enough against a quality opponent.

When we got to the steepest part of the descent, we did a series of switchbacks. Switchbacks are a zigzag pattern that enables you to combine traversing with descending. Although it slows down a climb, it is a safer and easier way to descend. The most dangerous part of a switchback is when a zig is about to become a zag. Your feet and body must get turned, often on a steep face, as you redirect your steps to continue the descent. During this part of the climb, it was Gruffy, Jenny, me, Sue, Renee, Pat, Dick, Marietta, and Ben. I noticed that ever since our snow-school experience, when I wrote in my journal about a climb, I was very cognizant of the climbing order.

> *We were in the middle of a switchback. I heard a foot slip behind me and someone was sliding. Almost simultaneously, the whole patrol screamed "Self-arrest!" Sue had slipped and because she had chosen not to strap her ice axe to her wrist, she lost her ice axe in the process. The slope was icy and steep. She was turned sideways and could not get her feet turned around to even slow her down. She gained speed and the pack pulled her out of control as she went head over heels pounding against rock, snow, and grass. I would estimate the distance of her fall to be 700-800 feet. I froze, and the only words that I said were, "Dear God, who is it?" I knew it was someone behind me, but we all look alike in our helmets and gear.*

The next hour was hectic. Ben climbed down to where Sue was and called up that she was alive. He asked me to come down to help him with first aid, knowing that I was a first aid instructor and probably had more training than he had. Fortunately, Gruffy talked me through the remaining descent and literally placed my feet in her handholds. I could not believe how paralyzing fear can be. The whole patrol was clinging to the side of the mountains and was afraid to move.

Stuff from Sue's pack was strewn everywhere, but both her helmet and backpack stayed on. It was probably the fact that the backpack stayed on that spared her life as it acted much like a roll bar might on a car and protected her neck and spine. We weren't sure if there were any broken bones, but I was confident that none of the injuries was life-threatening. As the others descended, we made a stretcher out of backpack frames in order to carry Sue and started to explore how we could safely get off the mountain.

By now it was 10:30 at night, and we were faced with steep boulder fields. Ben led us through the dark over boulders and snow and tried to find somewhere we could stop. It is extremely difficult to do this in daylight, but to do it in the dark seemed ridiculous. The only lights that we had to help us navigate were the headlamps on our helmets. Finally by about 11:30 we conceded that we would spend the rest of this night on the side of the mountain. We each started to arrange small rocks between big rocks to find a flat place where we could wedge in a sleeping bag. It had been a nineteen-hour day of some of the most physically demanding and stressful situations that could be imagined. I was so exhausted that I slept surprisingly well that night. I knew I would need my full strength to get out of there the next day, so I was grateful for the rest that I was able to get.

I truly discovered that day the inner strength that I possessed. I doubt that many athletes will ever be pushed to those kinds of limits, but I am confident that most people are capable of giving far more than they think they are capable of giving. As coaches, we need to be able to find a way to push our athletes without breaking their spirit. I think most athletes appreciate discovering the depths of their inner self as long as it is done in an educated and responsible manner.

When I tried to get up the next morning, I found it very difficult to move around. My legs would not support my body weight. I probably looked a little like a seal as I pulled myself around on the boulders and tried to get myself going. I believe that my leg muscles had reached a point of physical exhaustion. After an hour or so of self-massage on my quads, hamstrings, and lower legs, I became a little more functional. Following some coffee and oatmeal, the patrol had a meeting to talk about the day before and to explore our options.

Some were angry, feeling that our leaders had let us push past the point of acceptable risk. Others were simply appreciative that Sue had emerged from the accident without major injuries and we had made it through the night. Some simply just cried and let their emotions flow. Jenny cried the most. Gruffy was close to breaking as well. Her husband was a paraplegic as a result of a climbing fall, and this experience was eerily similar. Sue did not cry at all as I think the impact of things did not hit her until later.

We discussed whether we were afraid to climb on snow again. We were at least three days away from radio contact and felt like sending for help was not a reasonable option. We looked at the topo maps and tried to explore the best way out of our predicament. I said that I was exhausted and scared. I desperately felt a need to get off that mountain, but we needed to find a route that if someone made a mistake, it would not cost a life. As exhausted as we all were, mistakes were almost guaranteed.

After much deliberation, we chose a route that would get us to Trail Rider Pass. It was a good distance – about a seven to eight hour hike – with lots of boulder fields and some snowfields. However, it seemed to be the best of our choices.

The strength of my mind was severely tested that day. My body was screaming to stop, but my mind kept me going. We were trying to avoid snow traverses at all costs for the sake of all of us, but especially for Sue. When we reached the steepest part of the excursion, we chose a narrow strip on which the snow had melted to do the climb. It was so steep that there were times that I was crawling because there was no footing to walk. It was full of bushes and thickets and they were tearing at the pack and pulling me backwards. The climb was almost vertical. I think that most of the group cried somewhere during that ascent, as there were a lot of streaked faces when we reached the plateau. I know that I cried, and I was very relieved to reach the top. At this point, I believe the whole patrol felt that the worst was behind us.

As scared as I was and as exhausted as I was, I was able to derive strength from both my inner self and from the example set by Sue. Sue was badly beaten up and sore during this hike, so there was no doubt that it was tougher on her than it was on any of the rest of us. I have tried to keep that learning experience with me. We are capable of doing more than we think we can, and if there is someone who can set the example and we can model after them, it brings the task into perspective. The ability to dig deeply into our inner selves is a lesson that every athlete needs to learn if she ever wants to reach a level of excellence.

There were many other components to the Outward Bound trip, including lessons and challenges in rappelling, running a half marathon, doing an environmental service project, doing a final two-day excursion without any instructors, and just the day-to-day backpacking. However, I will expand more on our "solo" experience, which is another common element in all Outward Bound programs. I feel that this is where I was able to reflect on what I had learned, and it provided a capstone experience for me.

The standard "solo" consists of three days and two nights that you spend totally by yourself in the wilderness. You are left with no food, but you do have water. As Ben dropped us off one by one to hike to our solo sites, my imagination was running away from me as I conjured up pictures of wild animals and uncontrollable hunger. This was the part of Outward Bound that I had dreaded the most. I don't know how far apart we were from the other patrol members or from Ben, but we were given a whistle and assured that someone would be within ear shot if we got into serious trouble. I was nervous as I approached my solo site.

My home for the next couple of days was in a meadow, near a stream. I had a small tarp that I suspended between bushes to provide some protection from the elements. There was a big flat rock in the middle of the meadow that I used as my home base for catching up on writing my journal. I had no way to build a fire, so when night came, the only light was what the moon provided.

I was a little nervous when the first nightfall descended. As I huddled down in my sleeping bag, it did not take long for a family of marmots to start to bother me. A marmot is about the size of a ground-hog. They are aggravating because they are naturally curious and do not seem to fear people too much. They also like the taste of salt, so they will chew on anything that has salty sweat dried on it, ranging from leather boots to clothing. I kept a pile of rocks by my head just for the purpose of scaring them away, but they definitely disrupted what would have been a good night's sleep.

When I arose the next morning, I had to smile at the fear that I had harbored the previous night. I had made it through the darkness just fine, and worrying about things that go "bump in the night" now seemed pretty childish. As the day got underway, I took all my clothes to the stream and was able to wash them and hang them out to dry. It would be refreshing to put on clean clothes. We were also told that we had to bring back a gift for each member of our patrol from our solo experience. There were some pretty creative gifts ranging from drawings of wild flowers to pine cone bracelets. I decided that my gift would be a poem. I do not claim to be very adept at poetry, but regardless of the amateurish effort, the poem seemed to hit everyone pretty hard, as it captured the feelings that many of us were sharing. I entitled my poem, "The Battle of Self."

Whenever I meet a little adversity,
My soul displays its blatant diversity.
A tug of war occurs in my mind;
Should I push forward or fall more behind?

Just at the time that I'm feeling prolific
And all the things around seem terrific,
There's a part of me that keeps me constrained,
That dictates the joy be politely restrained.

When bravery seems to be what I need,
The cowardice in me says better take heed.
When strength is the answer to things I must face,
My weakness pulls me back in my place.

Whenever I feel that I need to push higher,
There's a little voice saying I surely will tire.
When the empathy in me says give her a hug,
Another part says fold your arms and look smug.

One side of the balance says always keep smiling;
The other end gloats on the frowns I'm compiling.
One yearns for adventure, the other stays home;
When this side says go, the other says come.

When one's going up, the other's descending.
When one's facing facts, the other's pretending.
When one's looking forward to seeing new things,
The other's afraid of what each new day brings.

So the tug of war in my soul battles on;
I must find a winner lest life's too far gone.
For my life will not make its final connection,
As long as my soul tugs in different directions.

A house divided will surely not stand.
The right must join with that flailing left hand.
United I stand and divided I fall,
Thus a whole, not a half, must answer each call.

Doubt must not linger when I make up my mind.
I can't strike out harshly when I ought to be kind.
If sincerity calls, then I can't appear hollow.
If the right foot leads, then the left one must follow.

I know I'll make progress if I pull as a team,
If I mean what I say and I say what I mean,
If the ends of the rope that have tugged me apart,
Are tied in a loop that encircles my heart.

Thus onward I'll go to meet life at its best,
Both halves will work, then both halves will rest.
I'll enter together and together come out,
I'll make a decision and leave behind doubt.

United, I'll fight all my cares and distress,
And double the strength that my soul does possess.
'Twas a battle of self but the war I have won;
Instead of a split, it's now all against none.

When our solo experience ended, we ate our first food in several days. The meal consisted of blueberry yogurt, flatbread, and coffee. Never had such a simple meal tasted so good. I did not know that eating could be so delightful, because I had never taken myself to such depths of hunger. I began to realize that to reach the highest peaks, you had to go through the deepest valleys. High reward only comes with high risk. I was beginning to understand the level of commitment that it would take to win a national championship. Somehow, I needed to continue to explore ways that I could communicate this message of commitment to my athletes. We must be willing to get out of our comfort zone to grow or to accomplish anything of substance.

~

Both my body and my soul felt totally refreshed coming off the solo experience. The thing that I had dreaded the most turned out to be the pinnacle of the experience for me. I reflected on the fact that the main reason that I took this course was to put myself back in the position of the athlete and to remind myself what it felt like to be really pushed both physically and mentally. As I thought about the pain and the strength of mind that it took to overcome the pain, I believed even more strongly in the value of this undertaking.

I have learned the value of group cooperation and commitment. Without the support and the example that the group provided me, I don't think I would have made it. The concept of "team" was strongly reinforced.

I have seen the impact of fear. There is nothing wrong with being afraid (perhaps fear is our innate guide to common sense), but fear is also paralyzing. If an athlete goes into a contest fearing either the opponent or the outcome, she will not be able to perform to the best of her ability.

I have learned to trust and rely on others to help me survive, but I have also learned that the ultimate responsibility for survival falls on me. Many of us associate maturity with independence. There is nothing wrong with leaning on others for help when we need it, but it takes wisdom to strike a balance between being accountable for our individual responsibility to perform and relying on teammates to bail us out when we fall short.

I experienced the feeling of some serious commitment. Once you make up your mind to do something, do not allow obstacles to stand in your way, regardless of the effort that it takes to overcome them. Again, it takes wisdom to strike a balance between commitment to a task and recognizing that a goal may have been set that is unreachable. Part of a coach's job is to help a team strike that balance.

I learned something about compassion for others. I was better able to empathize when another was scared or tired or hungry because at some point I had found myself in that same situation. I rediscovered how much an encouraging word could mean at the peak of emotional and physical stress. As a coach, I tend to be consistently critical of athletes when mistakes are made. For me, this technique provides the most rapid learning curve. However, I must not forget to counterbalance that with an occasional statement of support or understanding.

Outward Bound provided dynamic lessons on how paralyzing it is to dwell on the consequences of failure. The more I thought about the fact that I might fall on a traverse, the more difficult it became to push ahead. If I climbed to keep from falling rather than to get where I was going, it became twice as difficult to make progress. It reminds me of the statement that I have made many times to my teams, "You must play to win; you cannot play to keep from losing."

I discovered that I truly am a strong individual and I can hang in there under difficult situations. I am limited primarily by my mind. If you can control your mind, it is amazing to see the difficult things that can be accomplished.

Although there were a few things about Outward Bound that I would not want to experience again, I never regretted the time and effort that I invested in the trip. The lessons that were learned or reinforced proved invaluable as I continued my coaching career. I had grown as a person, and, as a result, I believed as the leader of my teams that I could transfer my growth to my teams, and together we could emerge as a stronger and more successful unit.

I began to rely more and more on my summer experiences to provide opportunities for my personal growth and to enhance my understanding of what it takes to excel in all aspects of life.

Chapter 5

The Accident

The ideal man bears the accidents of life with dignity and grace, making the best of circumstances.

Aristotle

The Outward Bound experience had been everything that I had wanted it to be and more. I had come back humbled by a renewed realization of how small a part I play in the overall scheme of nature and humanity. However, I also came back motivated to further excel in the world of coaching and determined not to let setbacks or discouragement overrule the desire to excel. I felt prepared to climb the next mountain, wherever it presented itself.

Things were continuing to go well in the coaching world. Both softball and basketball were having success. In 1983 and 1984 we had back-to-back seasons of twenty-three and twenty-five wins in basketball. In softball, we hit our first thirty-win season in 1986. I was getting a better grasp on how to recruit, and I was gaining credibility as a recruiter. No longer did I have to recruit by promising athletes the hope of great things that I wanted to accomplish or by promising them an opportunity to experience winning in the future. I could now show them that great things had already happened and that we were already winning. If they wanted to be a part of what we were doing, then Muskingum was a place that they should consider.

Field hockey was a struggle to produce winning seasons. Geographically, we were not located in an area where field hockey is a prominent sport. In earlier years, Muskingum attracted a fair number of students from Pennsylvania, western New York, and other areas that were hot pockets for prospective field hockey players. It seemed that our demographics had shifted, so that now we drew fewer students from those kinds of areas, and depended more and more on students from within the state of Ohio. As long as that continued to be true, it was difficult to produce a winning hockey team.

As I watched our men's teams compete in the Ohio Athletic Conference (OAC), I was envious when I saw how much excitement and added interest a conference affiliation brought to their contests. The women were not a part of the OAC, and at this time they were not wanted or welcomed as members. It was strictly a men's conference, and the women were left to fend for themselves.

There were several other female athletic directors throughout the state that recognized the need for a conference affiliation as well. I made several trips to Columbus to meet with others who were interested in exploring the idea of a women's conference. At this time, all women's teams were governed by the Association of Intercollegiate Athletics for Women (AIAW) at the national level. This was the women's equivalent of the NCAA. The NCAA was much like the OAC. The women were not part of their organization, and the OAC was fighting hard to keep it that way.

Since there were no conferences to produce conference winners, the ticket into post-season play was to win the state tournament. All women's teams in the state, regardless of the size of the institution, would compete in a season-ending tournament to establish a state champion and to move teams forward into post-season play. Both basketball and softball had qualified for post-season play within this organizational structure, but part of the drawback was that the AIAW had no funds to help out with expenses for any institution that qualified for post-season play. Whereas the NCAA produced Division I television revenue that was distributed throughout the ranks to offset the expenses of participating institutions, the AIAW did not have that luxury. I have less than fond memories of getting behind the wheel of a van and driving my team all the way to Pella, Iowa, to participate in the national finals in softball. We traveled on a shoestring budget and drained any money we had raised in order to make the trip.

After many meetings and deliberations, Muskingum did join with several like institutions within the state to form what was called the Centennial Athletic Conference. If the men did not want us as part of the OAC, it was time to step out on our own. It was difficult to convince the administration that the conference was necessary. Even though they thought it was a grand idea for the men to be part of the OAC, they were more than skeptical about the need for a women's conference. A new conference meant paying a new set of conference dues. It also meant the need to explain the new structure to alumni, fans, friends, etc., in a way that people would understand two different organizations with different rules, and to some extent, different philosophies.

The Centennial Athletic Conference had no sooner gotten off the ground than it was disbanded. Both the NCAA and the OAC recognized the fact that they were fighting a losing battle. Women were destined to become a part of both of these organizations, so rather than fight the issue, it eventually seemed more logical for the men and the women to join hands and find a way to unify the genders into one organization. Both men and women were reluctant to fully support the idea. The women feared their loss of autonomy and were not convinced that the men would always have their best interests at heart. The men were slow to let go of their "Good Ole Boys Club" and seemed determined to find a way to allow women to have membership without necessarily giving them equality of representation.

The early OAC meetings were often long and heated. It was hard to differentiate between when we were discussing and when we were arguing. There was much debate about which gender would vote on issues. Philosophically, it became quite challenging to merge the opinions of both sexes into a constitution and by-laws that would satisfy both. Gradually, however, the OAC became an institutional organization without deference to gender. The NCAA followed the same route, and by 1985, both our men and our women were members of the same athletic organizations.

One decision that the OAC made that directly impacted me was to add soccer as a women's sport at all the OAC institutions. Because soccer and field hockey were played in the same season, it quickly became obvious that both sports could not function on a campus of our size. The decision was made to drop field hockey as a sport and to focus on soccer. After twelve years of coaching hockey, I had given up coaching the sport. We had an interim coach that got us through one year, but after that, the transition to soccer began, and field hockey ceased to exist on our campus.

I then turned my attention to coaching basketball and softball. In 1987 we had another twenty-win season in basketball, and in 1988 we had our best season ever with a 29 - 2 record. We made it to the NCAA national quarter-finals that year in basketball, and lost in the final minute of the game to fall just short of the final four. We also won thirty-seven games that year in softball, winning the OAC and making it to the NCAA Women's College World Series.

Things were flying high for me and my coaching career. We had experienced unprecedented success for Muskingum, and I pretty much had all my players returning for the next year in basketball. I had visions of a national championship playing through my mind.

About the time you think you have arrived, other plans are revealed. Such was the case in November of 1989 as we prepared to open our basketball season. Expectations were high for this team, and everyone associated with the program felt that this would be the year that we would make it to the national finals and perhaps win a championship. Anything short of that would be a disappointment.

The season was scheduled to begin much like most of our other seasons. We usually opened up on the road at an out-of-state tournament in order to get a couple of games under our belt and to play some competition that we normally do not face during the season. We were headed to Frostburg, Maryland, to open our season at the Frostburg Invitational.

It was a typical winter morning as we loaded the vans and prepared to leave. The temperature was hovering around 32 degrees. There was a mixed bag of precipitation, ranging from light rain, to sleet, to light snow. There were no serious storm or travel advisories that had been issued. Although I would have preferred a bright sunny day to make the drive, the thought of canceling the trip because of the weather was not even considered. Any time there is any snow or ice, I get a little nervous as a driver. However, I have driven in some pretty bad conditions, so this light snowfall did not seem too alarming.

Oftentimes when we traveled by van, I would make my players change where they were sitting or even which van they were riding in. It is not cool, by college players' standards, to ride with the coach. It was not uncommon for the upperclassmen to crowd into the van that my assistant was driving and leave the freshmen to ride with me. There were few things that made me angrier much more quickly than this tactic. It tended to encourage cliques and create separation between freshmen and upperclassmen, and it was an irritating sign of immaturity on the part of the upperclassmen. I do not remember telling anyone to change where they were sitting for this trip, but I did tell them that we needed to balance out the numbers, as there were eight people in my van and eleven in my assistant's van. One person reluctantly switched over to my vehicle. I am grateful that I did not make a scene about it before we left, as I would have tortured myself forever about those decisions after the events of the rest of the day unfolded.

When we pulled onto the interstate to head east towards Wheeling, West Virginia, I was cautious. The roadway was wet, and as the temperatures fell and rose from slightly below freezing to slightly above freezing, the potential was there for slippery conditions. My assistant coach followed me in a second van. About the only place that I noticed any slipperiness was on the entrance and exit ramps. The roadway itself seemed ok, although there were sections where the snow was starting to stick to the roadway.

We were only about an hour into the trip when the accident happened. I honestly remember very little about the details of the actual accident. Perhaps that is because my mind has blocked it out, or perhaps it happened so fast that I was not able to comprehend exactly what happened. At any rate, as we were traveling on the interstate, the car ahead of me suddenly put on its brakes. I am not sure if they felt themselves sliding, if they hit black ice, or what caused their reaction, but as they braked, they forced me to brake. As I did so, the van began to slide.

The next thing I knew, it seemed that we had bounced from guard rail to guard rail. To this day, I am not sure if we actually did go from one side to the other, or if we were just jostled around. You often hear people say that during an accident, things seem like they are moving in slow motion. Such was the case with me. I had no concept of the time or distance involved in the accident. Regardless, there was a tractor trailer directly behind me that rammed us broadside as the van spun out of control. When things finally came to a stop, it was hard to discern exactly what had happened.

I seemed to be coherent and relatively uninjured. As I unbuckled my seat belt and turned around, I said, "Is everyone all right?" At this point, I had no idea how serious things were. (To protect the identity of my players, any names that I use in reference to the accident will be pseudonyms.) I heard one of my players say that Annette and Mandy had been thrown from the van. By this time a couple of players from the second team van had made their way to our van. They witnessed what happened, but fortunately they had not been involved. I asked these players to go to Annette and Mandy and see if they could be of help.

I tried to see what I would be able to do to help those in my van. The accident happened in the time before cell phones, so I was hopeful that a passer-by would call and get help on the way. I gave my attention to Darla, who was sitting directly behind my seat. She was in a great deal of pain. Her face had some lacerations and profuse bleeding, but mostly she was having difficulty breathing, and it created severe pain in her back anytime she tried to move. I tried to stop her bleeding while stabilizing and immobilizing her back. I feared that she had injured her spinal cord.

One of my uninjured players felt that one of the girls, Jackie, was not breathing. She asked me how to do mouth-to-mouth, and I explained the basics as I tried to deal with Darla. Fortunately, I had several players with me who had taken my first aid class as part of their academic curriculum, so I was blessed to have some with me who already knew what to do and helped to keep things calm.

There had been nine people riding in my van. The people in the front of the van, including me, were the least injured. Everyone else was pretty seriously injured. The situation was critical. I do not know how long it actually was before the first ambulance arrived. I know that I was worried about victims going into shock. I asked all those who had been riding in the second van to give up their coats and to try to keep their teammates warm.

When help finally arrived, the emergency personnel performed triage to decide who they would transport first. The ambulances were arriving one at a time, and it would take seven vehicles to transport the injured. I rode in the ambulance with Darla, as she was panicked and it was hard to assess how serious her injuries were. The stuff from our van was strewn on the highway and across the guardrail. I hoped that my assistant coach was able to care for the uninjured and handle that end of things.

I remember very little about what happened once I got to the hospital. I am sure that I was in a state of shock, and although I was trying to function, my mind was not operating clearly. I was not sure where each player was, or if the rescue workers had even brought them all to the same hospital. I do remember walking down a hallway, and one of the hospital workers grabbed me by the arm and told me that no one had been killed. I cannot describe the wave of relief that went over me when I received that news. However, it was only a few minutes after I received that news when a physician found me and said I needed to go to the morgue and identify two bodies. I collapsed on the spot in the hallway. I don't know how that type of information could have been miscommunicated, but in this case it certainly was. I never did make it to the morgue. I was so distraught and disoriented at that point that I honestly don't remember much of what went on for the next several hours.

Two of our players had been fatally injured in the crash. One of these was Annette, who had been ejected from the van. The other was Jenny, who was sitting on the end in the second seat and took the brunt of the impact from the semi.

"Bad news travels fast," as they say, and it wasn't long until parents and personnel from Muskingum began to arrive. I don't know at what point I was given a full report on all the injured. Several players were in critical condition, with at least two suffering broken legs as well as internal injuries. Darla had severe lacerations, several broken ribs, and some internal injuries, but at least she had not broken her back as I had feared. Others had a variety of internal injuries that were still being assessed.

The parents of the deceased players called. I was unable to talk with them as I was so overcome with grief that I could not even try to have a conversation. To this day, I remain deeply grateful to the kindness, understanding and forgiveness that these parents showed. I don't know if I would have made it through if it were not for the support that these two sets of parents gave me. At a time when they had every right to lay full blame on me and take out their pain on me, they were incredibly supportive and seemed as worried about me as they were the tragedy that had befallen their own families.

The events that night were a blur. I did not sleep, but continued to go room to room to check on my players. The college had sent a vehicle to take the uninjured players home. They would have to take care of each other until things settled down here. The parents of the injured sat up all night in waiting rooms, anxious to get results of surgeries or procedures that were being done on their daughters, and making an effort to comfort each other. I can remember that about dawn the next morning, I was able to take a shower and change out of the blood-stained clothes from the day before.

The parents of the injured players were also incredibly supportive of me. I was so emotionally fragile at that point that I do not know what I would have done if a parent had chosen to attack me. Fortunately, I didn't have to find that out. I still marvel at the understanding and graciousness shown to me by every parent that was involved.

I cannot recall when I returned to campus. Several of the players were being kept at the hospital as they were unable to be transported. I made daily trips to Wheeling to see them until they had all been released to either go home or to be moved to a hospital in Zanesville that was closer to campus. I can remember counting twenty-three straight days of visiting the hospital, as I was determined that I would go for however long we had players in the hospital.

Our campus is relatively small. Currently we have an enrollment of about sixteen hundred undergrads, but at that time the enrollment was closer to twelve hundred. It is hard to comprehend the impact that this type of disaster can have on a campus that is this small and closely knit. The memorial service that they held in Brown Chapel was extremely difficult. I remember walking across the quad to attend the memorial service, totally encompassed by my remaining team. It almost seemed like they had wrapped a protective shroud around me. Those who were seriously injured remained hospitalized, but everyone else was in attendance. I have never known our students to be as somber and respectful as they were that day. Brown Chapel was nearly filled to capacity with students, faculty, community members, and caring friends.

I was astounded by the maturity and caring that my team showed me for the next several months. I am the type of coach who does not allow close interpersonal relationships to be formed between me and my players while they are still playing for me. I care deeply for each of them, but it is not healthy to allow yourself to get so intertwined in their personal lives that it either interferes with your ability to be objective about their performance or gives the perception that you have "favorites." It is often after they graduate that I build a friend-ship with players, but while they are still playing for me, I keep them at arm's length. Young coaches who are similar in age to the players that they coach are often tempted to establish a "best friend" relation-ship or a "big sis" relationship with their players. Although this rela-tionship may satisfy a coach's need to be needed, it does not create a healthy environment for coaching. Making yourself available for pro-fessional advice is a necessity for a coach, but allowing yourself to get too close to your players is one of the biggest mistakes that coaches can make. However, in this instance, all walls were down.

It seemed that the only ones that I could talk to about how I was feeling were my players, and it seemed that the only ones that they could talk to were to each other and to me. I watched players ranging in age from freshman to senior both literally and figuratively wrap their arms around me and give support. The love that spread through the team was almost incomprehensible, and it was our mutual em-brace that held each other up.

The funerals were held on two consecutive days following the memorial service and were extremely difficult. The college chartered a bus for the team to travel to the funerals. This not only enabled us to stay together, but it also spared us the emotional agony of trying to ride in a van again. I do not recall many details about either of the funerals. I was still numb from all the events of the past week, and I feel that I went through the motions without really comprehending what was going on around me. Again, the families of the victims were incredibly supportive. Without their support, it would have been impossible for the healing process to begin.

~

We had suspended our season and held numerous team meetings with those who were able to attend to discuss whether we wanted to try to resume playing. We also had those conversations with the parents of both the healthy and injured players to see if they thought we should play basketball.

I was not sure in my own mind whether I could and would continue coaching. I drew the greatest comfort from being around my team, but at the same time, my mind was in such a tortured state that I did not know if I would be strong enough to withstand the trials that coaching through the season would bring. Not only were we dealing with the physical injuries, but just as significant was the emotional trauma that each player experienced. Even those that were not in the van that was involved in the accident struggled tremendously with how to handle things. To witness teammates being killed or seriously injured created severe mental trauma. Any of us who were not injured continued to question why we had been spared. The college provided psychological counseling for all those who wanted it, but it seemed most of us drew our solace from each other.

The team ultimately decided that they wanted to continue playing. We all needed something to try to take our minds off what had happened and we all needed a reason to stay together. If I could not continue coaching in the future, I would at least need a way to coach through the season. There is no way that I could abandon my team in this crisis. It would have been hypocritical to give up in the face of adversity after spending most of my coaching life preaching that you cannot give up. No matter how much the odds are stacked against you, you have to be willing to fight to win. The mountain that I was asked to climb came sooner than I thought.

I think now that too many coaches dismiss the impact of the example they set for their players. The easy way out is to say, "Do as

I say, not as I do." I have always been a believer in "do as I do." If I tell my players not to drink, then I will not drink. If I tell my players to stay in shape, then I will also take good care of my own body. If I tell my players not to curse, then I will not curse. If I tell my players not to cheat, then I will not cheat. If I tell my players to get to bed early and get their rest the night before a big game, then I will also turn in early the night before a game. No matter how trivial the issue, what you do as a coach speaks so loudly that your players cannot hear what you are saying with your mouth.

I sometimes wondered if this effort was lost on my players. Did they recognize what I was trying to do in providing them an example that they could follow? Looking for evidence, I found a copy of a paper that my team captain had written for a class, communicating some of the things that were in her heart following the accident.

> *"It is not so much the things that happen to you that determine your destiny, but how you react to the things that happen to you." This is a quote read to me and seventeen other friends of mine. These seventeen others were basketball players performing under one very special lady, Donna Newberry. She is the most spiritually sound person I have ever met and probably ever will meet. Her most essential attribute, though, is her willingness to practice what she preaches, even after an event which has scarred her life forever.*

I now believe that players absorb much more than we give them credit for. They can see sincerity, and they can see hypocrisy. They know the difference between a dedicated coach and one who is trying to give the appearance of dedication, but in reality is not willing to give at the level that this job demands. You cannot win championships while pretending to be fully invested. Players are around us enough to recognize honesty and dedication, and they will expose any shortcuts that you try to take. Sadly, the way they usually expose our deficiencies is to imitate them. However, they will also reward our dedication and life investment with imitation, and if they imitate often enough, it will become their own life's pattern and be rewarded with success at a high level.

I have heard many coaches dismiss the need to be an example to their players by simply saying that a player does not expect the coach to follow team rules. The rules are for the players. Coaches are mature enough that they can make their own decisions. This mentality is nothing more than an excuse to enable us to ignore the rules that we are asking our players to follow.

By choosing to be in a fishbowl occupation like coaching, you are agreeing to put your life in the public eye. Although some players might be willing to abide by team rules even if the coach does not, it will be much easier for them to swallow the rules if they know the coach will also follow the rules. This kind of coach gets much more respect from their team, and any coach that gets more respect will also get more production. If players see your work ethic and high commitment, it will naturally follow that as much or more is expected from them. Coaching is not a spectator occupation. You must be willing to involve yourself and invest yourself in where you want your team to go.

After the accident, the more I examined my own philosophies of coaching, the more I knew that I would have to continue coaching. To do anything less than that would have violated every principle that I believed in.

It took more than my own determination and resolution to keep me going. When tragedy hits, you cannot put a value on what your friends can provide. Although I had countless friends who supported me through this crisis, none was more valuable than my coaching rival at Ohio Northern University (ONU), Gayle Lauth. Gayle and I had been opponents ever since I began coaching. She was both the head basketball and softball coach at ONU, so we had much in common. ONU also had an outstanding program, so it seemed like it was either us or them who was consistently winning the league titles or moving on to post-season play.

It goes beyond comprehension to think that Gayle left her team and drove to New Concord to spend several days with me shortly after the accident. I had refused the offer of my family members to stay with me. It is not that I did not appreciate their offer, but I just felt that they could not relate to what had just happened and it would be hard for them to understand my perspective. I needed someone there who knew what it was like to get behind the wheel of a van with your team depending on you. I needed someone who understood the bond that is formed between players and coach. For Gayle to leave her own team just as they were opening their season to be of assistance to me is friendship without measure. She may have been my arch rival, but to this day I attribute her ability to get me through the darkest days of my coaching career as what kept me in the profession.

The other component that got me through was my spirituality and relationship with God. I was raised in a "church-going" family. Both of my grandfathers were preachers in the Church of Christ. My brother is still a preacher today. I spent my whole life attending church on Sunday mornings and Sunday evenings, as well as Bible study on Wednesday evenings. Going to church is not what makes one spiritual, but it definitely lays the foundation for faith. There came a time after I left home and began my own career that I had to explore my spirituality and decide what part it would play in my life. Fortunately, I assigned my walk with God as my highest priority. It would remain the foremost thing in my life, and other things would have to come second.

Were it not for the comfort that I derived through prayer and the strength that I gained by studying the Bible, praying, and seeking God's guidance, I doubt that I would have made it through this ordeal. My church family was extremely supportive. I found an internal peace that I probably would never have found with a lesser faith. It concerns me today that so few players have a spiritual connection. I am not sure if they will be able to handle things when they meet their first big test. God does not intend for us to go through difficult times alone, but there are far too many who establish no relationship with God in their lives, then wonder where He is when they most need Him.

Chapter 6

The Aftermath

You gain strength, courage, and confidence by everyday experience in which you really stop to look fear in the face. You must do the thing you think you cannot do.

Eleanor Roosevelt

In hindsight, I will be forever grateful that we decided that we should continue our basketball season after the accident, and that I decided that I should continue coaching. We decided to reactivate our season over Thanksgiving break. We normally hosted what was called the Muskingum Invitational Tournament on that weekend. We wanted to honor our fallen players by renaming the tournament the Muskingum Memorial Tournament, and we would let it serve as an annual reminder of the tragedy we suffered and the triumph of beginning play again.

The first practice that we held following the accident had a surreal feeling to it. The gym seemed eerily empty as we were missing seven teammates. I felt very weak physically. Some of that probably stemmed from lack of sleep and lack of appetite. I do not think that I acknowledged how physically worn out I was until I tried to get through that practice. The players were eager to do everything perfectly and were determined that they were going to do nothing that would upset me. I intentionally chose a series of drills that they typically performed well and tried to minimize the chances of a ragged or frustrating practice. Rarely have I seen them work so hard. It was one of those things that provided both relief and gratification when it ended, and it was a necessary step in moving forward in the healing process.

It would have been much easier to move forward if we had had the assurance from the college that the basketball team would never ever have to ride in a van again. All of us had a real "emotional hang up" when we even thought about having to ride in a van. I told the institution in a very adamant way that I would never again drive one of my teams anywhere. The simple task of getting behind the wheel of my own vehicle to drive myself to the grocery store seemed terrifying. To think of ever having the responsibility to drive a team again was overwhelming. Until you have had the responsibility of driving a van load of players, especially if it is late at night after a loss when you are both physically and emotionally exhausted, it is hard to empathize with the terror that the thought of ever driving my team again put in my heart.

I fully expected the college to immediately assure me that the basketball team would be on a bus from this point forward. I also thought that since I was the coach of softball, that the softball team would have that same option. I had numerous players who played both of those sports, so it seemed logical that the college would have the sensitivity and understanding to accommodate the physical and emotional needs of these teams. I quickly found out that it would not be this easy.

The first promise I was given was that the basketball team would be kept on a bus for their travels for the rest of the season. After much deliberation, it was agreed that the softball team would be kept on a bus for their upcoming season as well. There were five players who played both sports, and I, of course coached both, so at least this was a temporary solution to get us through the year. The larger issue was going to be much more difficult to resolve. At a time when I needed to find a way to get my mind off the accident, this new transportation issue gave me no reprieve.

I tried to be proactive by establishing a Memorial Fund on behalf of our fallen players. The parents of these players agreed to allow any money that was raised to be used to offset some of the transportation expenses that the college would not fund. Although this was a temporary and short term solution, it at least provided a little escrow to get us through an emergency. However, it was painfully obvious that this would be an inadequate way to solve the problem. The shortest bus trips cost at least $500.00, so it would not take long to drain any funds that we collected.

After many meetings with the administration and countless letters from the parents of the families that were involved in the accident, the college eventually agreed to keep the women's basketball
and softball teams on a bus until all the players that were involved in
the accident had graduated. Again, this was an unsatisfactory solution, but at least it bought some time to continue to fight for the busing of teams, busing that I thought would have been automatic after
the accident.

In addition to the busing issues, I had been indicted to appear
before a grand jury in Wheeling to see if the prosecuting attorney for
the county would be pressing charges against me. I had planned a
Christmas party for the team that we held in the lobby of one of the
dorms while we were there over the vacation period. The party was a
conscious effort to have the team together in an environment that was
not basketball-related, and allow us to enjoy each other's company
with hopefully no thought of basketball or the accident interfering
with our evening. It was a traumatic event when we were interrupted
during the party by a uniformed officer who pounded on the main
entrance to the dorm, and each player who witnessed the accident
was subpoenaed to appear in court. The idea of the party seemed to
have been working, but the timing for this could not have been worse.
It was extremely difficult to deal with the problems and emotional
grief of the accident, but to add all the legal concerns to that was
nearly unbearable.

I was completely out of my element when several meetings were
arranged for me with the college lawyer. These meetings forced me
once again to dredge up every detail that I could recall from the accident. This was a painful exercise for me, and I knew that the players
would have to deal with similar emotions when they were called in to
testify. I prayed that there would be some way that they could forego
this experience, but the prayer was not granted.

The court date was in February. To prepare for a game that week
was very difficult as we all had other things on our mind. It was yet
another lesson in mental discipline as we had to compartmentalize
the accident and all the things that were spinning off it in order to
function well enough to get through our day-to-day activities. The

accident was on my mind all day as it was the last thing that I thought of before I went to sleep at night, and the first thing that came into my head when I awoke each morning.

I continued to agonize for the families who had lost their children and for the families who were still nursing their injured children back to health. My thoughts would continually bounce from one player to the next as I worried about how they were dealing with things and how they were progressing both physically and emotionally. If I could have dismissed the legal issues and the transportation issues, it would no doubt have expedited the recovery process, but I was forced to deal with the reality of these two problems on a daily basis.

Rumors had spread that the prosecuting attorney for this county had publicly stated that he intended to find fault with every fatal accident in his county. He wanted someone to "pay the price" anytime someone lost his or her life. I do not know if this was true, but the thought of it definitely made me more apprehensive as the court date approached.

The court room smelled of old wood and furniture polish. The floor creaked as people moved about and spoke in hushed tones. For the most part, I was simply asked to tell the story of what happened and there were a few questions thrown in to clarify things that might have been confusing. There were two benches in the hallway that were full of players waiting to be called in as witnesses. It was an uncomfortable afternoon filled with apprehension and tension.

Each player was called in individually, and to this day I don't know what was said or what was not said by any of the players. I am guessing that it was much like my encounter in which I was just asked to recall what happened. It was agonizing to simply wait and feel that what my future held could be determined by someone else as each player entered and exited the court room.

When I received the word that no criminal charges were going to be filed, it was a huge relief. Although I was warned that a civil suit could be filed anytime during the next several years, I was at least relieved of the fear that I would be convicted on criminal charges. This part of my fears could now be dismissed. The college lawyer had prepared me for the worst possible news, which included serving as much as four years in prison for involuntary manslaughter charges. To receive good news was a lift to my spirits. I think my team was happier for me than I was for myself. If prison time could have changed the outcome or brought back the lives of my players, I would have gladly accepted the punishment. However, I think the best way I could serve my team at this time was to be accessible to them and to be part of their support system.

The battle now shifted back to the transportation issues. The ideal solution would be to put all of Muskingum's teams on buses when they traveled so that all athletes would feel equally safe on a road trip. The parents of my players really stepped up to the plate. They did a tremendous amount of research with the help of the National Safety Council involving statistics and the probability of a van vs. a bus accident. They surveyed other OAC institutions as well as other Division III institutions across the state and nation to see what their transportation policies were. They were relentless with writing letters and fighting for a cause that was deeply important to them. I was fighting the battle as well through regular meetings with the administration, but for the most part, the parents were taking the lead role. They were worried that I could lose my job if I pushed too hard, and they insisted on fighting on the front lines and taking the bullets for me. We were passionate about the cause, and we were determined to get a positive result. Muskingum's administration was not anti-busing. It just was discouraging to see how slowly things moved and to see other institutions moving faster as a result of our accident than we ourselves were moving.

There were many questions to be answered, and all of the other OAC schools began to try to answer them on their own campus as well. If nothing else, the accident raised the awareness for the potential of a van accident and involved each institution in a life-and-death soul-searching expedition. Where would the money come from to bus the teams? Should you only bus long distance trips, and drive the shorter trips? (Our accident occurred less than seventy-five miles from campus.) If you used a bus, should you charter the bus, or would it be more economical to buy a bus? Should coaches or anyone who drove a van be required to have special training before driving? Should students be allowed to drive a van? Should only winter sports where snow and ice is a factor be bused, but fall and spring sports drive? Should there be a certain number of people in the travel party before you take a bus? Should small teams, such as golf, be required to go by van? If the weather is questionable, how should the decision be made about whether a team should even leave campus and travel on roads that might become dangerous? Should all athletes be required to fasten their seat belts? (The accident occurred at a time before this was law.) Could a coach refuse to take a bus and go by van in order to save money in their budget and use it for other purposes?

If there were an unlimited supply of money, the answer would have been easy. The answer would be that of course we will bus every team so that we have a safe vehicle and professional drivers transporting every team. However, there was not an unlimited supply of money, and there were far more questions than there were answers. It was frustrating to see other institutions in the OAC implement travel policies and establish procedures that were very bus friendly, while Muskingum was slow to respond with anything but a temporary fix. It was gratifying to know that our accident helped other institutions install safer travel policies, but it was also frustrating that our own institution procrastinated when it came to making a decision about what to do.

At the time that I went through the Title IX battle on our campus, I thought that I would never have to go through anything again that would be as frustrating and difficult. However, fighting the battle about our transportation issues proved to be more overwhelming than what I experienced with Title IX. Perhaps it was the passion that was involved and the personal emotional demons that also had to be fought that made it so difficult, but it remains the one thing that disappointed me more than anything else during my career at Muskingum. It took far too long and required far too much pushing from me and from parents for the issue to be resolved in a satisfactory manner.

It took several years for a transportation policy to finally evolve that seemed to address most of the concerns about safety. The ultimate solution of busing for every team in every sport, regardless of distance, time of year, and size of team will probably never be reached.

However, the transportation policy that took effect had an overall positive impact. It encompassed more than just our athletic teams. All groups that traveled off campus, whether the trip was for athletics, music, theatre, academics, or other purposes, would now fall under common guidelines that would try to make the trip as safe as possible. There was no way to insure safety, but at least the awareness level had been raised to minimize the likelihood of another accident.

When our season did resume we started off by winning our own Memorial Tournament. Our first game back we defeated Methodist College of Fayetteville, North Carolina, by a score of 90 - 56. I was extremely nervous as I prepared for the game. The nerves had nothing to do with the apprehension of winning or losing the game, but rather had more to do with whether I thought I could even make it through the game. The thought of being back in the public eye so soon after the accident was unnerving. I felt like everyone would be examining each move that I made with a microscope. I felt like they had come to see me and how I was doing more than they had come to see the game, and I do not enjoy being that kind of a center of attention.

I coached with an almost detached persona. It seemed like I was hovering above the court, watching someone else coach. I had a difficult time focusing. As I looked down the bench, I would notice the absent players, and whatever concentration I had mustered would be snatched from me in an instant. The half-time speech rambled a bit, but the players did not seem to mind. They were simply relieved to be playing and to be together again as a team. Fortunately, it was a game that we had comfortably in hand, so what I did as a coach mattered very little and the outcome was never really in doubt. It was a relief to get the inaugural game behind us, hoping that each time we played it would be a little easier to deal instinctually with the emotions and feelings that seemed to surface most noticeably during competition.

We won the championship game against Adrian College of Adrian, Michigan, by an 85 - 75 score. Although it was nice to win the tournament, I do not think the scores mattered too much to anyone. The important thing was that we were playing, that we remained a team, and that we had the strength to continue to do what we all loved to do. Playing basketball was the greatest therapy we could have had to help us through these times. We finished this abbreviated season with a 14 - 8 record.

Coaching through that season took all the strength that I could muster. Every time we boarded the bus for a road game, I prayed fervently that we would arrive safely at our destination. There were games when my emotions would overwhelm me at the most unexpected times. My players never needed to ask what was wrong. They knew, because they had also experienced those uncontrollable moments. It was a constant battle to focus on the present. It was far too easy to let your mind drift to thoughts that were not healthy or productive. In the unity of that team, I found strength. It was sad when the season ended, as we temporarily lost the substance that kept us congealed as one spirit.

For at least a year, the accident was the last thing that I thought of before I went to sleep, and the first thing that I thought of when I woke up. I had always prided myself on mental discipline and the ability to stay focused on the present. However, it was not unusual to find my office tasks interrupted by flashbacks and tears. Even though I had been told that time heals all wounds, it was apparent that this healing process would be slow and painful. With God's help, I made it through, but I always lived on the fragile edge of what might trigger pieces of that memory.

The next year, 1990, did not necessarily bring high expectations for the team. Several key players had been lost as a result of the accident. For some, their careers were ended due to physical injuries that could not be overcome. For others, the physical injuries healed to the point where they could play, but the emotional scarring kept them from continuing as players. I was not sure how I would bounce back as a coach. I had made it through the previous year with multitudes of supporters, much prayer, and the adrenaline brought about by a highly emotional and stressful situation. I was not sure what things would be like a year removed from the crisis.

As the next season got underway, we were having surprising success. In spite of losing key players in the accident, and in spite of a difficult recruiting year, we were a very competitive team every time we took the floor. If it is possible that the whole can be greater than the sum of its parts, then such was true with us. When you analyzed each player and her capabilities, there were many times that we did not compare favorably to an opponent. Yet when you put us on the floor as a team, we had such chemistry and determination that good things were happening.

Our second regular season loss at Capital University in Bexley, Ohio, by a score of 69 - 72, seemed to spark a fire that we refused to let die. We won the next eight straight games to take us to the championship game of the OAC. At that time, Capital was ranked #1 in the nation, but we defeated them on their home floor 86 - 84 in overtime to win the tournament. Muskingum was ranked fourth in the nation at this time, so it was quite an unpleasant surprise to learn that the NCAA had matched us up with Capital the following weekend in a first-round game in an NCAA regional.

The NCAA first-round game was also held on Capital's home floor. To beat them once had taken a great effort. To beat them twice, especially on their floor, would be very challenging. However, we managed another win against them the next weekend in the regional tournament, defeating them 76 - 74. It was a beautifully played game that came down to the last second. Capital missed a shot, and we rebounded the miss, brought the ball up to half court, and called a time out with twenty seconds to go. After inbounding the ball and taking ten seconds off the clock, we ran a final play. The play that we called would have had Laurie Deal coming off a screen to shoot, but they had her well defended and she wisely dished the ball off. The ball swished through the basket as Toni Moone hit a baseline jumper just as the buzzer sounded (Figure 4).

There was a crazy celebration that followed, but by the time we left the locker room, our focus had already turned to the game we would play the next week. We were fortunate enough to get to host the Atlantic Sectionals the following weekend. Although I feared a letdown on the first night of the tournament, we played well and

Figure 4. The basketball team erupts off the bench as Muskingum beats Capital University at the buzzer in the first round of the 1991 NCAA regional tournament.

managed a 67 - 57 sectional win over Hartwick College of Oneonta, New York. In that game we had a very balanced attack with four different players reaching double figures.

That win allowed us to play the next night in the Atlantic Sectional final game. The winner of this game would join three other teams the following week with an opportunity to play for the national championship. Two times previous to this season we had made it to the national quarter-finals, only one win away from the Final Four. On both occasions we had fallen short in the final minute of the game. This time we were not to be denied.

Our matchup was against St. John Fisher College from Rochester, New York. They were a highly touted team, and the game would definitely be a challenge. When we came running onto the floor of our Recreation Center, it was overwhelming to see the size of the crowd and hear the noise level. We had to rally from a 38 - 33 deficit at halftime to defeat St. John Fisher 81 - 70. Our point guard and off guard came through for us as Michelle Harkness scored 25 points and

Kate Titus chipped in 18 points and recorded 11 assists. We were headed towards the opportunity to win a national championship.

The celebration as we cut the nets down was euphoric. No one wanted to leave the gym. All of those fans who had gone through such agony with us the year before, now just wanted to stay and drink in the joy of the moment. The only down side to the game was that Laurie Deal, our leading scorer and a survivor of the accident who had worked hard to recover from injuries so that she could play this year, had torn her ACL in the waning minutes of the game, and she would be unable to play at the national tournament. We had managed to climb the mountain and now only had a few more steps to go to be able to say that we had reached the summit.

The national tournament was being held on the campus of University of St. Thomas in Saint Paul, Minnesota. At the Division III level, teams usually do not fly to their games, so it was exciting to know that the NCAA would fly the team to Minnesota, and it was a relief to know that we were not looking at a long bus trip to continue our post-season run. There was much excitement as the team prepared to leave. We had already exceeded expectations, and I am not sure if anyone really expected us to continue to win. Regardless, there were a surprising number of fans who made the trip to Minnesota to support the Muskies.

Our opponent the first night was Washington University from Saint Louis, Missouri. All the scouting and film breakdown led us to believe that it would be a very difficult matchup for us. They brought a 25 - 4 record into the tournament. The calling card of this team was its fearsome full court pressure. They forced an average of more than twenty-one turnovers per game, and most of the turnovers came courtesy of the team's relentless pressure. If opponents could get the ball past half court, they picked you up with a rugged player-to-player defense. They allowed opponents only fifty-three points per game, which put them among the best in the country. Washington was big and experienced with great depth, and it would take our best effort to stay in the game with them.

Just before leaving the locker room to come onto the floor for warm-up, I had another of those moments where the flood of emotions was impossible to control. It seemed that the circumstances had triggered all of those memories from the previous year to again come to the surface and remind me of all that had happened. I am sure that the fans wondered where I was as I sent the team out to the floor and I stayed behind until I collected myself.

Regardless, it was one of those nights where we played with great precision and intensity. I do not know if we could have played much better. It seemed that the crowd and the atmosphere did not distract our players from the task at hand, and the Muskies were determined that nothing would deter them from reaching the national final game. By halftime we had a 36 - 26 lead. We committed only 11 turnovers and forced them into 29 miscues. Michelle Snow, who had replaced the injured Laurie Deal in the starting lineup, led all scorers with 23 points. We won comfortably by a score of 85 - 60. We had played the first game of the evening, so as soon as our players were showered and dressed, we settled into the stands to scout our opposition for the next night.

Being on the doorstep of winning a national championship is a long way from where we were the previous year, dealing with the aftermath of the accident and wondering whether we could muster the strength to coach or play our next game. When there is only one day to get ready to play again, the preparation is condensed and focused. As we went through our walk-through practice and shoot-around that next morning, it was hard to comprehend that we could conceivably be national champions by the end of the day. We would be playing St. Thomas, as they had won their game the previous night, which means we would have to deal with them on their home floor.

St. Thomas would be a formidable opponent and were currently ranked second in the nation. They had won 27 of their last 28 games, including their last 11 in a row. They had piled up 25 straight wins at home, with their last home loss coming back in 1989 with a season opening loss to Mankato. They had made the NCAA tournament for five consecutive years, so all of their players were tournament tested. They were equally capable at multiple things. They could run the fast break or patiently set up the offense. On defense, they stuck mainly to player-to-player but would occasionally mix in some zone.

Although they had a lot of capable scorers, their main player was Laurie Trow, an intimidating six-footer. She averaged 22 points a game, shooting 62 percent from the floor, and she grabbed ten rebounds a game to add to her credibility. They started a second inside player, Suzy Bouquet, who was also a six-footer and who led them in blocked shots. They featured a 5' 11" guard in Tonja England, who led them in assists. Their size advantage was formidable.

Our run for the championship came to an end that night. The crowd was large and heavily in favor of St. Thomas. The All-American center for St. Thomas, Trow, was more than we could handle as we had no answer for her size and overall athleticism. She ended the night with 33 points, hitting on an incredible 14 for 16 shots from the field. We were forced to rely on our perimeter shooters, and it was a cold night, as we barely managed to shoot 30 percent. We had three players in double figures and we fought valiantly, but it was a night where our shots would not fall and we were a bit overmatched. By halftime we were down by 10 points, with the final score being 73 - 55. The sound of the final buzzer finished things off just short of the perfect ending that we were seeking.

There had been a groundswell of support for the Muskies all season. The college and surrounding community recognized the strength that it took to make it through that season, regardless of the amazing success that we had. They recognized that no opponent could pose for the Muskies problems that were bigger than what the team had already encountered and risen above. The ending was bittersweet, but there was no one who had regrets about the effort, the mental and physical discipline, or the passion that was displayed.

The finality of the season hit the players as the awards were handed out. We had shown more resilience than anyone could fairly expect, and we were proud of the strength that we had shown in our ability to fight back after such tragedy the year before. The players were proud of the way they had represented their fallen teammates, and they knew that they had given everything they had to give that season.

It was nearly 2 o'clock Sunday morning by the time we got back to the hotel. I, along with three members of the team, caught a flight later that morning that took us straight to Orlando, Florida. Kate Titus, Jen Yontz, and Andrea Weininger were all members of the softball team as well and made up the bulk of my infield as our catcher, third baseman, and shortstop. The rest of the softball team had ridden the bus to Orlando with the baseball team, so they were there waiting for us to join them. We opened the season that afternoon.

Needless to say, I don't know what the trip home was like for the basketball team, and I did not get to enjoy the reception that was waiting for them when they arrived in New Concord. Those of us who were also involved in softball would not get to join in the celebration back on campus, but I am sure it was memorable for the rest of the team. One of the keys to success in Division III is the ability to multi-task and move quickly from one mode to another. The four of us who were obligated to both basketball and softball were exhausted both physically and emotionally, but it was time to move on and engage in another venture.

A few weeks later, it was announced that I had been named the NCAA III National Coach of the Year. Even though we had not won the championship, people from across the country recognized what we had done as a team by naming me the recipient of this award. I gave the following short but emotional acceptance speech when they flew me to New Orleans to receive the award.

> *It is indeed an honor to be standing in front of, and sitting with, so many prestigious coaches. I want to thank the WBCA and Converse for providing me the opportunity to be here and for making this kind of award possible.*
>
> *Last year if someone would have said to me that my team would be playing for a national championship and that I would be named the National Coach of the Year, I probably would have told them that they were crazy. If there is such a thing as a hell for basketball coaches, then last year I was in it. I didn't think there was anything that would ever make me want to give up coaching because I really do love it, but last year I did come very close. A tractor trailer on an icy patch of interstate slammed into the team van that I was driving, and I have been trying hard for the past year to just forget the*

things that happened on that day. I watched two of my players die by the side of the road. We frantically scrambled to keep four other players alive until we could get them to the hospital. In all, we lost six players to death or injury in that accident.

Sometimes those trite expressions that you use with your players come back to haunt you . . . things like not giving up or not quitting or sticking it out through tough times. Those were some of the things that my players threw back in my face when I was about ready to hang it up last year. I am very appreciative to them for that, because were it not for the example that they set for me and the encouragement that they gave me, I probably would not be here today. I was about ready to end my career at that point. They are not here to hear it, but I appreciate the wisdom that they displayed last year.

I guess what I need to say the most is that basketball is very important to all of us who are here today, but I think there are other things that put the importance of basketball into its proper perspective. Really in the whole scheme of things, basketball is somewhat insignificant.

I think sometimes the Lord finds ways of striking balance in our lives, and you don't always understand them. Maybe the success that my team has enjoyed this year and the success that I have enjoyed this year has in some way tried to strike a balance between last year and this year.

If there is a service that I could provide today, it is probably to simply remind you to enjoy your players while you have them and enjoy each other. Enjoy your career. Wins and losses are important but they by far are not the most important things in life.

It is with a great deal of appreciation and humility that I accept this award. Thank you very much.

Reflecting back on this accomplishment in my life makes me think about the challenges of coaching and the temptation to quit. I hate it when I see good coaches drop out of the coaching profession. Because I was so distraught after the accident, I nearly became a victim of that process. However, it saddens me even more when I see an athlete quit a sport partway through her career, even though she has eligibility remaining. Almost without exception, when a player comes into my office to quit, she gives me one of two reasons. She either says that she wants more time to focus on academics, or she says the sport is just not fun anymore. I believe that athletes recognize that these are two "reasons" that a coach cannot really question, but I often doubt if these are really behind why most athletes quit. When I saw some of my player's careers cut short because of their injuries in this accident, and I reflect on players who throw the rest of their careers away for various reasons, it is difficult to accept the decision that players make who arbitrarily discard their remaining playing years.

There were a couple of young players from our national-runner-up team who came into my office after the season ended to tell me that they would not continue playing the next year. As I thought about the players who had either lost their lives or who had been so severely injured that they could not continue playing, I had a hard time resolving the opportunity that these quitting players were turning down. Compared to what any one of the players who had been deprived of that opportunity would have traded for another chance to play, it just seemed incomprehensible that a player would willingly give up what others yearned to have. Although I am certain that there are occasionally legitimate reasons for dropping out of a sport, I just hate to see players give up when they are discouraged, disappointed, or short of their goals. As a coach, I always struggle with whether I should "talk them into staying" or just let them walk. If there were some way to communicate to players how much it hurts to see them throw away an opportunity, perhaps they would be more reluctant to walk away from a sport they love.

Maybe I am overestimating when I think that players get as much from playing sports as I do from coaching sports. However, in most cases, I think they get more. No other challenge that players undertake can replicate the competition that they experience in sport. Sport requires a true balance of physical, emotional, intellectual, and social skills that is unmatched by any other type of competition. In a team sport, not only do you have to master these areas yourself, but your teammates have to achieve that mastery as well to reach excellence as a team. There are many aspiring athletes who have the needed mentality to excel, but who simply have not been blessed with the physical tools to excel. There are others who have the physical tools, but lack the work ethic and commitment needed. Sadly, there are some who are blessed with all the necessary ingredients, but they choose to quit or end their careers early. I will probably never understand the mentality of those who choose to throw their opportunities away, and I applaud all those who remain for the full duration of their playing career. I can only attempt to teach young athletes the lessons that I believe sport has to offer, and hope that I provide them with the type of experience that will encourage them to remain engaged in the sport and not give it up prematurely.

Chapter 7

Life with the Indians

Solitude is painful when you are young, but delightful when one is more mature.

Albert Einstein

In the 1980s, I made my girlhood dream come true when I completed work on a log-cabin home, a cozy place on a gentle, wooded hillside outside New Concord. I had saved money for years, scouted out and invested in the land, drew up all the floor plans, and served as my own general contractor during a summer of work, overseeing the process of putting things in place inside the walls of White Pine that I had purchased from an Amish timber company in Sugar Creek, Ohio. When I moved in I had almost nothing, just two lawn chairs in my living room, but I loved nothing more than sitting on my deck with my dog, a Boxer named Diamond, who had been a gift from a basketball player. Diamond and I listened for the owls, deer, and turkey in the surrounding forest. Once, even a bear would come to visit at my back door.

My love of nature was connected to my desire, each summer, to try to make a trip somewhere or undertake some type of project that would help to expand my horizons. It did not matter to me if the trip was not directly connected to softball or basketball. I simply took advantage of some of my time off in the summer to attempt to broaden my understanding of the world and to gain insight into people that I might not otherwise get to know. There is not room in this book to elaborate on all of those trips, but there were some that were more meaningful to me than others.

In the fall of 1991 I read an article in *Outside* magazine that introduced me to a North American Indian tribe. The Koyukon Indians, a part of the larger Athabascan language group, are perhaps one

Figure 5. Coach Newberry's cabin in the woods, on five acres just outside of New Concord.

of the most primitive tribes left in North America. This tribe lived in Huslia, Alaska, where the Koyukuk River flows into the Yukon River. The name of the tribe came from merging the names of these two rivers. For the most part, they still lived off the land and depended on animals for both clothing and food when I visited with them. The primary concessions that they had made to civilization was that they now used a rifle for hunting instead of a spear or bow and arrow, they used a chain saw to cut their wood instead of an axe, they used motors for their boats instead of paddling canoes, and some of them had chosen to use "iron dogs" (snowmobiles) instead of dog sleds. Other than that, many of their ways and material goods remained unchanged from years ago.

The *Outside* article described how the Koyukons are best known for their knowledge of hunting, trapping, fishing, and tracking of animals. The information they have stored in their heads could fill volumes of books about animal habitat and habits. In addition, they are experts on plants and the patterns of nature. The possibility of accessing their tremendous knowledge about plants, animals, and nature intrigued me.

The article said that the Koyukons had decided to open their tribe to five "white people" for two weeks over the summer. They felt that they wanted to expose their tribe to what they called "the lower 48." The article said that if you were interested you could write a letter to the designated address, and the tribe would notify you if you had been chosen to be one of the five.

I was now reaching that mid-life stage of life, as the previous November I had turned forty years old, and I was continually evaluating the worth of my life. Could I be doing something more, should I be doing something different, and what was the meaning and contribution that my life held in the bigger scope of things? My summer excursions seemed to be a salve that soothed my uncertainties on an annual basis, and I looked forward to the escape they provided and the wisdom that they generally imparted to get me through another year and confirm that I was doing what I should be doing.

I had not yet decided where I would go or what I would do for the following summer, but I was intrigued with the thought of a trip like this. Sometimes the best opportunities present themselves when you are least expecting them, and what had started out as an innocent reading of an interesting magazine article was beginning to transform itself into an idea for a summer experience. The key to providing experiential learning opportunities is to keep one's mind open to possibilities that initially may appear intimidating, unrealistic, or too far out of your comfort zone.

There were many reasons *not* to entertain a trip like this. To travel that far alone without really knowing what I might be getting into was reason enough to dismiss the thought as quickly as it entered my head. It was also a convenient excuse to think that I was probably not the type of person that they were looking for, so I would likely not be chosen anyway. Excuses provide comfortable pillows that absorb all those elements of fear, hesitation, and lack of confidence, and thus make it easier on the conscience to ignore opportunities. It takes a good deal of wisdom to differentiate between excuses and legitimate reasons that might necessitate a more conservative approach.

I began to imagine the trip in my mind's eye, including both good and bad images. I was teaching the camping and recreation course at Muskingum, and I had always loved the outdoors. I decided that it would be a wonderful adventure to get to experience a new culture and absorb everything that they could teach me, so I overcame my hesitation and wrote the letter. The article listed no criteria and said nothing about what kind of person they would choose to come to the village, but I figured that I had as good of a chance as anyone else.

I sent the letter off, and a couple of months went by without hearing anything. I had almost forgotten about it, when, unexpectedly, I received a letter that was postmarked Alaska. I was excited as I tore it open. The letter informed me that I was one of the five. It gave me the date that I was to be there and told me to be at a certain address in Fairbanks, where a bush pilot would be waiting for me to fly me to the village. The letter was typed but was not written like a normal business letter. Instead, it contained nothing more than this basic information, and it said that they looked forward to seeing me in August.

My excitement quickly turned to apprehension as I realized the magnitude of this type of trip. To do something like this with a travel partner would be a little unnerving, but to travel as a single woman to such an unknown destination was a little scary. I decided that the best thing to do was to write another letter and ask them about what to pack and, for the most part, what to expect. I did not realize at the time that many of the older Koyukons did not speak English, so I probably did well to receive the first letter. After two attempts at following up with them to get information, yet hearing nothing back, I decided that I would either have to make the trip on good faith and believe that the bush pilot would show up at the designated place and time, or I would have to cancel. I had always believed that usually the most worthwhile things that we do in our lives involve an element of risk and reward, so I decided to proceed with the trip and tried not to worry about all the negative possibilities that could occur.

I arrived in Fairbanks and checked into a motel room my first night there. The next morning, following a hearty breakfast at Denny's, I called a cab to take me to the designated address. I was extremely apprehensive as I approached the destination. My mind was entertaining all the worst-case scenarios ranging from the bush pilot not showing up, to an Indian tribe that would be less than friendly to a single white woman.

Thankfully, the bush pilot was there as scheduled. He introduced himself and said that we would basically be following the Alaska pipeline visually to take us to the village. He explained that the village of Huslia was located 350 miles from the nearest road. He flew into the village once a day, usually hauling cargo consisting of mail, alcohol, and goods needed to stock the small general store in Huslia. Seldom did he carry any passengers in the plane, but he cleaned off the second seat so that I would have room to sit. He equipped me with headphones so that we could communicate, and he explained that anytime he was not talking he would share his love of Irish music with me and play it over the headphones.

The two-seater seemed a little rickety, but the flight was delightful. To begin to get to see the rough beauty of the Alaskan wilderness by air was a treat, and as we followed the pipeline, my pilot had plenty of Alaskan history to share. As we approached the village, he made sure that I could hear the radio dispatcher who was talking to us from the ground. The "airport" was nothing more than a dirt landing strip that had been leveled off for the bush plane. It really did not look long enough for the plane to come to a stop, but the pilot assured me that it was adequate. As we were preparing to land, they radioed from the ground that we would need to continue circling because there was a bear on the runway and we could not land until they either shot it or chased it away. Obviously they chose to shoot it, as they had already begun the butchering process when we landed. If this was an indication of what the trip would be like, it was definitely going to be interesting.

When I disembarked from the plane I was immediately introduced to Huey and Eleanor. I did not know if these were their Indian names, but these were the names that I was instructed to use during my stay. They both spoke relatively good English, and they explained that they would be my guides while in Huslia. Huey would teach me the things that the men specialized in, and Eleanor would teach me the ways of the tribal women. I was surprised to see that they were dressed in blue jeans and flannel shirts. Although they still made much of their own clothing from the furs and skins of animals, they usually saved the handmade dresses and shirts for special ceremonies like weddings or funerals. In their day-to-day activities, it seemed that blue jeans were the standard choice. When I asked them where they got the jeans, they simply smiled and said "L. L. Bean."

I had interpreted the article about inviting five people to their village to mean that there would be five of us there together. When I asked about when the others would be arriving, Eleanor and Huey seemed quite surprised. They then explained that everyone was coming at a different time. It was a little unnerving for me to realize that I would be the only non-Indian there during my stay, but I had to quickly adjust my mentality to accept the situation as it was, even though it differed from what I had expected.

Eleanor said that the first task was to go to her house and gather food for my stay. She explained that we would not be staying right in the village, but rather we would be going about an hour up river to camp on the banks of the Yukon. Each day they planned to spend time teaching me the history and stories of their tribe, and we would also make daily trips in the boat to other rivers and locations that they thought would be of interest. Each night, they said, a group of Indians from the village would come up river to sit with us and also tell tribal stories. It sounded like a great plan to me.

I had only been in the village for a short while, but I quickly understood the need for wearing a head net. It looked more like something you might see people in Africa wearing to protect themselves from mosquitoes or other insects, but in this instance the problem was gnats. Apparently, I was there during the time of year that gnats were a major problem. Anytime you were outside, it was critical that you donned your head net, as this was the only way to prevent the gnats from flocking to your eyes, ears, mouth, or nose. As aggravating as it was to constantly wear the protection, it was still much better than trying to deal with the gnats. Figuring out a way to eat without getting a plate full or mouth full of gnats was difficult. You had to keep your plate covered with a cloth, then lift one corner just enough to allow your fork to get to the food. You then had to quickly move the bite of food to your mouth before the gnats descended while re-covering your plate with the cloth. This was annoying at first, but as you got used to it, it became second nature at meal time.

There were really only two ways to get relief from the gnats if you were outside. The first was to create a breeze. For example, if we were in the boat and moving at a certain speed, the breeze created by the moving boat kept the gnats at bay. It was a luxury to be in the boat and not have to do constant battle with the gnats. The other way was to burn multiple pans of punk at the campsite. Huey taught me to identify a fungus called "punk" that grew on cottonwood trees. They used burning punk much the same way that we would use citronella. We would have at least a half dozen punk fires burning at our camp-site throughout the day and not only did it repel gnats, but it also seemed to keep the bears away as well. It was a repugnant odor, but in choosing the smell or the gnats, the smell was definitely the better choice.

The quick visit to Eleanor's house was interesting. I learned that the Koyukons were somewhat nomadic and lived at four differ-ent places during the four seasons. The main house was where they lived during the summer. All of these homes were log homes that had been built with timber that was cut nearby, and Eleanor's house was the largest house in the village. In the fall, they moved to a temporary shelter at their hunting camps. In the winter, they moved on to their trapping camp, and in the spring they lived at their fishing camps through the run of the salmon.

In Eleanor's back yard there was a large pile of moose racks and caribou racks. There was a huge dump right outside the village that was to be used specifically for moose racks, but these racks had not yet been taken there. The fact that there were world-trophy-sized moose racks in their dump pile did not seem at all important to her. I was to learn a lot more about their hunting and fishing rules and beliefs later, but she gave me a quick explanation about the racks. There was some bitterness in her voice when she explained that the white man hunts their moose primarily for the trophy of the rack, but for the Koyukons, this is the only part of the animal that is not useful. They would never kill an animal without going through the necessary tribal rituals after the kill, and then once they killed it, they would make sure they used every part of it, even down to the hoof, the intestines, and the nose. To do anything less than that would curse their luck with the hunting gods.

She walked with me around the village for a short time, and the thing that was most noticeable to me was the overwhelming smell of fish. Every house had multiple rows of dried chum salmon (also called dog salmon) suspended above their dog pen, much like you would have several rows of clothesline to hold all of your laundry. In the spring when they were at their fishing camps and catching salmon, they would separate out the chum salmon and dry it so that it could be used for dog food. This would provide their dogs all the food that they needed throughout the long winter. Each day in the winter they would go out and cut down strips of the salmon for the dogs to devour. It was not unusual for a house to have ten to twelve dogs, and each house would have a dog sled sitting in the yard just waiting for the winter months. Some of the Koyukons put wheels on the sled runners in the summertime so that the owners could keep the dogs in shape for winter travel. A few fortunate villagers owned an "iron dog," but for the most part, these were not within the economical reach of the Koyukons.

As we walked, I saw lots of children and women, but I noticed that the only males that I saw were young boys or old men. I was curious why there did not seem to be any young adult males. Eleanor explained that about the only income the Koyukons have comes from fire fighting during the summer months. Each year, the government comes to the village to certify all interested young men as fire fighters, and they then go to California during the summer to fight the wildfires. The Koyukons have become known to be some of the best and fiercest fire fighters in the world. They are only allowed to work three weeks at a time, then are forced to take some time off. Usually, they can fit two three-week shifts into their summer, and they get paid $3,000 for every three weeks they work. This is about the only income the Koyukons have except for what they might earn mining for gold. Huey had missed the training last year and was not able to go, so he was a middle-aged man stuck in the village for the summer because he did not have the needed certification.

Eleanor walked to her storage shed behind her house and pulled a rusty saw blade from the wall. She asked me to go to the kitchen with her to help cut some of the meat that we would be taking on our trip. She had a large slab of both bear meat and moose meat stored, and she began chunking off generous portions of the meat for our upcoming meals. I had never eaten either of these meats before, but I was more concerned about the saw than I was about the meat. I am pretty good at adapting to situations, and clearly I was going to need to adapt to a number of things to get through the next couple of weeks.

We eventually got the boat packed with food supplies and other necessary items and prepared to go up the river to camp. The trip was incredible, as there were miles of uninterrupted beauty and it seemed like the only three humans that were alive on earth were me, Huey, and Eleanor. When we pulled into a small alcove of the Yukon, I could see that they had already set up most of the camp. There were four tents consisting of a large mess tent with all the food, an equally large tent for me, and two smaller tents for Eleanor and Huey.

It was already evening, but now that we had unloaded and settled into our tents, I asked Huey if there was a chance that I might see a moose tonight. He smiled and motioned me to go to the boat with him. We puttered up the river, and it was only a matter of minutes until I saw my first moose swimming across the river. It was hard to comprehend how massive these animals were when they were submerged, but once they ambled out on the banks, it was almost unbelievable to see their size. During this time of year they spent a lot of time in the water for the same reason that we were wearing head nets, needing a way to keep the gnats off their body. In all, we saw seven moose that first night in about an hour's time. Huey said we should head back to camp.

In early August, there were twenty-four hours of daylight. It got a little dusky at around 3:00 A.M. or so, but there was never a time I needed a flashlight. It did not take long to learn that the Koyukons paid little attention to time. When I awoke the first morning, it was about 7 o'clock. Somehow, I thought Indians would be early risers. However, when I peeked out my tent flap, neither Huey nor Eleanor was stirring. Wanting to be a good guest, I decided that I would stay in my tent until they made the first move. By the time 10:00 A.M. rolled around, I was getting pretty restless, so I quietly slipped out of my tent and made my way to the banks of the Yukon. I washed my hair and washed off the grime from the day before and felt pretty refreshed as I went back to my tent. I was restless in my tent and wanted to get started with the day, but it was about two hours before Huey and Eleanor started to move about.

They did not wear a watch and seemed to have no desire to know the time. It was a difficult adjustment to make for me to put away my watch and not worry about when it was time to eat, get up, or go to bed. We ate when we were hungry, slept when we were tired, and got up when we were rested. What a novel idea! For the most part, breakfast was usually around noon, lunch was around 5:00 P.M., and dinner was around midnight.

The concept of not being bound by time was an uncomfortable adjustment for me. I have always been obsessed with punctuality, whether it involves me or those who play for me. Generally speaking, if you are not early, then I consider you late. The lesson of punctuality is probably the first lesson that freshmen who play for me learn. It is so disrespectful to make people wait on you, because it seems to say that you feel that your time is more valuable than their time. It also represents carelessness, lack of attention to detail, and lack of planning. Time is a precious commodity that we need to handle with care and value each moment that we have. It is a waste of this commodity when we keep a group or an individual waiting because we did not pay enough attention to time.

Even though I feel strongly about this issue, it did not take me long to not only understand why they functioned that way, but to even enjoy and support the idea. By the third day, I had stopped looking at my watch, and by the fourth day I had taken my watch off and did not wear it again until the day that my flight was scheduled to leave. The Indians were so in tune with nature and the rhythm of nature that they trusted their instincts far more than they trusted any manmade instrument. They did not need a clock to tell them when to get up or when they were hungry. They listened to their bodies and did not disrupt the flow of the day until a need became urgent enough that it was time to do something about it. It is a liberating experience to allow oneself to be unconscious of time. I found it to be one of the most peaceful parts about this trip. Although I do not believe that this attitude would fit well into the academic and athletic environments where I normally function, it was a great experience to let go of the hands on the clock and instead grasp the hands of the rhythm of the day.

After we had our first breakfast, Huey turned his attention to making sure that I stayed safe throughout the trip. He asked me if I knew how to shoot a gun. When I said yes, he pulled out what I think he called a "mini fourteen semi-automatic weapon."

I quickly said, "But I don't think I know how to shoot that gun!"

He explained that he could fix it to shoot three consecutive rounds or ten consecutive rounds, and asked me which way I would rather have it. It seemed logical to me that ten was better than three, so I told him ten rounds. I started to get a feel for his sense of humor when he laughed heartily and said, "If you can't hit what you are aiming at in three rounds, it will probably be too late anyway."

He was kind enough to make sure that I knew how to use the gun properly, and we did a little target practice. He was not joking around, however, when he emphasized that the gun should be at my side anytime that I was not on the water in the boat. Even though most of the bears were in the mountains rather than by the river at this time of year, there was a good chance that we could bump into one. He said to take the gun with me when I went into the edge of a thicket for a bathroom break, and to keep it within reach when I slept at night. The closest I came to using the gun was when a porcupine startled me and I took aim until I realized what it was. Fortunately, we had no need to shoot anything during my stay.

I learned that the life of the Koyukon Indian represents living in harmony with nature and animals. They do not try to change or influence their environment; they simply want to live peacefully with it. Most of the stories that they told me about man's relationship with animals, the role that animals play on earth and in conjunction with man, and the origin of the very existence of man seemed like pagan teachings to a Christian's ear. It seemed that it was filled with superstitions and mythological characters. However, as they spoke, they believed what they were saying and would have taken great offense to my listening if they thought that I was either skeptical or patronizing.

They, in turn, asked me about my beliefs as a Christian. Although I am quite certain that they totally disagreed with much of what I was saying, they listened with much eagerness and attentiveness. They were also very curious about our societal practices, and in particular they were amazed at the role that I played as a female in a college setting. They had a hard time comprehending a female teaching males or a woman coaching an athletic team.

However, regardless of the divergence of beliefs, they had a unique ability to be completely accepting to what I said, even if they disagreed with it or misunderstood it. They never gave me the sense that made it seem like they were right and I was wrong, or that their ideas were good and mine were bad. They seemed to be able to move back and forth between Christian beliefs and pagan beliefs, between our society and the Indian society, and between very primitive living and more civilized living without appearing uncomfortable or out of place.

They seemed to believe that different belief systems could co-exist because each is independent of the others and is self-contained. Koyukons are not troubled by the idea that everyone should believe the same thing or that one belief can only be accepted at the expense of another. I termed them to be "biculturally fluent." There probably is not such a term, but it is the only way I found to describe what seemed to be an amazing ability and willingness to absorb another's beliefs or culture without judging it, rejecting it, or accepting it. To them, diversity was truly an asset.

I tried to have that same level of receptivity when I listened to their stories. I tried to keep an open mind, but I do not believe I absorbed and valued what was shared to the extent that they did. It would be a wonderful lesson in diversity for education if somehow we could take the openness that the Koyukons showed by nature and with no training, and incorporate it into our society. It would definitely make us a more tolerant and peaceful people.

The Koyukons showed great reverence to animals and believed that animals have a spirit, much as many of us believe that humans have a soul. One of the most talked about animals was the raven. The raven is a revered and spiritual bird. They did not seem to fear what the raven was saying to them as much as they feared the message of some of the other animals, but they were very in tune with watching and analyzing the raven. One of their stories of creation involves the raven taking the four corners of a sheet and unfolding it to reveal the north, south, east, and west of the earth.

When we were out in the boat and Huey spotted a raven flying, he would cut the engine to eliminate any noise and then gaze at the raven until it either flew out of sight or landed. He would then tell me what the raven had said to him. By looking at the flight patterns, the Indians get different messages as the bird swoops, glides, flies, and turns. After the raven had sent its message through flight, the Koyukons could go from happy to immediately distraught if the raven was bringing bad news or warnings of impending danger. It was not uncommon for Huey to change our destination and follow a raven in the boat if he wanted to know more about what the bird was saying.

At the very top of the list of animals that the Koyukons revered was the wolverine. Because this was a secretive and solitary animal, they feared its spirit and believed its message, although they seldom talked about the wolverine. Unless a wolverine was seen, there was no way that they could receive its message or interpret the signs that it might be sending. Unless an Indian happened to catch a wolverine on their trap line, there was not a reason for it to be brought into a discussion.

The bear, however, was a different story. They clearly held the bear in great reverence and were cognizant any time a bear was seen, heard, or hunted. It was second to the wolverine in spirituality but was discussed far more than any other animal. At the time of year that I was there, most of the bears were still in the mountains, as the berries were ripe there and the salmon were not running in the river. Regardless of that, it was not unusual to see a bear along the banks of the river, and as soon as we did, the Koyukons' mood became very somber.

The first bear we saw immediately caused Eleanor to turn her head and cover her eyes. Almost any type of female interaction with a bear, unless a woman is beyond the age of menopause, will curse an Indian's hunting luck. I was allowed to look at the bear along with Huey because I was not a member of their tribe, but any viewing by Eleanor would have brought us many problems. Huey explained to me that if I were confronted by a bear and did not have my gun, the quickest way to get rid of the bear would be to drop my pants and expose my private parts. He said that no bear would look at a young woman under these circumstances and that he had seen his grand-mother use this tactic several times to cause a bear to flee into the woods and no longer be a threat.

There were many strict rituals that a hunter had to follow when a bear was killed. If any one of the rituals was violated, it could curse the hunter's hunting luck for years, or, worse yet, it could curse their family and bring bad luck or even death. I should clarify that their bear hunts would not resemble what hunters would do who shoot down a bear with a gun. The best known method for hunting the bear was to wait until the bears hibernated, at which time their coats would be thick and they would have a good layer of fat that was built up for the winter. The Koyukons were adept at identifying bear dens (Huey gave me a couple lessons on how to find the dens) and would have several bear dens identified by the time the snows came. Once a den was located, the Koyukons would burrow into the den until they heard the bear breathing. They could estimate the age of the bear just by the breathing that they heard, and they also insisted that they could hear the heartbeat of the bear and used that to identify the age as well. The younger the bear, the more its heart would speed up as you slightly disturbed their sleep. The older bears tended to sleep right through a disturbance and it would not affect either their breathing or heart rate. It took a brave hunter to do this, but a spear would be thrust into the bear while it slept. When they were sure it was completely dead, they dragged it out by a rope with only men pulling the rope. To use a chain or get the assistance of an iron dog, no matter how heavy the bear was, would curse their hunting luck.

A bear had to be left for a designated time at the site of the kill before it could be skinned and eaten. The hunting gods required that a certain amount of time elapse between the kill and what you did with an animal following the kill. The first few bears that were killed each year required a "bear party" that was usually held at the site of a kill. To risk bringing it into the village would risk inadvertent interaction with women, and this would be a curse. The men would cook huge pots of bear meat. They were careful to cook the heads in one pot, as there were certain rituals that had to do just with the head and the brains. In another pot would be meat with lots of bear fat on it. The most prime parts of the bear were the paws and the nose, and you could usually find these roasting on a stick over the fire. Only the men and the boys were allowed to partake in these bear feasts.

The less desirable parts of the meat would be taken back to the village, where the women would be allowed to eat. The women past the age of menopause were allowed to eat some parts that the other women were not, but so as not to risk violating the rules of the hunting gods, the men would usually only bring into the village the meat that any of the women could eat to minimize the chances of making a mistake.

You will never find a bear rug on the floor in the village of Huslia. It could bring a major curse for a woman to step on or over a bear skin. If the bear had been dead long enough (usually over ten years), it would no longer matter, but again to avoid any potential problems, the Indians did not take a chance. If a bear skin was used for anything in the house, it might be used as a hanging partition in a doorway or in between rooms. In many cases the men would cut the hide up in small pieces and leave it for other animals to destroy, rather than take it back to the village and make a mistake with it.

There were so many beliefs and rituals associated with their hunting and trapping that I am not sure how they kept them all straight, but the teachings were handed down through each generation, and most of the Indians seemed to fully understand what was expected. Regardless of how cold it was, animals could not be brought inside as this would violate their spirit. Even if the animal were a pet, such as a dog, it must not be brought under a roof. On very rare occasions, when it was so bitter cold that the Indians felt that they had to take an animal inside to skin it, they could get by with it if they placed a bag over the dead animal's head so that the spirit of the animal could not see where it was.

Perhaps my favorite part of the trip was the day that Huey spent most of his time teaching me how to track animals. We identified many different types of animals by the prints that were left in sand by the river. We tracked a timber wolf for quite a while but never caught sight of it. We also tracked a bear for a distance until we lost the trail in the thicket. Anytime we were walking through brush or a thicket, Huey would make sure that we were rattling the brush with walking sticks or making adequate noise. One of the worst things that you can do is to surprise a bear or a moose. If they see you first, they will usually go the other way, but if you surprise them, there is no predicting what they might do.

Another attempt to track a bear led us to one of the hunting cabins belonging to one of Huey's friends. The bear we had tracked earlier in the day was a black bear. This bear, however, was a brown bear or grizzly. I definitely hoped that we would not catch up with it, as the Indians had already told me too many brown-bear stories. As it turns out, we only caught up with the aftermath of this grizzly. According to Huey, the bear likely detected the smell of bacon grease from inside the empty cabin, then broke through boarded up windows and literally tore the cabin to shreds. A bed and mattress were ripped apart, the cupboards were torn down and busted, and everything else had been overturned. We made the trip that evening all the way back to the village in order to inform Huey's friend that his cabin had been ransacked and virtually destroyed by a bear.

The solitude and peacefulness of the trip almost exceeds description. We would go all day down different rivers and never see another human. At night it would be so quiet that you could hear the call of a wolf from miles away, yet it would sound like it was nearby. The crack of a beaver's tail on the water would sound like a gun shot in the silence of the wilderness.

I value solitude and quiet above many things that others might find desirable. My log home sits on approximately five acres of ground, and I am content to sit in my porch swing and watch the sunset or to be at my house all day and never have a conversation with another person. The sound of silence is a sound that many people find intolerable and uncomfortable, but to me, the only way to get to your inner thoughts is to still the outer noise long enough to be able to hear what else is going on within you.

When I was younger, I spent a good deal of time playing the guitar and trying my hand at song writing. My Alaskan experience brought to mind some of the words of a song that I had written many years before.

> *Now my thoughts are the only thing that's making a noise.*
> *I know that's not a sound everybody enjoys.*
> *For solitude will cry out loud, one is company, two's a crowd*
> *Listen to the sound of being alone.*

> *Silence is the sound that I love best.*
> *I've learned to love it more than all of the rest.*
> *For silence is the only sound that won't drown out my thoughts I've found,*
> *Listen to the sound of being alone.*

As a coach, I have seen that, by contrast, most of my recent athletes are uncomfortable with solitude and being alone with their thoughts. If they are not constantly communicating with someone by texting, cell phone, e-mail, Facebook, or some other form of contact, it seems they almost start to go through withdrawal. Many young people have nearly lost the art of face-to-face communication. I have watched many of my recruits squirm in their chairs as they struggle to keep both eye contact and concentration for the duration of a visit with me. For an athlete to enjoy a conversation seems more unusual every year. They would rather text me than talk to me. The only thing that makes them more uncomfortable than being asked to communicate face-to-face is to ask them to be alone and cut off from all communication except listening to their own thoughts. Most of our college athletes have not yet learned how to be alone without being lonely.

When you juxtapose the perceived need for our younger generation to communicate constantly through technology with the desire of the older generation for peace and quiet and a slower, more personal style of communication, there is little wonder that these differences contribute to the generation gap. To successfully communicate with my athletes, I have to remain receptive to their pace of life and their constant tweeting, texting, and other modes of communicating that are simply not a part of my lifestyle. I must do it without judging or condemning, and in return I expect that they will reciprocate with openness towards my lifestyle that values solitude and the art of meaningful conversation.

It is an unfair assumption to believe that "your way" is right and "their way" is wrong. That thought process is probably the biggest wedge that is driven into the generation gap. Each of us is capable of learning from others in a diverse setting, whether that diversity is represented by age, or race, or social and economic status, or whatever. Diversity should be a source of growth and broadened understanding rather than a source of opinionated frustration. As we age, the experience and knowledge that we gain should provide a richer pool of information to share with our athletes than perhaps they can provide to us. However, there still is a need to learn from each other without compromising our principles. This is one of the key steps to gaining respect from an athlete.

I treasure the moments of solitude that I can steal from what is often a hectic lifestyle. With coaching, it seems like a work day never ends. Between recruiting, preparing for games, traveling and playing games, practicing and preparing practices, and dealing with your athletes one-on-one, there is very little time left over for yourself. A coach needs to learn how to accept this lifestyle without resenting the time that it consumes. Stealing the quiet moments when you can makes coaching seem calmer.

I am still working on the ability to keep my mind quiet. I make the most of opportunities to keep my surroundings quiet and peaceful, but the only true way to achieve the full peacefulness of solitude is to have the ability to quiet one's mind in addition to silencing one's surroundings. The noise of our thoughts can be more disconcerting than the noise of our environment. As I continue to mature, I have progressed in my ability to turn off this background noise created by my own head, but I still have a ways to go in this regard.

~

In my time with the Koyukons, I learned about many traditions that I thought were useful and unique ideas. When a funeral was held it called for a "potlatch." In many ways, a potlatch resembled our pot luck dinners. However, the least important part of the event was the preparation of food. Koyukons would spend many years preparing for the potlatch held for a loved one. On the day of the funeral, a good friend of the deceased would dress in the clothes of the deceased and make his way around the crowd who attended, telling each person how much he appreciated him and the impact that he had in his life. The spouse or closest of kin would also give a gift to those who attended. The gifts could be things such as moccasins, mukluks, gloves, or other handmade items. It took much effort and time to store up enough gifts for a potlatch, and many of the women in the village spent a large part of their adult life making gifts for the inevitable potlatch of their loved ones. A Koyukon funeral was truly a celebration of their life. It was a joyous time rather than a time of mourning, and those who attended the funeral felt enriched rather than saddened.

Eleanor spent the better part of one day in a sort of show-and-tell for me. She displayed a variety of items that she had made, ranging from cookware to clothing to jewelry. As she showed me each item, she explained in detail how she made it, the problems that she dealt with while making it, and the time that it took to make it. By the end of the day, she had certainly earned my respect by her knowledge and mastery of the various skills that she displayed in order to be able to hand-make a wide variety of items. She was particularly proud of a purse that she had made because she not only had fashioned the purse and all of its beadwork, but she also had shot the moose, skinned it, and tanned the hide that she used to make the purse. Although the women played somewhat of a subservient role in the tribal traditions, they were very strong and could certainly have survived on their own with no help from a man if they needed to do so.

My most memorable night of this trip was on the Monday before I was preparing to leave, and a boat full of Indians came to camp around midnight to tell me stories about their tribe. This in itself was not unusual, as they had done this same thing on several other occasions. I had found the Koyukons to be great storytellers. On those long cold winter nights when they were in their cycle of twenty-four hours of darkness, they became proficient at passing the time sharing stories, and many of them had become expert storytellers as a result. They could keep you spellbound for hours as they told tribal tales and stories of their ancestors.

On this night, however, Huey interrupted their storytelling with a request to tell the story of his great-grandmother, Anna Biffelt. Before he began telling the story, he prodded me in a kidding way to tell me that I would have met my match in his great-grandmother. After I heard the story, I agreed with him.

In the early 1900s, there were a number of white men who moved to Alaska to seek their fortune mining gold. A few of those men liked the environment and lifestyle and chose to stay there. One of these men was named Ned Regan.

Ned had built a cabin just a few miles from the cabin of Anna and Victor Biffelt. Anna and Victor were married, although marriage in Koyukon terms simply meant finding someone with whom you were compatible and living together. Anna and Victor had two small children, and for the most part they carved out their survival by hunting, trapping, and fishing.

Land boundaries were much like the marriages, in that they were not clearly defined but they were clearly understood. The territory that an Indian claimed for his own was precious because his area provided the space needed to hunt and fish, and therefore it was his ticket to survival. To violate the territory that belonged to another Indian was a serious violation.

Ned Regan was not fully respectful of the Indian ways. He did not consider it a major problem if he inadvertently wandered onto the land of Victor Biffelt during the course of a hunt. On more than one occasion, Ned and Victor had words about this issue, and the more often it occurred, the more heated the words became. On this day, it had been a very heated argument with both men threatening to do harm to the other.

That same evening, Victor and Anna were sitting at their table drinking tea, and both children were tucked safely in bed. A knock was heard on their cabin door which of course was very unusual with the closest neighbor being miles away. When Victor went to the door and opened it, there stood Ned Regan dressed in his warm parka with a ruffed hood pulled over his head. As the door opened, Ned pulled a shotgun out from underneath his parka, leveled it at the head of Victor, squeezed the trigger from less than eight feet away, then slowly turned and walked away in his snowshoes.

Anna was overcome with both shock and grief. Her husband's head had been nearly blown off, and he lay motionless in a pool of blood at the door of their cabin. Anna cleared her head and was stricken with fear. She reasoned that because she was the only witness to the murder, Ned might likely return to kill her and perhaps even her children since she was the only one who could connect him to the crime. It did not take her long to decide that she needed to take her children and get as far away from the cabin as she could. Victor had turned the sled dogs loose that night, and she knew that she would be unable to round them up. Her only alternative would be to pull the dogsled herself.

She loaded the dogsled with some supplies and food, then tucked both of her children underneath some furs and skins to keep them warm. Anna then grasped the dragline that would normally be for a dog and put it around her shoulder to begin the journey up the Hogatza River toward her father's house. Fortunately, the river was frozen at this time of year, but it took her five days of pulling the sled on the ice to reach her destination. This would be difficult for anyone, but Anna was a tiny woman, weighing slightly more than ninety pounds, and the fear, cold, and fatigue took their toll. She reached her father's house, faint from exhaustion and hunger.

She told her father about the murder, and it both saddened and angered him. He said, "It would satisfy me to kill him myself. But the white man's law says that we may no longer kill our enemies. Let us see, then, how they will deal with one of their own."

He sent his son, Hog River Johnny, to find Ed Monson, a white man who ran a trading post and whom most of the Indians trusted.

When Ed heard the story, he got the word to a U.S. marshal in Nome, and within a couple of months, Regan had been captured and arrested. After a time, two men were sent to fetch Anna so that she could be a witness at Regan's trial. Anna did not want to go because it would separate her from her babies, and she would be in Nome, a thousand miles away and in Eskimo country. However, she was told that Regan would go unpunished if she did not go to be a witness, so they took the last steamboat of the summer and arrived in Nome in September of 1904.

Nome was a bewildering and agonizing place for Anna. There were thousands of people here, and she was used to a small village. She did not understand the language and she felt completely lost. A white couple was paid to house her and take care of her. Although they treated her very well, all she could think about was returning home.

The trial was held in February of 1905. Regan denied everything. Anna did not speak well, and there was no one there to translate her language. Whether it was because of that, or whether a jury of white men would not take the word of an Indian, Ned Regan was freed of all charges. When this was explained to Anna, she was heartsick as she returned to where she had been staying.

She began gathering her few belongings and told her hosts that she was going home. They insisted that she at least stay until the spring thaw so that she could take a steamboat back home. There was no way that someone could walk that distance in the dead of winter, and in addition she would have to cross through Eskimo territory. When you travel by river, the trip to Nome is over a thousand miles. When you go cross country as the crow flies, the distance is about four hundred miles, but it is still nearly an impossible trip. The Eskimos were bitter enemies of the Indians, so even if she survived the harsh conditions, the Eskimos would kill her if they found her.

When they realized that they could not stop Anna from leaving, they gave her food and a note that explained who she was, that she was trying to return home, and asked for help from anyone she met on the trail. They wished her well as she headed out with no clear understanding of where she was going, except that she knew that she needed to head north. She believed that if she reached the Kobuk River, she would eventually recognize the territory and find her way home. She had travelled annually with her father to somewhere along the Kobuk when he was trading with Schilikuk, an Eskimo trader that he trusted.

Anna would travel from dawn until dark, then build a small fire and burrow into a snow bank to stay warm until morning. She would snare rabbits along the way, and occasionally she would come upon a prospector who would help point her in the right direction. There were a couple of roadhouses that she came upon where she could obtain food, and even though she offered them her gold coins, they would read her note and refuse payment.

In early spring, she reached a place called Candle, where a miner had heard of her plight and asked his wife to take her in. She stayed there for many days so that she could make herself some new boots, as her boots were totally worn out. It also allowed time for her frail and shriveled body to recover somewhat.

When she headed out again, the travel was even more difficult as the snow had started to melt. Her footing was now in mushy, loose snow instead of the firm footing of frozen snow. As the ice started to melt, she had some harrowing experiences of trying to cross a river or stream, or being caught in marshes that would have been easily passable if they had been frozen. As the sun became hotter, mosquitoes became a constant problem. There were many evenings where she lay down to sleep and would writhe in pain from the unripe berries that she had eaten during the day.

She travelled with the constant fear of wild animals. However, her greatest fear was the fear of being discovered by an Eskimo. She had no doubt that she would be killed on the spot if she was discovered. Her worst fears were realized one morning when she awoke and saw an Eskimo boy in a kayak not more than twenty feet away staring at her as she lay under a bush along the river bank. The Eskimo boy disappeared quickly, and Anna knew that he was headed back to his village to bring the news that an Indian was in their territory.

Anna did her best to find a way of escape as she moved as quickly as her strength and stamina would allow. The Eskimos saw her before she saw them, and when she realized the situation that she was in, she was too tired to run. She simply waited with sadness, knowing that her life would end without her being able to see her children again.

The young boy had brought his father. It was immense relief when she recognized the Eskimo to be Schilikuk, the fur trader friend of her father. Schilikuk brought her back to his village, and he and his wife took her in to nurse her back to health. As she grew stronger, she insisted that it was time for her to get back on her journey. Her Eskimo friends insisted that she wait until the next spring so that she could travel with them when they went to trade furs, and after that, they would see to it that she would make it home.

Anna was restless and often talked about her burning desire to be home and to be with her babies again. It was a useless argument to convince her to wait until the next spring, so they decided the next best thing would be to persuade Anna to at least wait until the first snow came. When the rivers froze again and the ground was more firm, it would make for easier travel.

Anna could barely contain her excitement when the first snow came. Her Eskimo friends loaded the dogsled for travel to take advantage of trapping season as they accompanied Anna on her journey. Anna traveled with the family as far and as long as she could, but eventually she had to again set out on her own. It seemed that her first night was full of bad omens as the sky darkened while the clouds became thick, and it seemed the stars were flickering out one by one.

She got back into her routine of going as far as she could in one day, then hunkering down for the night in a snow bank. On more than one occasion she was confident that she was in familiar territory, only to find that her mind had played tricks on her and what once looked familiar was still totally unfamiliar. However, there finally came a day that she saw snowshoe tracks in the snow and she knew that someone had to be nearby. As she looked around, she began to recognize spruce trees and knew that she was within a few miles of her father's cabin.

After another half day's walk, she felt a surge of relief overwhelming her when she came across the top of a hill and saw her father's cabin in the distance. As she approached the cabin, she could see the silhouettes of her children through the window. She did not want her children to see her tired and worn from her journey, so she took the time to snare a rabbit and eat the scraps of food that remained in her pack.

As Huey concluded his story, he said, "A year and two moons after she had left, my great-grandmother, Anna Biffelt, walked into the cabin straight, and tall, and proud." The reunion was emotional for everyone, but especially for Anna. She had accomplished what everyone had told her would be impossible. The love for her children had motivated her in a way that gave her almost superhuman strength and determination. Her story has now been passed down for several generations, and Anna is an inspiration to every Koyukon today.

Later in my coaching career, when I was inducted into the National Fastpitch Coaches Association (NFCA) Hall of Fame, I told this story as part of my induction speech. I had always wanted a female role model who could inspire me to greatness, but, more importantly, who could teach me toughness and perseverance. I wanted someone who could show me that if you don't give up, anything is possible. I found that role model in Anna Biffelt. Ever since my trip to Alaska, I have thought about Anna when times got tough and I needed to quit feeling sorry for myself. If I had gotten nothing more from this trip than the feeling that I had after listening to Huey tell me about his great-grandmother, the trip would have been worth it.

When I left for my Indian adventure, I had no idea what I would get from it or what parts of it I would be able to weave into my life after I digested it. The ability of the Indians to be biculturally fluent is something that I have tried to imitate. I increased my respect for those who have little formal education but who are incredibly intelligent with life experiences. My appreciation of nature and its beauty and magnitude rose to new levels. The peacefulness and solitude that were part of their everyday life in Huslia is something that I have had a hard time reproducing here, but just the thought of it recharges my batteries.

I am not sure if my stay with the Koyukon Indians made me a better coach, but I know it made me a better person. As I was waiting on the bush plane to fly me back to Fairbanks, I asked Huey and Eleanor what made the Koyukons decide to open their village to me and the others. I felt almost ashamed that I had invaded their privacy and intruded upon their peaceful lifestyle. Huey had a very simple answer. He said, "The Koyukons wanted to prove to the white men that they were more than a bunch of savages living on a chunk of ice." Indeed, they certainly proved their point to me.

Since that trip, they invited me to return to Huslia in the winter. They wanted to teach me how to mush the dog teams, and then we would travel by dogsled about one hundred miles to the hot springs. They have cabins spaced twenty miles apart on the path to the hot springs, so our goal would be to mush twenty miles each day and stay at the cabins at night until we reached the hot springs. At the springs, they promised me that you could lie in the hot water and listen to the timber wolves howl while enjoying the aurora borealis. How could anyone turn down that kind of offer? I guess I knew I was a dedicated basketball coach when I had to say no to the offer because it was during my basketball season. If I ever recover my health, it is still something that I would love to do.

Chapter 8

The Betty Ford Center

Life's errors cry for the merciful beauty that can modulate
their isolation into a harmony with the whole.

Rabindranath Tagore

In coaching, the years can go by quickly. You reflect and wonder where the first ten, and then where the first twenty years of coaching have gone. More than twenty years had elapsed in my career, and although I was having a great deal of success, I still felt that I had much to learn. A quote that I have shared with players many times is, "When you are through improving, you are through." The quote applies to coaches as well as to players.

One of the keys to longevity in coaching is to be able to adapt to the younger generation without trying to become part of the younger generation. We have an obligation to try to understand their problems and relate to their way of thinking without necessarily trying to imitate some of what they do just because they might think it is cool or might more readily accept us. It is far too easy for coaches to err in the direction of either ignoring players' issues because these issues seem so trivial or absurd that you wonder how players could be concerned and involved in such things, or going too far the other way and forcing our beliefs on them just because we are the boss and we refuse to view an issue through a younger person's eyes.

There is a need to assert ourselves as a positive influence without necessarily trying to micromanage the lives of our young athletes. It is difficult to keep the separation needed to maintain the proper respect from and rapport with our athletes, but at the same time provide enough of a comfort zone that they feel they can come to you when they need advice or help in dealing with problems. The longer I stayed in coaching, the more I needed to remind myself that when

Top) Clockwise, from left rear: Dave, Diane, Debra, and Donna Newberry pose in front of heir father's sporting-goods-store truck, about 1959. (Bottom) The Newberry family – left o right: Diane, Donna, Juanita, Dale, Dave, and Debra – at Dale Hollow Lake, Tennessee, n the summer of 2010.

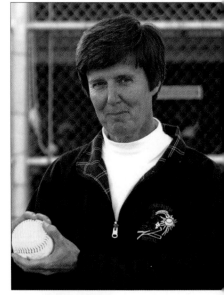

Portraits of Donna Newberry (upper left) upon graduating from South Parkersburg High School in 1969; (upper right) with her 1991 NCAA Division III Coach of the Year in basketball trophy; (lower left) around 2000; and (lower right) holding a softball in 2003.

The amazing 1991 Muskie basketball team lifts Coach Newberry in celebration after defeating St. John Fisher College in the NCAA Division III Atlantic Sectional Finals.

PHOTO GALLERY 4

(Top) During Coach Newberry's stay with Alaska's Koyukon Indians in the summer of 1992, a bug net and a semi-automatic rifle – necessary for warding off mosquitoes and bears – were her constant companions. (Bottom) Coach Newberry with Ann Gordon sometime during the late 1990s, in the television station Ann managed in the village of Kwakwani, Guyana.

Top) Coach Newberry with the 2001 team at the start of the season. Pitching Coach John Vells, standing at far right, passed away during the World Series tournament later that year. Bottom) The 2001 Muskingum softball team celebrates winning the NCAA National Championship after the final out in the 2001 Women's College World Series in Eau Claire, Wisconsin.

Photo Gallery 6

Coach Newberry before and during softball games in (top) 2004 and (bottom left and right)
2006. The bottom left image was taken on May 13 during the NCAA regional tournament
at Salem, Virginia, and the bottom right image was taken on May 19 at the NCAA World
Series tournament at Raleigh, North Carolina.

Top) Coach Newberry delivers her acceptance speech at the National Fastpitch Coaches Association Annual Meeting in December 2008, where she was inducted into the NFCA Hall of Fame. (Bottom) The 2010 Muskingum softball team in another milestone moment after Coach Newberry recorded her 900th win at Marietta College in April.

During her thirty-six years of coaching softball at Muskingum, Coach Donna Newberry' teams won eighteen OAC championships and made eighteen appearances in NCAA pos season play, including eight trips to the Division III Women's College World Series. 2001, her team won the NCAA Division III National Championship.

athletes had problems, the problems provided me with an opportunity rather than providing me with another source of frustration.

We must play a role in shaping the lives of our athletes. It is too easy to allow them to make mistakes and then just pick up the pieces of the aftermath. We must be proactive enough to try to keep them from falling off the cliff in the first place when we see them racing towards sure disaster. The shaping process takes a lot of energy, insight, and wisdom. This process is often where I see coaches wear out the quickest. You get so tired of dealing with problems that you finally succumb to just letting the problems exist and ignoring most of what is going on, or you simply get out of coaching because it is draining to constantly fight the battle, and often the efforts are resented rather than appreciated even when you do make the effort.

I believe it was these very issues that, in 1995, motivated the NCAA to send out a letter to coaches who had the experience of twenty or more years in college coaching. I received a letter encouraging the older coaches to update their knowledge on drug and alcohol abuse. The NCAA believed that many of us were likely outdated with our knowledge and understanding of these types of problems, even though it is probably one of the biggest issues that we face in coaching young athletes. Whether it was ignorance, naïveté, or just a lack of desire to try to relate to the athletes about problems of abuse, there was clearly a need to find a better way to help young people deal with the problem. The letter included a list of articles, seminars, videos, and books that were recommended by the NCAA, and it encouraged each coach to update her knowledge of identifying and dealing with the problems associated with drug and alcohol abuse.

The most extreme option listed was an invitation to contact the Betty Ford Center (BFC) to seek permission to be admitted to their Professionals in Residence (PIR) program. If you were accepted, the Betty Ford Center allowed you to be admitted to their treatment facility as a patient and experience the life of an addict and alcoholic in their rehabilitation program. Because of my fondness for the experiential learning approach, it seemed like an unbelievable opportunity to update my knowledge. Although I was apprehensive about what I was getting into, all it took was a letter of request, and before I even had time to give it second thoughts, I received a letter of acceptance with my arrival dates and all the necessary details enclosed.

In order for the reader to better appreciate my experience at the BFC, I will give a little background on the history, rules, and policies of the facility. The BFC is one of the few treatment facilities in the country that treats 50 percent men and 50 percent women. Other facilities treat predominantly men, but Betty Ford's influence has obviously helped us to recognize that many women need treatment as well. The BFC was founded in 1982 by Betty Ford and Leonard Firestone to treat alcohol and drug dependence. It is located in the foothills of the San Jacinto Mountains in Rancho Mirage, California. Its campus consists of seven buildings connected by winding pathways and is encompassed by majestic scenery and an almost serene atmosphere on its fourteen acres. The BFC sits adjacent to the Eisenhower Medical Center and is adjoined on the opposite side by the Sinatra Child Abuse Center.

The dorms are called "units." There are four units which house twenty patients each, forty women and forty men in total. The length of stay can vary, but the average stay lasts for twenty-eight days. Nearly every day, patients are being dismissed from the BFC, and new patients are admitted from the waiting list. As patients come and go, the actual make-up of each unit is in a constant state of flux. All the rooms are two-person rooms except for one room in each unit that holds four people. The interaction and healing process that develops from the camaraderie between roommates mandates that no patient has a single room.

The name of the BFC generally conjures up images of high-profile clients and celebrity patients. Although they do get more than their share of these types of people, the BFC quickly extinguishes the mystique that fame and fortune have brought. There are clients from all walks of life and all income levels. The one thing they all have in common is their desire to overcome their addiction, and beyond that, nothing else much seems to matter.

No one is forced to enter the BFC, and no one is kept there against her will. Although numerous patients are there as a result of intervention from others, or finally "bottoming out" and seeing this as a last resort, they always have the choice to be admitted or not, and they can leave at any time, even though it might be "AMA" (against medical advice). An important lesson to be learned is that treatment cannot be effective unless the individual really wants help.

Four admissions counselors field up to three hundred calls per day. They assess the problem to see if the BFC is the appropriate treatment center for a potential patient. Patients with other medical problems besides addiction can be accepted as long as they are ambulatory and functional. Once admitted, each client goes through a full battery of tests including a physical exam, psychiatric evaluation, social evaluation, and drug testing. Based on the composite results of these tests, an individual treatment program is developed for that patient.

There is a long list of policies, rules, and procedures. I will not attempt to list all of them, but I will list some of them to give you a better understanding of what a stay was like.

1. Substance – Unauthorized use of any medication or chemical substance is forbidden. Patients are checked when they enter to make sure they have no drugs, including all over-the-counter medicines like aspirin. Even caffeine is hard to come by, as all tea, coffee, and soft drinks in the cafeteria are decaffeinated.

2. Gambling – Gambling in any form is forbidden.

3. Attendance – Patients are expected to attend every session. Anyone too ill to attend a session must be assessed by the nursing staff. One must attend all lectures, meetings, and meals with other unit members. Interestingly, before a unit leaves the dorm for an activity, another rule is that members give a unit cheer on the patio before departing the unit. The Dupont Hall cheer consisted of circling up and stomping our feet in rhythm to the following cheer:

"1, 2, 3, 4
We're the girls from Dupont Hall
We don't do no drugs at all
We don't need no booze, no powder
We got us a higher power
1, 2, 3, 4, – 1, 2 DUPONT!"

4. Dress – Appropriate dress is required. Shoes and shirts are required at all times. Excessively tight fitting clothing, low cut, or revealing blouses are not appropriate. Undergarments must be worn at all times, including bras for women. Only walking length shorts may be worn. Dark glasses and hats may be worn outside only. (Trying to enforce the dress code at the BFC reminded me of the same problem that occurs while trying to enforce a dress code at a school, church, camp, etc. The patients pushed the rules to the limit and tried to get away with wearing or not wearing what they wanted, rather than what they were supposed to wear. This behavior was a constant source of aggravation for both the staff and the patients.)

5. Books and Television – Books for leisure reading are not permitted. Selected reading materials are given to you as assignments and are expected to be completed within designated time limits. No television is permitted except on Saturday from 5:00 P.M. through Sunday at 11:00 P.M. (The only television is in the living room of each unit. Most of the viewings permitted are movies that the patients vote on from a selected list of choices.) The BFC believes that television detracts from concentration on the recovery process and thus discourages patients from communicating with each other.

6. Visitors – Visiting hours are from 1 P.M. to 5 P.M. on Sunday only. Visitors cannot enter patient areas, and patients must wait in their hall for a visitor to be announced. All visitors must sign a confidentiality agreement to protect the privacy of all patients.

7. Housekeeping – Each patient must maintain the cleanliness of her own room and bathroom. Beds must be made by 8 A.M. Each patient is also assigned a community job (Therapeutic Duty Assignment) that must be performed daily. These duties range from vacuuming the hallways, to cleaning the patio, to working in the dining hall, etc.

8. Telephones – Telephone hours are from Saturday at 5:00 P.M. through Sunday at 11:00 P.M. This also seemed to be

a source of friction between patients and staff. Each unit has one phone, and one has to sign up for phone times in fifteen-minute intervals. In many cases, the phone calls are monitored.

9. Fraternization – Patients are expected to form meaningful relationships with patients and staff within their own unit. Patients are not to involve themselves with patients in other units. All lectures, meals, recreation, etc., are attended as a group. Of all the rules that patients tried to violate, this was probably the hardest to enforce. At first, I did not understand the need for such a rule, but the longer I was there, the more sense it made.

Although there are plenty of counselors and facilitators on staff, much of the healing process for these patients comes from other patients. The more camaraderie that can be established in a unit, the more the patients can help each other. Because it is difficult to bond with a group of twenty people, any communication outside your group distracts from focusing on your group. The BFC attempts to establish an almost sorority- or fraternity-type atmosphere within the units.

Fraternizing with the opposite sex is sometimes seen in clandestine settings at opportune moments. If caught, a patient could be dismissed. As a staff member put it, "Besides being against the rules, you're fishing in polluted waters." Note-passing on cafeteria napkins, prearranged meetings, and even nighttime rendezvous activities occurred all too frequently. This is an important rule at the BFC, but the patients reminded me of overgrown juveniles as they tried to devise ways to violate it without getting caught.

Besides the rules and policies, there is also a daily schedule that had to be followed. Although there might be slight variations in a patient's schedule, for the most part each day is identically structured. Having a daily routine and responsibilities that have to be met are part of the treatment process.

A typical daily schedule at BFC would be as given on the following pages in Table 1.

Table 1. A typical daily schedule for patients at the Betty Ford Center, as experienced by Coach Newberry

Time	Activity
6:00 A.M.	Wake up
6:30 A.M.	Therapeutic Duty Assignment – Patients perform the cleaning duty they have been assigned.
7:00 A.M.	Breakfast
8:00-8:30 A.M.	Meditation Walk – No talking is permitted. There is a leisurely stroll around the grounds or surrounding area to help get your thoughts focused for the day.
8:45-9:20 A.M.	Lecture – All patients assemble in the auditorium for a lecture by a physician. Topics vary, but include such things as "Signs of Addiction," "How Alcohol Affects Your Body," "Forgiveness," "The Nicotine Habit," "Relapse," etc.
9:30-9:45 A.M.	Peer Processing – Patients assemble back in their units, and each one shares what she gets out of the lecture.
10:00-11:30 A.M.	Group Therapy – The unit is divided into two groups of ten. Each group meets separately with a counselor acting as the mediator. In group therapy, the emphasis is on feeling, confronting (not advising), and leveling (responding to the confronter).
11:45-12:45 P.M.	Lunch
12:50-1:50 P.M.	First Step and Peer Feedback – Whoever is due to give the first step from the AA recovery process shares with the group and the group gives feedback. Step 1 states, "We admitted we were powerless over alcohol and that our lives had become unmanageable."

2:00-2:50 P.M.	This time slot varies daily. Some days it is Step 2 and Step 3 of AA. Step 2 states, "We have come to believe that a greater power than ourselves could restore us to sanity." Step 3 states, "We have made a decision to turn our will and our lives over to the care of God as we understand Him." There are other days when this time slot is used for a community meeting in the dorm, a time for visits to the med center, or for psychological assessments.
3:10-4:00 P.M.	Activity Therapy – You can choose a physical activity such as aerobics, swimming, running, or weight lifting.
4:10-5:00 P.M.	Specialized Groups – Each person is assigned to an appropriate group. Some of the group choices are grief groups, stress management, abuse survivors, body image, and relaxation.
5:15-6:15 P.M.	Dinner
6:30-7:00 P.M.	Lecture
7:05-7:20 P.M.	Peer Processing
7:30-8:30 P.M.	AA meeting or NA (Narcotics Anonymous) meeting
8:30-9:30 P.M.	Goodbye Ceremonies – If anyone from your unit is to be dismissed the next morning, a very moving ceremony is held for her that includes each person in the unit giving parting words of advice. It concludes with the patient's admissions papers being burned on the patio while the remainder of the group does the hokey pokey around the burning urn.

∽

By sharing with you some of the stories of the lives of the patients that I met, I hope that you can gain a better understanding of the wealth of understanding that this type of opportunity provided me about dealing with drug and alcohol abuse. To protect the privacy of the patients, only pseudonyms will be used.

I arrived in Palm Springs the night before I was to be admitted to the BFC. After a quick continental breakfast at the hotel, I was nervous as I waited for transportation to arrive to take me to the BFC. On the ride over, the driver casually asked me if I wanted to make a stop anywhere before we got to the facility. I really did not know what he meant when he asked the question, but I politely declined. It was then that he said most patients who gave him the BFC as their destination asked to stop for one last drink before arriving. I guessed I had a lot to learn about living the life of an alcoholic.

Upon arrival, you are immediately fitted with a medical identification bracelet much like you would wear in a hospital. Even though the staff knew that I was not really a patient, the other patients knew nothing about me. I felt myself tugging on my long sleeves to try to cover up the bracelet. The stigma attached to wearing a bracelet that categorized me as an addict was almost more than I could stand. For me, the whole experience was only "make believe." I can't imagine how traumatic and demeaning it must have seemed for the patients who were truly there for treatment. I began to appreciate how difficult it must be for people to admit that they were an addict and to seek help.

When a new patient arrives at the BFC, a buddy is assigned to him or her. Your buddy is someone who has been there a while and who will "show you the ropes" as you try to acclimate. I was very fortunate to have Lehla assigned to me as my buddy. What an intelligent, delightful lady. She reminded me of Angela Lansbury. Lehla was a sixty-six-year-old financial consultant who had made most of her money through a successful book and writing a regular column for *Cosmo* magazine.

Lehla was close to the end of her stay at the BFC. She had broken her foot prior to going in, so she used a wheelchair if she had to walk far. I could just about predict the time before each meeting that she would yell, "Donna, can you give me a ride?," meaning she needed me to push her wheelchair. She had become hooked on tranquilizers and then had started washing them down with alcohol. Her hands still shook so much she could hardly light her cigarette. Her mind, however, was very clear. I don't know if I have ever spoken to anyone so intellectually stimulating. She could talk endlessly about politics, religion, philosophy, economics, and countless other topics. About the only thing that I found that she was not comfortable discussing was sports. Since that was the one thing that I felt most comfortable discussing, I learned to listen rather than speak. I've been around very few people who could articulate the way that Lehla could.

I doubted that Lehla would stay sober after she was released. I suspected that she was such a strong and independent woman that after she got out she would believe she could take a drink and still be able to control it. It would never work.

Lehla illustrates the sadness of the disease of addiction as she would likely die a premature death, and I suspected her mind would deteriorate before her body. Lehla illustrates how cheated society is when good people are lost through abusing drugs and alcohol.

When you enter the BFC, all substances have to be turned over to the medical personnel. The only exception that is made to that rule is that patients are allowed to keep their cigarettes. The BFC has had no success in trying to withdraw patients from nicotine while dealing with their other problems.

Most of the conversations where I learned the real truth took place on the patio. The patio was a hangout area outside where the patients could smoke. As I saw it, it was also sort of an oasis where they could get away from the watchful eyes and ears of the technicians and counselors. I would estimate that about 80 percent of the patients were heavy smokers, and it became clear to me that if I wanted to engulf myself in conversation, I would also have to engulf myself in cigarette smoke.

It amazed me how quickly I became one of the gang. After determining that I wasn't a med student and that I wasn't there to analyze or judge, as far as they were concerned, I was a patient. It was scary that at times I took on an almost invisible presence. Once they decided that I was not there to rat on them, they didn't hesitate to discuss openly anything from prostitution to their most recent plots to break the BFC rules. I might add that I also heard more profanity in a week than I've probably heard in a lifetime.

I met Danita on my first day while eating lunch. Danita was a Jacinto Indian from a nearby reservation. She bore most of the typical features of a Southwestern Indian, including the dark hair and complexion, stocky build, and dark piercing eyes. I immediately knew that we had several things in common, including the fact that we were admitted on the same day, and since I had spent time living with the Koyukon Indians in Alaska, maybe we would have some things that we could talk about. I made up my mind that I would strike up a conversation with her.

We talked for an hour at lunch, long after everyone else had left the cafeteria. Danita had been using speed when she was stopped for a traffic violation. She swore that it was her first arrest, but she said her sister had used her name and ID on seven previous occasions when she was in trouble. Apparently, the police didn't buy her story as she was given a choice of inpatient treatment at the BFC or jail.

Danita was very frightened. She had not been around white people before and had never been off the reservation without her husband. She desperately missed her children and was very worried about them. She said she had never had a white friend before today.

Danita had not used drugs or alcohol until two years before, although her brothers and sisters were heavily into both. Danita preferred to focus her energy on her family, and it was the death of her mother that had triggered her using drugs. Danita was the primary caretaker for her mother, and one day two summers before while driving her mother across the reservation, she panicked when her mother suddenly stopped breathing and died in the passenger seat of the car. Not only did Danita struggle with the death of her mother, but her sister, among others, resented and criticized her heavily for the way she handled the funeral.

Her mother's death was followed shortly afterwards by the death of a brother. With the close family ties that most Indians have, it was really difficult. She said that she might as well have adopted his son (her nephew), as he now lived with her and looked to her for comfort. Her nephew was really tormented over the death, and she said that for the last few months that he had been sleeping in the cemetery between the graves of her mother and brother.

After she finished her story, she said she was surprised that she hadn't gotten emotional. It was the first time that she had been able to speak of their deaths without crying.

We began to compare the way the Jacinto Indians conducted their funerals to the Koyukon Indians with whom I had lived. She was very curious about their customs and was equally willing to share her own customs. She said her father was a bird-singer and then said she'd learned most of the songs herself. A bird-singer tells the story of the different flights of a bird through its life journey, with a new song for each place it alights. The death song is sung when it alights for the final time. At a funeral, the bird-singer chants much of the day and the final song is sung as the body is placed in the ground. Danita said she couldn't stand the thought of another death in the family.

She shared some of her tribal history and even explained how she survived financially. All the adult Indians born prior to 1949 were "given" forty acres of land by the U.S. government. Hers happened to be where a part of the Palm Springs resorts were now built. The city of Palm Springs rented the land from her, and she apparently was financially comfortable.

Later in the day, Danita sought me out to lend me a tape of her father's bird-songs, and then explained what I'd be hearing. I gratefully took the tape and listened to it throughout my exercise workout. It wasn't until the next day when I was talking with one of the counselors that I had any idea that this gesture by her was at all unusual. The counselor said the Indians never share that part of their culture with whites, and she was amazed that Danita was willing to share it with me.

The next morning as we prepared to meet for group therapy, Danita was absent. Our counselor appeared distraught, and finally said that she would share with us why Danita was not there since she knew we'd find out anyway. The Palm Springs police had found her nephew's body in the streets of Palm Springs the previous night, and they had pulled her out of therapy to break the news to her. I couldn't believe my ears! About fifteen minutes later, I knew she had just been told. I heard her mournful wails and sobs echoing down the hallway, and later I saw them taking her off the grounds. I have no idea if she shared with the staff any of the information she had told me, but I doubt it. She had just gotten there the day before.

That night, I made sure I had access to a television at 11:00 for the Palm Springs news report. There was a long segment on the death. The newscaster called it a "random shooting with no known suspects." The camera spent a long time filming his dead body sprawled in the street. It was not like me to cry through a newscast, but that night I did.

The counselor explained that they would allow Danita a few days for the funeral, and then hopefully she would return to the facility. Regretfully, my stay was up before she came back, or for all I know she may have chosen to go to jail. I sent her a letter after I got home, but I have no idea if she got it, especially since I only knew her first name for the address.

The memory of my short acquaintance with Danita haunts me more than anything else I experienced there. I know that she chose therapy over jail because she didn't want to become like her addicted brothers and sisters. She honestly seemed to be struggling to live a decent and honest life, but her story reinforced my belief that life isn't always fair.

Danita's life illustrates to a larger degree the risks that I have seen so many college age students take. Using drugs or alcohol one time or occasionally seems perfectly harmless to a student, but as one thing leads to another, the scenario can get much worse. Property damage, arrests, blame, and even death can be traced back to a careless decision to drink too much or to use drugs at a party. After the damage is done, hindsight does not help much. I heard so many of the BFC residents reflect on "if I only had it to do over again."

Although there were many patients that had sad stories to tell, another that stuck out in my mind is the story of Judy. Judy was a beautiful woman. She was probably about thirty-five, had a dark complexion with long dark hair, full lips, and what most people would probably call a voluptuous figure. She was normally attired in tight velvet dresses, or skin-tight pants with a halter top that had fringe hanging down to cover her navel. Regardless of the rest of her outfit, she wore platform shoes and lots of dangling jewelry. She changed her clothes several times a day.

Seldom did you find her without gum in her mouth and chewing as if she was mad at the world. She was so out of it when she entered BFC that she could not talk and could hardly walk. When she spoke it was obvious that she is intelligent, but as a result of drugs, she suffered from memory loss and had a very short attention span.

Every patient at BFC is required to do "First Step" with their unit. "First Step" refers to the first step of the twelve steps of AA that states, "We admitted we were powerless over alcohol—that our lives had become unmanageable." A full hour is set aside for the patients to face the group, admit they are unable to control their addiction, and then tell their life story that shows how unmanageable drugs have made it.

Judy had been hooked on all types of drugs since junior high age. She remembered sitting in the middle of the school football field smoking pot. In high school she remembered not getting invited to a friend's party and she became so angry that she broke into her friend's house and stole several thousand dollars' worth of jewelry and used it for drug deals. At another point in high school, she and her boyfriend beat up an old man on the street and took $700 from him.

Following high school, she began getting her money through prostitution. Much of the time, she would commit the act but would have her boyfriend hiding in the closet. After the act, her boyfriend would jump out, and they would beat up the client and steal everything he had. Judy really seemed to enjoy prostitution, but spoke with great remorse about being abducted and raped during a drug deal in Florida then being dumped off in a black neighborhood from which she barely escaped with her life.

While in New York she met and married an Israeli and went with him to Tel Aviv, where she continued to live. They had four children. She was the owner of a renowned and fashionable boutique in Tel Aviv. Her husband appeared to be an addict as well, and it seemed since her marriage that her life had gotten continually worse.

It almost seemed to me that she really didn't care if she died. She and her husband had shot up with drugs on the top of the World Trade Center in a very dangerous scenario. Judy had jumped out of a second story window and had also tried to hang herself while on drugs. She and her husband fought violently, and she told a chilling story of a high speed chase in Tel Aviv when her husband was angry. She jumped in the car while trying to escape from him and he followed in his truck. They wove in and out of traffic at nearly 100 mph until she slammed on her brakes and slid her car into a 180-degree turn. She said she had the accelerator to the floor as she rocketed toward a head-on collision with her husband. He veered off at the last minute, although she said she had had no intention of stopping.

She had smuggled drugs in and out of both Israel and the U.S. One of her stories involved going into the bathroom of a United Airlines plane while they were preparing for takeoff and shooting up with heroin. After she came out she became violent and was using a lot of profanity while spitting at the flight attendants. United expelled her from the plane and the other airlines refused to fly her as well, so she had to charter a private jet to get back to Tel Aviv from New York.

Although her boutique remained very lucrative, most other aspects of her life were in shambles. She still had quite a lot of time left at BFC, but I worried that she would be unable to turn things around. She was a contrast in extremes. The night before she did her First Step, she sat on the patio with me and a few others and we sang old television theme songs. She was the only one who knew all the words to the Brady Bunch. The next day when she told us about her crime, drugs, and sex with no hint of emotion in her voice, I could hardly comprehend that she was the same person who had been singing the Brady Bunch song. It was amazing how the patients could fluctuate so dramatically. One minute they would seem like endearing, child-like people and the next they would be sharing sordid stories of criminal activities.

Once in a while when Judy let her guard down, you could see how frightened she was and how much she wanted to get well. At other times, she seemed really hard-nosed. I saw her celebrate when she got the results of her AIDS test back and it was negative, as she fully expected it would come back positive. Most of the time in her group therapy, her comments were flippant and funny. I'm sure it was only to hide her true emotions. I was relatively sure that Judy was sneaking out at night and meeting a guy from another unit. I also saw her give a male patient what I suspect was drugs that she had managed to hide from the staff. Strangely, the only time I saw her cry was when word came to the unit that Anna, a woman from our unit who had been discharged five days before, had already relapsed. Judy said she was so sure that Anna would make it.

Judy was a typical patient. She never meant for her life to spiral out of control, but the more she drank and the more she used drugs, the less control she had over her decision-making ability. What once seemed like a good time had now gotten such a grip on her life that she was unable to make good decisions. It was not only ruining her life, but it also was ruining the lives of her children.

I heard the story over and over again. It all began with one harmless drink. Gradually it took more beers or harder liquor to achieve the same kind of buzz. You progress from being the life of the party, to being the one that others have to babysit because you are out of control. By the time you realize what is happening, things have spiraled so far out of control that the only way you can salvage your life is to give yourself over to a rehabilitation center to see if they can help.

The group therapy sessions were emotionally torturous for me. Probably the most emotional session was a day that the counselor came into the room with ten of us who were in that group and distributed five pieces of blank paper to each of us. She instructed us to write down the five most important things in our lives by writing one thing on each piece of paper. When we began to ask whether she meant for us to write down names of people, or if she meant earthly possessions, or exactly what she meant, she simply said to write down whatever five items that we deemed to be the most important items in our lives and to stop asking questions.

After each of us had our five papers complete, she then instructed us to rank order the papers from the most important to the least important. I later learned that one of the women had written down the five names of her children on her five papers, but all of us struggled to come up with a rank order that made sense.

Once we finished our ranking, the counselor began with the first one of us sitting in the circle of chairs. She said each of us would be asked to wad up the paper with our lowest ranked item, throw it into the middle of the circle, and verbalize why that item was what we had chosen to give up first. We didn't make it too far around the circle before protests were being launched by the participants. How could you be asked to choose one child above another, or to choose your spouse above your children, or to choose your parent above your health? We were being told to throw it in and get rid of it, but it did not make it any easier to justify letting go of something very important in your life.

A couple of the patients became belligerent and refused to give up their paper. The counselor would not listen to their protests and refused to move on until they gave up a paper. Round 1 was difficult, but Round 2 and 3 became almost impossible. Somehow a figurative exercise had become very literal to all who were there, including me. I think everyone in the circle was crying.

Finally, we got to Round 5 and the third person in the circle had saved her most precious possession for last. She threw in her paper and said that she had written "Sobriety" on it. The exercise was over, as this was the acknowledgment that the counselor was waiting for. The point of the whole exercise was for the patients to realize that sobriety had to become the most important thing in their lives, because if it was not valued above everything else, everything else would be lost anyway. Parents had already lost their children, spouses had lost their mate, workers had lost their jobs, and patients had lost their health. In my own experience, I have witnessed college students who have lost their opportunity to play sports or more importantly to get their degree, just because drinking had become more important than studying.

As I reflect back, I wonder how we all could have gotten so caught up in something that was just an exercise in group therapy. However, I guess that the purpose of group therapy is to find exercises that will cause one to be honest and to get to the core of the problem. The therapy on that day had definitely done its job, as all of us were emotionally shaken when the counselor stood to depart from the room. One of the rules of group therapy is that you are not allowed to touch another patient, so it was difficult to comfort one another when you were required to "keep your distance." The box of tissues that was kept in the center of the circle was well-used that day, and I believe everyone was relieved, yet appreciative when the session was over.

One of the TDA jobs was to clean up the therapy room after a session by sweeping, straightening the chairs, and making sure it was ready to go for the next day. When the person who had been assigned that duty began to sweep up the wads of paper from the floor, I gently grabbed her arm and in a surprisingly irritated voice commanded her to "Wait a minute!"

I got down on my hands and knees until I found all of my slips of paper. It became very important for me to put my parents, my siblings, my work, my dog, and my health back in my pocket, as no one was going to strip me of those five valuable things quite that easily. I will not reveal the order that I ranked those things except to say that I held onto my health for the final round. I am sure that health was a priority for me as I had gone to the BFC only a couple of months after having a bilateral mastectomy as a part of my first battle with breast cancer.

There were several patients who joined me in the search for their wads of paper. The significance of the exercise just completed had not been lost on even the worst of the addicts. The BFC is often the last resort for patients, and they succumb to treatment there only after trying everything else that they know to do to shake their addiction. They clearly knew what was at stake in their lives if they were not able to overcome their addiction, so it was a relief to each of us who retrieved our papers and kept our life's treasures from becoming trash.

~

Mary was one of the older patients, and by superficial appearance, she could have been my mother. She was a well kept, attractive woman in her early sixties whose most noticeable characteristic was that she was always smiling. I don't know if I had ever met anyone who seemed to be so perpetually happy.

The more I was around Mary in group therapy, the more I came to realize that she had one of those "pasted cheerleader smiles," and for the most part, it was her way of disguising a lifetime of hurt and disappointment. During a particular exercise one day in group therapy, we were asked to write some things down and hand them to the counselor. While all the rest of us were writing, Mary meekly spoke up and said that she could not complete the exercise. When the counselor tried to find out why, she finally admitted that it was because she did not have a dictionary with her and she was afraid that she would spell a word incorrectly. When the counselor tried to convince her that we really didn't care if she spelled a word wrong, Mary still refused to write. She eventually confessed that this stemmed from the fact that her husband had been calling her a "dumb drunk" for years, and one of the ways that she tried to refute his statement was by writing grammatically correct sentences with no misspelled words.

For about the next twenty minutes, Mary went on a tirade about how miserable and boring her life had become. Her youngest son, who was nearly thirty, still lived at home and treated her terribly, and her husband would not let her get a job or have friends of her own. Most of the day, after her son and husband had gone, she would pull down the shades and drink.

It occurred to me later how I could see some of my athletes in the life of Mary. In spite of the fact that she was a lovely woman who could carry on an interesting and intelligent conversation, her self-esteem was about as low as it could get. Mary had deeply internalized the "dumb drunk" label and had no confidence in her ability to live her own life. I have talked with so many students who think they are not good enough to excel or reach their goals, simply because they have been told so many times by their parents or others that they lacked whatever it took to be successful. As was the case with Mary, too many of these students simply use alcohol to cover up their disappointment, despair, and hopelessness. Instead of learning to stand up for themselves and prove those around them to be wrong, they choose to drink or use drugs, and gradually evolve into a life of addiction.

It seemed like Mary was changing during her stay at the BFC. Shortly before I was dismissed on my last day, she pulled me aside and said, "Do you know what I am going to do when I get out?" I feared that she was going to tell me that she was just waiting for her first big drink. Instead she said, "First I am going to divorce my husband, and then I am going to get a job!" I was dumbfounded, but found myself inwardly smiling at the first hint of determination that I had ever heard in her voice as well as a definite fire in her eyes.

When I first entertained the idea of going to the BFC, I was mostly afraid of going because I felt the patients would be so unlike me that I could never relate to them, and I would be uncomfortably out of my element there. As with any worthwhile experience, we need to expand beyond our comfort zone to grow. I have never tasted alcohol or smoked a cigarette in my life, so to think that I would live the life of an addict for a few days was almost laughable.

As I reflect back, it is a revelation to see that I had written in the journal that I kept while I was there this statement: "It is scary to realize that these people are more like me than they are unlike me." Somehow, I think I had perceived addicts to be some subculture of humanity. I viewed an addict in a stereotypical way that included the image of low-life, uneducated, unmotivated people who wanted to do nothing but escape their troubles. However, I discovered that when they were sober, they were exactly the same type of people I would enjoy having as friends. I valued their wit, conversation, intelligence, and insights.

I previously had viewed the irresponsible use of alcohol as a lack of self-discipline and a way of escape for the weak of heart. I had little tolerance for students who turned to alcohol or drugs when they entered college, and even less tolerance if that student happened to be an athlete. I could not understand why anyone would risk her health and career to indulge in something so frivolous. My theory always had been that if you don't take the first drink, you will never become addicted.

Although that statement is true, it is an oversimplification of a situation that has many ways of getting started. I began to understand that addiction was a disease that had a variety of causes and a very difficult cure. Even if I disagreed with the actions, I developed empathy for those who were locked in the addiction vice, and I became more proactive in dealing with those who suffered from the disease. It was a breakthrough when a campus fraternity invited me to their fraternity house to speak about my experience, and I was able to deliver a message that they not only heard, but embraced.

My stay made me more appreciative of all the things that I never had to deal with while growing up. I did not have parents who were alcoholics, I was never sexually abused, I did not have a husband who mentally or physically abused me, I did not have financial problems, and I was under no great pressure to succeed and live up to someone else's expectations. It also made me more appreciative of all of the things that I did have, including spiritual direction, a loving family, a college education, and a job that I truly enjoyed.

None of us is problem-free, and even the problems that we do have are sometimes hard to identify as they often come disguised in different costumes. We have all had our share of adversity. I am not excusing or justifying the addictions that stem from these problems, but I began to appreciate how vulnerable some people are to such obstacles if they have no coping skills. As a result of my BFC experience, I am more empathetic to the things that an addict must face, and I am more educated about the treatment process.

The addicts that I spoke with advised me about the early warning signs of addiction. The younger your age, the less likely it is that the threat of long term health problems will be a deterrent. At a young age when you feel invincible, the threat of a future disease is too far removed to have much of an impact. The warning signs that need to be heeded are things like a feeling of disappointment when alcohol is not served at a party or having anyone who is really interested in you, such as a roommate or girlfriend or boyfriend, criticize your drinking. If you have started to drink when you feel physical discomfort or feel tense, the disease has already started to progress.

If addiction problems can be identified at these early stages, as coaches we need to help an athlete who has a sense of self-responsibility to take these signals seriously. At this stage, an individual can often overcome the progressing addiction through his own efforts and through self-discipline. Those who choose to disregard these warnings often face an impending spiral of increased dependence on the drug and all the consequences that are connected with addiction.

It was indeed a surprise when the patients in my unit held a goodbye ceremony for me the night before I was to leave. I was not expecting it since I had not been there for a full stay, and more so because I believed most of them knew that I was not really an addict. A medallion that has the BFC logo on one side and the AA prayer on the other side was passed from person to person. As people held the medallion, they gave me their parting words of advice. When the last person handed me the medallion, she said something like, "And if you ever fail to hear the words that we have said to you, it is not because we have stopped talking, it is because you have stopped listening." I keep that medallion in my bedroom as a perpetual reminder of the things I learned at the BFC.

It ended up being a very emotional experience that night. Several of the patients that I had spent a good deal of time talking with pulled me aside later to talk with me privately. My greatest fear was that the patients would resent my presence there when they discovered that I was there to learn rather than to receive treatment. I thought that they would feel like lab rats, and they would think that I was there to observe and analyze their predicament.

Once again, I did not give them enough credit. I was told how deeply appreciative they were that I was willing to take time out of my life to try to broaden my understanding of addiction. They felt that if my visit there could keep just one person from becoming an addict, then everything that I did and anything that they did to share their insights was worth it. They promised to write to me and let me know how their rehab was going once they were released. One even asked me to be her "nicotine buddy" by phone. She was trying to kick her cigarette habit among other things and wanted to call me when she needed encouragement or a deterrent. They were actually very sorry to see me leave.

When I checked out, I got my flight home and resumed my normal lifestyle. Unfortunately for the patients, the check-out was just the beginning of the process. They have a rehabilitation program that they need to follow the rest of their lives in order to avoid relapse. It includes ninety AA or NA meetings in ninety days. After that, you are expected to attend three of these meetings each week for the rest of your life. For some, it means a halfway house for a time after being discharged and additional outpatient therapy. An addict is always in recovery and never cured. The BFC saying is, "It's alcoholism, not alcoholwasm." If a discharged patient fails to follow instructions after leaving, relapse is almost inevitable.

I think the NCAA would have been pleased with what I learned at the BFC. My eyes were opened to athletes' problems that I had previously chosen to ignore, simply because I did not know how to deal with them or how to approach the athlete. To this day I am a firm believer that it would be best for people to never take that first drink so that they are never tempted to do it again if they find it pleasurable. I have seen so much property damage and so much damage to students' lives on college campuses, just because alcohol and drugs were abused and students got out of control. Usually there are deeper problems that prompt a student to drink, or especially to drink irresponsibly.

If for no other reason, I think some athletes have been receptive to some things that I have said to them about alcohol because they know that I had taken time out of my life to try to study and understand the issue. I cannot force my values, morals, and beliefs down the throats of my players, but I can provide a solid example and try to be a positive influence. If they fall short, or disappoint me, or struggle with the best way to handle their problems, it becomes my job to mentor them and provide an adult source of information. A team who is winning on the court or field will only be considered successful if they also properly learn to handle themselves off the court or field.

My stay at the BFC was very enriching. If I came away as even a slightly better person and coach, then it was worth it. The concern about wins and losses can sometimes make coaches lose sight of why they are really coaching. Ultimately our goal is to find a way to help shape better people out of the moldable clay that we are provided. There were several sayings engraved on plaques and stones around the BFC grounds. The one that stuck with me the most was the reminder that, "The best things in life aren't things."

Chapter 9

The End of an Era

Letting go doesn't mean giving up, but rather accepting
that there are things that cannot be.

Anonymous

It was February, 2000. I was now twenty-six years into my career. That was a long time to be doing one thing, especially one thing at the same place. The inevitable question seemed to pop up more and more from colleagues, friends, family, and especially from recruits. How much longer are you going to coach? Are you thinking about retiring anytime soon?

The answer always remained the same. I get tired *from* it more quickly than I used to, but I am not tired *of* it. When I get tired *of* it, then it will be time to get out. It took me more than anyone else by surprise when close to the end of the 1999–2000 basketball season I seemed to hit a wall that told me I could no longer continue to coach two sports. I never saw it coming, but I was so physically and mentally exhausted as the end of the season drew near that I questioned if I would have the strength to even make it through the upcoming softball season.

I don't think it was the coaching that fatigued me as much as it was the recruiting. The time demands for recruiting seemed to increase exponentially every year, and it was an intimidating proposition to be coaching softball at the same time you were still having basketball recruits visit the campus. One minute I would be preparing a pregame or postgame report, and the next minute I would be trying to close the deal with a basketball recruit or juggling to find a day that I was not off campus for a game so that a recruit could visit.

Recruiting can be a draining ordeal at the NCAA Division III level. Because you don't have athletic scholarships to offer student

144

athletes (all of the aid at Division III comes through academic performance, need-based aid, or awards of special circumstance), you have to be able to sell your program in other ways. Constant contact needs to be maintained. There is always a risk that you can spend an inordinate amount of time on a student athlete, only to have her snatched away at the last minute with an intriguing money offer from a Division I or II institution having both full and partial athletic scholarships. The student may not even be one of their top choices, but if the promise of book money, or partial scholarship, or the encouragement to "walk on" and then maybe next year there will be money is enticing, you may lose a player who was critical to your future plans to an institution who has encouraged her to come as an afterthought. The process can be discouraging and cause even the most dedicated coach to lose some of her initial enthusiasm.

Not only are you competing against schools that are NCAA Division I and II or NAIA offering them money for their playing abilities, but you are also competing against many other Division III schools that are often trying to recruit the same athlete that you are recruiting. Ohio creates real challenges when it comes to recruiting, as there are about twenty-five other Division III schools in this state alone, creating a bigger demand for quality student athletes than the state is able to supply. The secret to success is to find the athlete who wants the Division III environment, who is very skilled, whose ego is not directly tied to saying that she got an "athletic scholarship," and who has parents who are willing to navigate the financial aid process to find a package that makes the education financially affordable.

To locate these athletes, take time to see them play (in many cases multiple times), establish a relationship with them, get them to visit the campus, and eventually seal the deal, is a time-consuming and energy-draining endeavor. If they decided to go somewhere else at the last minute when you feel you did everything that you could do to recruit them, you have to be strong enough that you are not devastated to the point where you take it personally or become too discouraged to forage on. It is easy to let self-doubt enter in, wondering what is wrong with your program or with you that the athlete chose to go somewhere else. It takes a tremendous amount of tenacity, self-confidence, and perseverance to be a successful recruiter, and I had to admit that doing it for two major sports for that many years had started to wear on me. Good recruiting is a critical component of winning, and I did not want to see either of my sports suffer because I did not have enough time to devote to recruiting.

The thought of dropping one of my two sports was not a thought that I had been entertaining. As much as I loved coaching both sports, it was suddenly painfully clear to me that if I continued to try to coach both, the quality of both would suffer. Not only could I not devote the needed time to recruiting, but with increasing age came a waning of energy that prohibited me from keeping the pace that I was used to keeping.

There was also the challenge of maintaining coaching continuity with my assistant coaches. The assistant coach for basketball was a full-time position that was linked with being the head coach of women's golf. Most people who held that position were using it as a stepping stone to a head basketball position. Two or three years were pretty much the maximum lifespan for that job. Once I got someone trained and familiar with my system, it was time for her to move on. Softball was even more challenging, as the assistant coaches were graduate assistants who vacated the position every two years as they completed their Master's degrees. I could count on the assistant coach being young and eager but in need of a good deal of mentoring, and I also knew that the better they were, the more likely it was that I would lose them quickly.

If I had been able to keep an assistant for a long period of time where I felt more comfortable delegating some of the responsibilities that I reserved for myself, it might have made it more likely that I could sustain both sports for at least a couple more years. But the constant cycle with my assistants of hire, train and mentor, and watch them evolve into a head coach, ultimately put most of the coaching and recruiting burden on me.

I innately knew that something was going to have to change. I didn't know if softball or basketball was the sport that I should drop, but the reality of needing to do what was necessary to maintain the quality of both programs while enabling me to have continued

146

longevity in the coaching profession dictated that something would have to go.

I had other duties at Muskingum as well. I was a full professor in the Physical Education department, and although I did not teach a full faculty load, I taught a couple of courses each semester as part of our physical education teacher training program. I love teaching, and I did not even consider dropping teaching in order to free up more time for coaching. If I had wanted to be only a coach with no other types of responsibility, I would have probably looked for a job at Division I or II, where the duties are focused on just coaching. Administratively, I was the assistant athletic director and I had some responsibilities that touched both the men's and the women's program. I am passionate about my teaching and truly enjoy my administrative duties, so I definitely needed them to remain a part of my job. The most time-consuming part of my job were the coaching duties, and I was acutely aware that one of the two sports would have to be handed over to someone else in order for me to keep going.

During the 1999–2000 season, I had gone over four hundred wins in basketball. I had more wins than any other coach in the OAC, and we had made regular appearances in NCAA post-season play. Our success seemed to be trailing off a bit, however. It had become more and more difficult to recruit quality players, so I had to find ways to work both harder and smarter in order to maintain and improve the program. Anything less than the pursuit of excellence did not satisfy me.

I wrestled for many days with the decision of which sport to give up. I wasn't even sure if the college would be amenable to shrinking my duties down to one sport, but I knew that I could not keep going at this pace, so one way or the other, one of my two sports had to be handed over. I wavered back and forth in my decision-making process. I truly still enjoyed coaching both sports, so it was not a matter of being tired of either one. I knew that as soon as I made the decision and got it approved by the administration, I would immediately tell my players. Even though we had a few games to go in basketball and a whole season to go in softball, I was not going to pretend once I reached a decision. Pretense is something I despise, and I felt that my players knew me well enough that they would understand my decision-making process and respect me for my honesty.

I found coaching basketball to be more strategically challenging, simply because I believe that a coach has more control over strategy in a basketball game. In softball, there are only so many variables you can control. In basketball, you can switch defenses or disguise defenses, changing things up almost every time down the court if you so choose. You can control the clock, get the ball into the hands of your shooter, put on a full court press, run special plays for special situations, change your offensive sets, run subs in and out, and continually manipulate strategic variables to help determine the outcome.

I am not saying that many of those opportunities don't exist in softball, but where they do exist, it is to a lesser degree. You can still change defensive sets, call time out, substitute sparingly, and control some other strategic areas, but to a large degree, once the game is underway it is in the hands of the players. I love matching wits with other coaches, and I believed that I could influence the outcome of more games as a basketball coach than I could as a softball coach. Maybe basketball would best utilize all the coaching experience that I had accumulated.

Both teams had a sizeable number of freshmen, so it was going to be hard to break the news that I might be leaving after I had recruited them, telling them that I would be there all four years of their career. I value nothing more highly than the integrity of one's word, and it was breaking my heart to think about telling a group of women that I had planned to be there for them throughout their career but suddenly things had changed. I would have given them fair warning and been totally forthright with them had I known how I would feel at the end of the 2000 basketball season, but it caught me by surprise as much as it did them.

Both teams had upcoming seniors to whom I felt a great deal of loyalty. Quitting on them now would hurt them as much as it would hurt me if they were to walk into my office and suddenly announce that they were too tired to play their senior year. Both teams had a bright future. The basketball team had a chance to build around a first-year player, Jessica Gates, one of the best players to come out of our local area in many years. She was an athletic post player who could score at will, and I was only beginning to tap into her potential as a freshman. The softball team had more players with experience. There were some promising freshmen, but there were also six juniors who were looking forward to their final two years of play.

Basketball was more challenging to me from a coaching perspective, but softball was more enjoyable. The season was not quite as long and it was played outdoors where I could enjoy being outside. We worked extremely hard in softball, but the conditioning demands were not as overwhelming as they were for basketball. About the time "spring fever" hit every year, we got to take our softball trip to Florida, and despite the trip's being a lot of work and preparation, I began looking forward to the next year's trip the day we returned from the current one.

My mind vacillated between the pros and cons for days, and the final decision still did not seem to be clear in my mind as I tried to finalize things. The deciding factor for me went back to the accident that we had in basketball season. Even though we now traveled by bus throughout the basketball season, every time we had to make a trip with any snow on the road, my heart would be in my throat from the time we left campus until the time we safely returned. I dreaded any kind of recruiting trip when the weather was bad before I left or was threatening to turn bad while I was gone. The fact that basketball is a winter sport, and every trip dredged up unwanted memories of our accident, finalized my decision that I would keep softball and give up basketball.

The very next day, I called the president's office to see if I could meet with her and get this proposed change approved. We had just gone through hiring a new president, so I was not looking forward to introducing myself under such circumstances. Our new president did not know me and knew very little about me, except for whatever she might have read about me in college publications.

I was extremely nervous when I walked into her office. Anne C. Steele was trying to settle into a new situation and position, but was very gracious when she greeted me and immediately put me at ease. I had rehearsed how and what I wanted to say to her, but to hear myself say aloud for the first time that I wanted to resign as head basketball coach created more emotion than I was able to control. I struggled a bit with composure, but she patiently waited until I said what I had come to say.

When I left her office, I left with the assurance that she would talk with other members of her cabinet and would get back to me as soon as possible, and I was told to keep things under wraps until we were able to resolve all issues and decide exactly what needed to be done. I had a real difficult time coaching at practice that day, as I felt that I had betrayed the team but was not allowed to confess to them yet that I was done coaching them. It seemed that I was violating many of the rules that I had preached to them regarding hypocrisy, loyalty, honesty, and dedication. However, as much as it rubbed against my nature and made me feel uncomfortable, in my heart I knew that my decision would not change and I needed to stick with my decision and prepare to live with the consequences.

I had made it a practice of telling recruits that, ultimately, my goal was to win a national championship in basketball. I wanted to build character in my players, I wanted to build citizenship and an understanding of what it was like to be a contributing member of a larger community, and I wanted to increase their work ethic and perseverance. But combined with all that, I wanted to win a national championship. We had come close on three occasions, making it all the way to the championship game once and to the national quarterfinals two additional times, only to lose in the final minute of both of those games. It was torture to think about falling short after making a goal public, knowing that I never reached that goal.

Only a few days had elapsed when President Steele called me back to her office to say that the college would regretfully accept my resignation as Head Women's Basketball Coach. In lieu of those duties, I was asked to assume oversight of the intramural program for the college. Intramurals was in need of a major overhaul and desperately needed someone with credibility who would assume responsibility for it and get things moving in the right direction. I welcomed the challenge of getting our campus more involved with intramurals and recreation, and began laying plans for releasing the news of my resignation.

The Muskie grapevine has a way of spreading information around campus quickly. Usually the news is somewhat accurate, but it is often exaggerated or tainted with some inaccurate information. I wanted my team to hear it from me and not through the rumor mill, so I arranged to meet with the basketball team, followed by the softball team, that very night.

Maybe I am overly analytical, but I gave a lot of thought to where and how I wanted to talk to the team. I decided that the locker room was not appropriate. It was a locker room used for basketball, and then softball moved in when basketball was done with it. Right now, we were in basketball season and it was strictly a basketball locker room, so I felt like the softball players would resent having the news broken in someone else's living room.

I thought about using a classroom, but that just seemed too formal. I did not want the players to feel that they were being lectured to, and I just did not want the sterility of the classroom to destroy the interaction that needed to happen. I wanted to talk with my players rather than talk to them, and it seemed like a classroom would not facilitate that type of environment.

I eventually decided to use the area we called the VIP room. The VIP room is an elevated lounge area with a glassed-in front that overlooks the Rec Center gymnasium. It contains casual furniture that can be arranged in a conversational friendly fashion, and has lamps and lighting where you can control the intensity of illumination, so you don't feel like it is an interrogation room. It is a private area that I knew would not be interrupted by a wandering student, and it had a waiting area outside where the team waiting to come in could hang out if they were early or my presentation went late. The students sensed that it was something important when I called a meeting in the VIP room.

My heart was in my throat as I spoke that night. It is hard to say goodbye to a piece of your life that you have dedicated a quarter century of work to develop, and it was even harder to think of the ramifications that my absence would hold for those players who had chosen to come to Muskingum because I was the coach. I broke the news as tactfully and honestly as I knew how, and the team was in shock as a whole when I was done speaking. They had not seen it coming, and neither had I. After twenty-six years at the helm, I had to admit that it was time to bring things to a close and say goodbye to a team and a sport that I truly loved. I spoke to the basketball team first, and as they filed out, the softball team filed in. There were a few players who played both sports and stayed for both meetings.

Emotions were mixed that night. Some students cried out of empathy, while some cried out of anger. There was not as much inter-action as I had hoped there would be, as many of the players seemed to be avoiding eye contact. It was almost like an out-of-body experi-ence for me. I heard myself talking, but it seemed like I was the one listening rather than the one formulating the words. I imagined what thoughts of betrayal and disappointment might have been going through their minds. I felt like I was standing in the front of a court room, having just confessed to a crime, while I had my accusers in front of me, staring blankly, as they wondered what had possessed me to do such a thing.

A press conference was scheduled the next day to announce to the public that I would be stepping down. This was far easier than telling the players, as it was a business matter rather than an emo-tional investment. All of the predictable questions were asked, and it was mercifully over within a matter of fifteen minutes or so.

My final basketball season was not a particularly memorable season as far as the record goes, finishing at 12 - 14. I truly hated bowing out after a losing season. It was gratifying to upset highly favored Mount Union in the OAC tournament, but we ended up los-ing two nights later to Baldwin Wallace to bring my basketball career to a close. As the school year progressed and we entered softball sea-son, the college had a retirement reception that acknowledged every-thing that I had done for women's basketball. The OAC coaches also gave me a wonderful acknowledgment at the final game of the OAC tournament. Although it was appreciated, it did not take the sting out of giving up a sport that I so dearly loved. I believe the players even-tually understood my need to whittle my duties down to one sport, but in my own mind I knew that I had let them down as I was unable to bring home the national championship that I wanted them to experience.

Knowing when to let go is a decision that is gut-wrenching and requires a great deal of wisdom and maturity. I don't know if it is harder on a program for a coach to leave it too early, or for a coach to try to stay involved too long. To this day, I do not know if my timeline was right, but my mental anguish over giving up on an incomplete job was eased by knowing that I gave everything I could to basketball while it was still under my tutelage. Although I would no longer have the privilege of coaching the basketball team, I knew that the players that I had coached were loyal and proud graduates, and I knew that my job now was to turn my attention to softball and try to raise the level of excellence there.

Chapter 10

We Are the Champions

Those that know how to win are much more numerous than
those who know how to make proper use of their victories.
Polybius

Although I was still mourning the loss of basketball, the 2000 softball season was good to me. We finished the season with a 45 - 5 record. We sailed through the OAC season, going undefeated, and followed that with an undefeated showing in the OAC tournament as well. It was a disappointment to lose twice to Alma, Michigan, in the NCAA regional tournament, 3 - 0 and 4 - 0, but it seemed like their pitcher had our number.

We had six key juniors who would all be returning the following year. The primary graduation loss was our number one pitcher, Jennifer Segner. She was both an athletic and an academic All-American, and her athletic and academic work habits were off the charts. When she graduated, she held the NCAA III career win record with 117 wins, as well as the NCAA record for most wins in a season with forty. When you consider that Division III is limited to playing forty regular season games and you can only exceed the forty game count by playing in the post-season tournament, it makes that feat seem even more remarkable. Jen was primarily a drop-ball pitcher. She struck out her share of batters, but mainly she depended on forcing batters to beat the ball into the ground and then allowing her defense to make a play.

With so much emphasis on pitching, it was little wonder that people were skeptical about our chances for success after Jen graduated. The only other pitcher that we had with any experience was Dani Keiffer. Most players would have quit long before they got to the point in their career where Dani was. Dani was a freshman during

Seg's sophomore year and she had waited patiently behind Seg for three years. Seg pitched every important game for us, and Dani was spotted in against weaker opponents or when we had enough of a lead that giving up a couple of runs would not matter. Over her first three years, she had pitched a total of 118 innings. Her cumulative won-loss record was 11 - 3 with an ERA of 2.61. Probably her least impressive statistic was that she had only struck out thirty-three batters, while she had given up a total of 123 hits. Dani was not what you would call a dominant pitcher.

But Dani had some innate qualities that most other people lacked. She was eternally optimistic and never let her disappointment in not getting to pitch show through to her teammates. Her unselfishness was a quality that was admired by everyone who knew her. Even though Dani had not been tested in big games, she had supreme confidence and never seemed to doubt her ability to get a hitter out. She was one of those hard workers that you are glad to have on your side and that you admire immensely, but she was not one who you would think could carry a team or maybe even carry her share of the load. It was not that I didn't trust Dani, it was just that she was an unproven entity and it was a little worrisome to think that the future of my team rested on her arm.

For the first time in many years, I was not tired when softball practices got underway in 2001. I did not realize how much of a difference it would make by not coaching basketball, but it was definitely a refreshing feeling to start a season with plenty of energy. I could hardly wait for our spring trip.

We opened our season at the Lead Off Classic in La Grange, Georgia. The Lead Off Classic is held once every three years in NCAA Division III, and, in theory, the top twenty-four teams in the nation are invited to participate. Although there is no way to guarantee that the best twenty-four teams are actually there, you can be certain that the competition will be very challenging. It is probably not the best way to open a season when you have no experienced pitching.

The results were pretty predictable when we opened our season 0 - 3. Our opening game was against Cabrini, Pennsylvania, and we lost 7 - 4. The next game pitted us against St. Mary's of Minnesota, the defending national champions. Thank goodness for the mercy rule as the game ended 10 - 1 in the fifth inning. That was followed by yet another loss to LaGrange, Georgia, 8 - 7.

However, the mark of a good team is the ability to bounce back, even when your confidence has been shaken. We followed our less than stellar beginning with thirteen straight wins. This streak included our home opener, a 13 - 12 eighth-inning win over Case Western Reserve University that was highlighted by a three-run homerun in the bottom of the seventh inning with two outs. Second baseman Shelly Delucas hit a deep drive to center field that looked like the game's final out, when the ball popped out of the center fielder's glove and over the fence. Maybe this was an omen of things to come.

It seemed that things were still not in sync. We lost our next three games 2 - 1 and 6 - 4 to Denison, followed by a 1 - 0 loss to Baldwin Wallace in our conference opener. However, following this we reeled off twenty-four straight victories, including seven one-run wins. We closed the season at 37 - 6, winning the OAC and the OAC tournament for the fourth straight year. We totally dominated the tournament, winning three games by a composite score of 30 - 3.

We once again were in the NCAA regional tournament. It was being hosted by Denison University, designated as the number one seed, due in large part to their sweeping a double header against us earlier in the season. I was glad to see Denison was the host, as their campus was less than fifty miles from our campus and it would be a convenient site for our fans.

It was a difficult matchup for us in the first round, as we had to play Alma, Michigan. We still had a bad taste in our mouths from losing to them the previous year, but we managed to hold them scoreless and won the game 3 - 0. We then had to play Case Western Reserve University. The regular season matchup had been a slug fest, but this time we handled them fairly easily, winning 9 - 4. Because this was only a five-team regional, if we stayed in the winners' bracket, we only had to win one more game and we would be able to punch our ticket to the national championship tournament.

Denison came out of the losers' bracket, so we were destined to face a team that had already beaten us twice during the regular season.

Denison had an outstanding pitcher in Courtney Zollars. Her specialty was the rise ball, and she threw it with both good velocity and movement. I was having a hard time getting my hitters to lay off that pitch and not chase it out of the zone. By the third inning, I was already frustrated with how many of my hitters were striking out.

With two outs and a runner on first, our center fielder, Chantelle Andrews, walked to the plate. Chantelle was a small player at 5' 5" and about 110 pounds, and she was definitely not a home run threat. She immediately got behind in the count 0 - 2. Knowing that Zollars would try to get her to chase a rise ball out of the zone when she was that far ahead in the count, I decided I would give Chantelle a take sign on an 0 - 2 count. Although she looked at me like I was crazy, she did what she was told and did not swing, and my hunch was rewarded with a pitch that was up and out of the zone. I was pretty confident that Zollars would still give her nothing to hit, so I gave her the take sign again. I am sure Chantelle was frustrated, but to her credit she froze her bat and let another high pitch go by that was the same pitch Zollar had used for her strikeout pitch on several other batters. On the next pitch, I gave Chantelle a green light. She turned on a pitch and sent a line drive sailing just inside the left-field foul pole for a homerun.

We were elated to have a 2 - 0 lead, but the fifth inning was when we finally put the game away. With two outs and runners on first and second, our second baseman, Shelly Delucas, hit a routine pop-up to their second baseman, who lost it in the sun, allowing the runner at second to scamper home and kept runners at first and second. Mandy Carnes, our All-American, drove her twelfth homerun of the season deep over the right field fence. We were now up 6 - 0 and coasted home for the win.

We celebrated on the bus as we drove back to New Concord, knowing that we had now earned our spot to play with the final eight teams in the nation. We had been to the World Series on three other occasions, with our best finish being fourth place. After you have been there once, it is such an awesome experience that it gives you tremendous incentive to get there again. However, when you consider that there are nearly four hundred softball teams in Division III, the likelihood of returning can seem pretty slim. Our seniors had been there as freshmen, so they recognized the magnitude of this accomplishment in 2000 and looked forward to making the best of the opportunity.

Dani Keiffer had pitched every single pitch in the regional tournament. In the final game she had done an outstanding job, striking out three, walking no one, and giving up only five hits. There were several times during the course of the tournament when I thought about taking her out, but it seemed like every time I went out to talk with her, she said something that convinced me that I should leave her in the game. In spite of the fact that she did not dominate the opposition, it seemed like the "bend but don't break" rule worked well for her as she shut out two excellent teams and defeated the other to pitch us into the next round.

This is the best time of year to be playing softball. Classes and finals are now over, and summer jobs have not yet begun. For the players, it takes them back to a younger age when all you have to worry about is playing ball and enjoying your summer vacation. Most of the students have gone home, but the ones that remain, along with the community and faculty, are buzzing with excitement.

The turnaround time between the regional and national tournament is very short. You no sooner get home from the regional tournament than it is time to leave again. You are able to get the team laundry done and repacked, hold a couple of press conferences with local media, fit in a couple of practices, and before you know it, you are ready to depart.

A Division III head coach does not have the luxury of assistants or administrators who are assigned the responsibility of making travel arrangements or collecting scouting information, so these couple of days felt like a whirlwind of activity. I was not doing all the work myself as I was blessed to have two quality assistant coaches. Sandra Sanford was in her second year of being a graduate assistant. She was a graduate of the University of Connecticut and her main duty for me was as a hitting coach, although she performed many miscellaneous duties as well. She was as organized, knowledgeable, and professional as any assistant that I had ever had. John Wells was more of a volunteer assistant who was a dear friend and had worked with my pitchers for over a decade.

In spite of the fact that I had great assistants, things seemed even more hectic this year because the national tournament was being held in Eau Claire, Wisconsin. If a post-season site is within five hundred miles of your institution, the NCAA requires that you travel by bus. However, if it is over five hundred miles, then they will fly the team. Salem, Virginia, is often the site for the national tournament, and when it is held there, it is well within the five-hundred-mile radius and we conveniently travel by bus. Eau Claire fell outside the five-hundred-mile radius, so this time we were flying. Because we seldom fly to a game, there were a lot of details to deal with that I was not used to handling.

There was a small group of well wishers who helped us load the bus and wished us luck as we headed for the Columbus airport. We had several players who had never flown, so they were a little anxious as we checked in and went to our gate to wait for our boarding call. It was unfortunate that a major thunderstorm hit shortly before our flight was scheduled to take off. There was about a two-hour delay before they began boarding, so it definitely did not help the nerves of those who were already apprehensive. The predictable kidding and joking became even worse as the expert flyers (anyone who had flown at least once in her life), tried to expose any signs of weakness in the novice flyers.

It was nearly 2:00 A.M. by the time we landed, got our luggage, reloaded a team bus, and made it to the team hotel. I was shocked that our local host, Jo Ellen, had hung in there, and was still waiting for us when we arrived. She was the former softball coach at the University of Wisconsin-Eau Claire, and although she was no longer coaching, she still taught in the Physical Education department. It did not take much coaxing to get the players settled into their rooms and in bed. It had been a very long day, and at this point, the fatigue superseded the excitement.

The first day at the national tournament does not include competition. There are two hours set aside for each team to practice, with the most important part of that practice being the one-hour time slot that you are allowed to be on the competition game field. I am not sure how much good a practice does at this time of the year, but the opportunity to acclimate to the game field and surroundings is invaluable.

Most of the rest of the day is devoted to socializing and team activities. The activities vary from site to site, and one of the activities sponsored by Eau Claire was a tee-shirt exchange. Every player was instructed to bring a softball tee shirt representing her institution for the event. When the trading floor was open, everyone was negotiating trades to get the tee shirt that she wanted to take home as a souvenir. The tee shirt in greatest demand was a St. Mary's shirt, as they were the defending national champions. The event was supposed to be fun, and for the most part it was enjoyable. However, there were a few disgruntled Muskies who left disappointed because no one wanted to trade for their shirt, so they exited the trading floor with their Muskingum softball shirt still in hand. I guess most of those who were there did not consider a Muskingum shirt to be of much value.

The culminating event for the first day is the NFCA All-American banquet. It is quite an impressive event as the best players in the country in NCAA III are assembled in one room. We were fortunate to have two players named to the All-American team. As a sophomore, Mandy Carnes was named to the first team for the second consecutive year as a designated hitter. Mandy had a .490 batting average, which included 16 doubles, 12 homeruns, and 52 RBIs. She eventually became the only player in Muskingum's history and one of only a few nationwide to ever be named a first team All-American for four consecutive years. Her final two years, she garnered the award at the first-base position and still holds the Division III record for most homeruns in a season, with twenty-four, and most homeruns in a career, with fifty-nine.

Carla Kampschmidt was named a third-team All-American at the first base position. This was her senior season. When she was a freshman, I decided to move her from the shortstop position that she had played all the way through high school to the first base position where I felt she could strengthen the team. To her credit, she willingly accepted the change. For the season, she hit .402 as a leadoff hitter, including 11 doubles, 2 triples, and 23 RBIs. Perhaps more importantly, she had committed only one error in 450 chances and had become one of the best defensive first basemen in the country. She not only was an outstanding athlete but was also an outstanding student as she was named an Academic All-American as well.

As much as you wanted the players to enjoy the festivities, we all understood that the reason we were there was to crown a national champion. We met that evening after the banquet in a meeting room provided by the hotel to go over the scouting report one more time on our first opponent, William Patterson University of Patterson, New Jersey, and to make sure everyone was focused going into the game tomorrow. I could already see signs of nervousness with the players as they shuffled scouting papers and had a faraway stare, only pretending to give me the eye contact that I always demanded. They were still in their banquet clothes, but in the privacy of our meeting room they had abandoned their lady-like posture. I am sure they felt just like I did; the quicker we got to play the game, the happier we would be.

The biggest concern for me remained our pitching. Dani had been doing a great job all season, but as we kept winning, we had elevated again to another level of hitters that she would have to face. We also had developed little pitching depth, as I had come to depend on Dani much like I had depended on Jen Segner during Dani's first three years. Angie Burnside was a freshman change-up artist, but she was not ready to pitch in the big games. If Dani had a bad game, we would disappear from the scene quickly. I kept telling myself to control the controllables and to stop worrying.

It was a feeling of relief the next day when we finally approached game time. We began our warm-ups about an hour-and-a-half ahead of game time. There was a practice field that was adjacent to the game field, so it provided a space to take adequate batting practice and to complete the rest of our warm-ups. Our pitching coach, John Wells (Figure 6), usually pitched batting practice to at least our starting lineup. It always amazed me how he could seemingly throw forever and never get tired. He had such good control that the players could always get a lot of good swings in against him without waiting on wasted pitches, so we had really come to depend on him for this service.

161

Figure 6. Pitching coach John Wells during the 2001 season.

After the game prior to ours had ended, the game field was dragged, relined, and it was announced that it was time for Muskingum to take their eight-minute infield warm-up. We looked sharp during our warm-ups, and I was grateful that my pregame speech would not have to lecture them about proper intensity and focus. They were clearly ready to play.

When the game got underway, somehow we got a little off track. We were on the verge of losing the game in the first inning when William Patterson loaded the bases with only one out. We managed to escape that jam without giving up a run but found ourselves in trouble again in the fifth inning as they put runners on second and third, but still could not score. They had an RBI single in the sixth to push across their only run.

The third inning gave the Muskies their first lead when Carla Kampschmidt doubled to right to plate our freshman left fielder, Erin Zupko. Another run was added in the fifth when third baseman Megan Monsman scored from third on a two-out wild pitch. The score was 2 - 1 going into the bottom of the sixth, and a Julie Ryan RBI single created some breathing room and the final margin of 3 - 1.

If there is such a thing as an ugly win, this game would have qualified. We were constantly in and out of trouble, and every inning seemed to bring a new adventure. Dani had pitched well, scattering six hits with two walks and no strikeouts, defeating All-American pitcher Diane Naugle, who had fanned seven and given up seven hits. Our usually reliable defense made a couple of errors and kept the game far more interesting than it should have been.

To have a realistic chance of winning the national tournament, you have to stay out of the loser's bracket early in the tournament. With the format being an eight team, double elimination tournament, going into the losers' bracket early creates a scenario where you have to win a substantial number of games to climb back out. This is a tall order for any team, but when you are primarily riding the arm of one pitcher, it becomes critical to minimize the number of games that you have to win. So regardless of how ugly and stressful the win over William Patterson seemed, it was a beautiful and necessary win to keep our hopes alive.

That win set up a match with St. Mary's University of Winona, Minnesota, the defending national champions. The St. Mary's team had been coached the previous year by highly regarded John Tschida, but he had left the school to take a position at St. Thomas, Minnesota, his alma mater. Although most of the same players were back, they were under a new coach.

Preparing for this game created some mixed feelings when you consider they had mercied us 10-1 in the second game of the season. In some ways our players were anxious to prove that they were a better team than they appeared to be in that game, but at the same time they were reluctant to admit that the possibility existed for us to be embarrassed again, only this time it would be on a national stage. The best strategy for us was to not dwell on the past, but simply play an out at a time and see where it took us.

While we might have been battling a chink in our confidence armor, St. Mary's was highly favored, and the coach was probably having an equally hard time selling the idea to her team that this would be a challenging game. I felt that she was plenty confident about their chances of winning when she won the coin toss for home and away, and chose to be away. The NCAA has a formula to even out home and visitor opportunities in post-season play, and she had already calculated that if they were visitors in this game, it would assure them of being home in the semi-final game if they won. I guess she thought her chances of winning were pretty high as she was saving her opportunity to be home team for the next game.

The game was scheduled for early evening, and we were fully into our warm-up routine. For batting practice, I had split the team into two groups so that the starters could hit batting practice off John Wells, our pitching coach, and the others would follow a different routine to get in their swings. I fully trusted my assistant coach Sandra Sanford with the hitters, so she and John were getting our main hitters primed and ready while I turned my attention elsewhere.

We were not too far into batting practice when one of the players raced over and, in between her gasps for air, managed to tell me that there was something wrong with John and I needed to get over there quickly. When I turned around, I saw that John had sunk to his knees, and I thought perhaps he had been hit by a pitch. As I ran over, I tried to get the story of what happened from the players who witnessed it, and about all they could tell me was that he said he did not feel well, and suddenly went down.

I asked the remaining players to vacate the area and call for additional help, and as I turned my attention to John, he lowered himself face forward towards the ground. I could hear him say, "Give me a towel," and he was sweating profusely. I called for a player to give me both a wet and a dry towel, and I slowly rolled John onto his back. He grabbed his chest, and it was pretty apparent that this was a heart attack.

I could already hear the siren as the ambulance was nearly to the entrance of Carson Park. John asked for a drink of water, and by the time I was ready to moisten his lips, the paramedics had arrived. I glanced at the players while they stood huddled together and watched paramedics work on John and load him into the ambulance. Within a moment, the scene we had just witnessed disappeared with the distant wailing of the siren.

I felt sick to my stomach. I teach the first aid class at Muskingum, and have lectured many times on the signs and symptoms of heart attacks. John was one tough guy, and anything that took him to his knees had to be serious. Having seen his onset of symptoms, watched the skin change color, witnessed the extreme shortness of breath and profuse sweating, not to mention the look in John's eyes, there was not much doubt in my mind that we had lost him. It was one of those things that I needed to deny in my emotional mind, but in my logical mind, I had to admit that the reality was that John had suffered a heart attack that he would be unable to survive. I am not qualified to diagnose, but his death seemed like a medical certainty to me.

I looked over at the players who stood some distance away, and even from a distance, I could see the look in their eyes that said, "Please tell us that it is not true." They stood close together, maybe hoping that strength could be derived from unity, and looking for me to say something comforting or wise as I approached them. I was choking back tears when I directed Sandra, my assistant coach, to take the team to a quiet area and keep them together until I could figure out what to do. I told them that things did not look good, but it was too soon to jump to conclusions about the condition that John might be in.

I saw a couple of members of the National Softball Committee walking towards me. It was now about forty-five minutes until the scheduled game time. They reassured me that I could take all the time that we needed, and if we needed to cancel the game and play it tomorrow, we could do that. They were very understanding and anxious to help.

My main concern was that nothing would be broadcast on the radio about what was going on, as I knew that Jane, John's wife, was tuned into the game back in Ohio, and I certainly did not want her receiving the news over the air. I didn't even know if information on what had happened had reached the broadcast booth on the main field as we were still on the warm-up field, but the committee assured me that nothing would be said publicly until matters had been taken care of privately. We had not yet decided if we were going to go ahead and play the game, or if we would postpone until tomorrow, but either way, the radio announcers would have to find some way to explain why the game was not on the air at the scheduled time.

I asked for a phone and a private area so that I could call Jane. Not only was Jane John's wife, but she was also my best friend. She was a senior the first year that I arrived at Muskingum and was a wonderful athlete. She was only one year younger than I was, so after she graduated, we became quick friends. She was from the area and got a job teaching math in New Concord. We played summer softball together for several years after she graduated, and as we both got older, we had become avid golfers and were part of a regular foursome. She usually traveled to post-season play with John, but because this trip was so far, she had stayed behind to take care of things at home.

I had no idea what I was going to say when I called, and both my hands and my voice were shaking. I don't know if I was relieved or disappointed when Jane did not answer, but my sense of urgency increased to contact her as soon as I could. I was not thinking real straight, but the next person that I decided to call was Debbie. She was part of our golfing foursome and I had her phone number memorized, so I tried to get through to her. Joel, her husband, answered the phone and I left the message with him. I tried to convey the sense of urgency to him that we needed to get the word to Jane before she inadvertently heard something over the radio. Joel found Debbie, and ultimately they decided that the best avenue was to find Jane's sister, Jill, who lived nearby and have her talk to Jane.

With that behind me, I went back to the team to talk with them and discuss what we wanted to do. There were mostly tear-smudged faces and blank stares as we tried to talk through the pain. Their minds were clearly at the hospital with John, but their bodies were at the ball park. The seniors somewhat took charge of the conversation, and eventually decided that they wanted to go ahead and play because that is what they thought John would want us to do.

I cautioned them that if we were going to play that we would have to resume warming up right away, and I reminded them that our opponent would not be interested in surrendering to us out of sympathy. If we were going to choose to play, then we needed to "be here now."

The "Be Here Now" phrase was one with which they were familiar. I lecture on it at least once every season, trying to get players to understand the uselessness of having your mind in one place while your body is another (be HERE), or the frustration of having mind and body together, but letting your mind race ahead to possible consequences or to reflect back on regrets (be here NOW). It would take all the discipline we could muster to piece together any kind of performance that would give us a chance to win the game.

I stayed away from appealing to their emotions by saying things like, "Let's win this one for John." I did not want players to feel regret or to feel that they had let John down if we were unable to win. This was a time to take every ounce of self-discipline that they had within them and use it to stay focused on the task at hand. I told them that as soon as the game was over, we would have a team meeting and try to sort things out.

I was especially worried for Dani Keiffer. All of the players loved John, as he brought a sense of humor and light-heartedness that was a great counterbalance to my intense and serious personality. He was quick to smile, he could always find something positive to say to a pitcher, and he was thoroughly addicted to fast-pitch softball. But he had a special relationship with the pitchers, and tonight Dani was going to have to carry the torch as she took the field for the first time in her career without John on the sideline.

I am not sure how far behind schedule we were when the game started. Time seemed to have been standing still for a while, but I suppose that it must have been an hour or so. We had not received any official word that John had passed away, although I knew in my heart that he was gone. I don't know if the players were clinging to hope or if they had resolved themselves to the gravity of the situation, but I wasn't sure how much leadership I could provide for this game as I was having my own difficult time of "being here now."

As the game got underway, the focus in our players had shifted from playing St. Mary's, the defending national champions, to conquering themselves, regardless of what the opponent was doing. The first two innings we matched zeroes as neither team could get anything going offensively. Each inning that Dani went out she would do what she always did when she pitched. When she got to the pitching circle, she would draw a smiley face in the dirt with her index finger to remind her that everything would be all right, then she would pick up a piece of dirt or pebble, throw it toward their dugout, and say something about the other team like, "Three and out! This inning is over," to remind herself that she was in charge of the hitters.

The third inning was good to us again as our number nine hitter, freshman Erin Zupko, led off the inning with a single up the middle. Carla Kampschmidt smacked a slap bunt right back at the pitcher that was too hot for her to handle, and suddenly we had two runners on with no one out.

The St. Mary's coach decided to make a pitching change, and brought in Jill Hocking, a rise-ball artist. I suspect that her scouting report told her that we had a hard time laying off the rise ball. Chantelle Andrews had a great at-bat, and with two strikes, she fouled off four straight pitches to eventually draw the walk.

We now had the bases loaded with no outs, and our number three hitter coming to the plate. Julie Ryan promptly singled up the middle to plate Zupko, and Mandy Carnes followed her with a run-scoring single to left field that scored Carla. Hocking retired the next three batters, but the damage was done as the Muskies had scored two runs.

It was during the fourth inning when one of the Muskingum administrators who was present at the game motioned me to the fence beside the dugout. I was given the news that John had been officially pronounced dead at the hospital. The only player who was within hearing distance of the conversation was Dani Keiffer. Even though I knew that she knew, we both pretended to be uninformed until the game was over.

St. Mary's had already stranded several runners, leaving two on in the first, third, fourth and fifth innings. Their final threat came in the seventh inning when Jennifer Meyer hit a one-out single up the middle. Jill Hocking followed with a single to left, giving them two runners with one out. Jackie Huegel reached base on a fielder's choice, putting runners on first and third with two outs. Their final batter smashed a hot ground ball up the middle. It looked like a sure hit, but shortstop Julie Ryan made a diving grab and flipped it to second baseman Shelly Delucas for the final out.

Keiffer had scattered ten hits, stranding twelve runners and striking out one batter. Muskingum had managed only six hits, but we found a way to get them when we needed them. It was bittersweet as we went through the line to shake hands, then immediately cleaned out the dugout and headed for a meeting room that had been provided for us by the tournament administrators.

The room was concrete block, much like an unfinished basement. There were some folding chairs as well as some folding tables. I asked my assistant to try to arrange the room in a circle or in some fashion that was not formal rows, and I would soon be in to talk with the players. I had also invited the parents to the meeting. We had quite a large contingent who had followed us to Eau Claire, and I thought I might need their support as I did not know how their children would handle an unexpected death. There were also a couple of other college administrators present, and although they stayed in the background, they were there for any support that was needed.

As the players and parents filed in, I walked around by myself for a few minutes, trying to collect my thoughts. I decided the best approach was to be direct and forthright, but to also be tactful and soft spoken. When I finally walked in, everyone's eyes were fixed on me as if they were waiting for some words of wisdom that would make everyone feel better. I had no such words.

The first thing that I did was to tell them that we had received official word that John had been pronounced dead at 6:35 P.M. at the local hospital and that he had died of a massive heart attack. I don't think they were surprised with the news; it was just hard to hear someone say it aloud. As long as you are only thinking it, there is something about the silence that validates hope. But once you finally say it, wishful thinking suddenly seems silly. We took a few minutes after the news had been broken to allow players to hug and comfort each other, or to cry into the arms of their parents, who looked as helpless as I felt.

I reminded all the parents that they had just witnessed one of the most amazing feats that they would ever see, and it was performed by their own children. At the peak of despair, they had displayed the strength and discipline needed to defeat the defending national champions. Never have I been more proud of a team than I was at that moment.

I gave the parents and their children some additional time together, and then I respectfully requested that we be allowed to load the bus and get back to the hotel. We were both physically and emotionally exhausted, and the evening was far from over. We needed to shower, eat, have a team meeting, and try to make sense out of the day.

The bus ride back to the hotel seemed eerie. John always sat in the first seat right behind the driver, and I always sat in the first seat on the other side of the aisle directly opposite John. Part of our routine was that we would share the stat sheet with each other after a game, and I think we both looked forward to analyzing the game on the way home to see if our foresight was as good as our hindsight. But on this ride, John's seat was empty. There was no one to talk with about the intentional walks, or the missed steal sign, or the Texas leaguer, or the ball that had eyes. There was no one to talk with.

There was an uncomfortable silence all the way back, and it almost startled me to hear my voice over the bus microphone announce to the players that they needed to shower while I ordered pizza, and then we would meet in my room to eat and talk. John's room was just down the hall from mine, and I wasn't sure what or how to say something to the front desk to let them know that we didn't need the room anymore. I decided I would postpone that task until tomorrow. Maybe it wouldn't seem like such an unpleasant thing to do then, so I was thinking that procrastination on that night would be my ally.

The pizza and the players pretty much arrived simultaneously. For once, they didn't complain about the toppings that I had chosen or the lack of napkins, nor did they question why I had gotten Dominos instead of their favorite brand. I wish they would have complained, as it would have broken the silence as they filed into the room, picked up their paper plate and drink, and found a spot on the floor or the edge of a bed. Most of them were in their favorite sleeping attire of mesh shorts and a tee shirt. The room smelled like shampoo and a variety of fragrant bath soaps. There were cascades of wet hair in the room. It almost seemed like no one even wanted the sound of a hair dryer in their room to disturb the blanket of silence that seemed to have descended to give us comfort.

I finally broke the silence when everyone had finished eating and began to sneak expectant glances at me to see what should happen next. I spoke for a few minutes in order to break the ice and to share my thoughts. "Dying is a part of living," I said. "If John could have picked the way that he wanted to die, it would have probably been similar to what just happened. He died with the team that he loved trying to achieve the pinnacle of success. He died doing what he loved with his cleats on his feet and his ball glove on his hand. Although it was unexpected, he didn't suffer, and if he could see what happened tonight, I know that he is smiling."

For some of them, this was the closest person that they had ever lost through death in their young lives, so it was hard for them to sort out their feelings. The seniors eventually chipped in, and although they were hurting in a way that many of them didn't even recognize, they said all the right things to comfort themselves and their teammates. The conversation was not about softball that night. It was about life and death and trying to make sense of a tragedy that didn't make sense.

John was sixty-two years old when he died. He had worked with our pitchers for the previous fourteen years, but in the past six or seven years, he had become even more involved with our program by traveling with us on our spring trip and making it to most of our road games. He had always been a volunteer coach and refused any money for his services, as he would always insist that I use it for the girls. I used to kid him that I would double his salary by giving him two coaching shirts.

John made his living by being the maintenance supervisor for the East Muskingum School District. His paycheck came from the school district, but his passion was working with pitchers. Even at age sixty-two, he still played some competitive fastpitch, but he had diverted most of his softball focus to teaching players how to pitch. He ran free clinics on Sunday afternoon for any interested player and also served as the pitching coach for John Glenn High School in New Concord.

John was a joy to be around. He had a quick wit and a mischievous grin that made you think he was always up to some practical joke. He had the perfect personality for a pitching coach, as he always found a positive way to help a pitcher who was struggling with confidence or who was frustrated because she just could not get a pitch to work. John would often come straight from work over to our practices, still attired in his blue jeans and work boots. The softball field seemed to reinvigorate his energy. His truck would roll into the parking lot after a long day that had probably started well before daylight, but you could see him relax and regain his energy as he worked with the pitchers and then pitched an hour or so of batting practice to our hitters.

Besides being their coach, John was somewhat of a grandfather figure for many of our players. Some of them shared stories of things John had said to them that had helped them when they were struggling. The pitchers, of course, seemed to be hit the hardest, but there was not a single person on the team who did not enjoy having John as part of our coaching staff.

The conversation continued until no one had anything else they wanted to say, and then the night ended with an obligatory announcement about what time we were meeting for breakfast.

I knew that I would have a hard time sleeping, and as much as I would have liked to just be by myself and reflect on the tragedy of the day, I felt like I needed to work on the scouting report for Central College from Pella, Iowa. They were the top-seeded team in the tournament, the #1-ranked team in the nation, and they had won their first two games to advance in the brackets and earn the right to play us for a spot in the national championship game. Although we had prepared some information on them, thinking that we might play them, there was a whole different level of preparation needed when we knew we *were* going to play them. Maybe by completing this task tonight, I would have the time tomorrow to prepare mentally for the game and face the reality of coaching without John.

It was a very restless night. I know that at some point I went to sleep, but when I got up the next morning, I did not feel like I had slept at all. The moment I awoke, my mind immediately raced back to the tumultuous happenings of the day before. It had almost seemed like a bad dream, but the morning brought the reality of the situation back into focus.

We had made it through the game against St. Mary's, but at least from a player's perspective, I suspected that some of what we had accomplished was due to riding the emotions and resulting adrenalin. With the emotional shock and the resulting adrenalin wearing off, I questioned whether we would be able to channel our thoughts and energy to focus on playing the game. Having twenty-four hours to let the tragedy sink in was not likely to have a positive effect on our play, and I wasn't convinced that we would have the mental discipline to minimize our emotional roller coaster while maximizing our physical level of play. I guessed we would have to find that out at game time.

John, Sandra, and I always sat together at breakfast. It was a good time to hash over strategy and make sure our game plan was in order. On this morning, the chair across the table from me was empty. It was uncomfortable to order my meal as I knew exactly what John would have ordered if he were there. The waitress was the same waitress from yesterday, and she had been the victim of some good-natured kidding from John when she could not keep his coffee cup filled fast enough. When she asked me if we were waiting on the gentleman from yesterday to arrive before ordering, I had to tell her, "No, he won't be coming today." The conversation between Sandra and me felt empty, as it seemed John should be chipping in with his comments at any moment.

There was a large message board in the lobby of the team hotel where players from different teams could leave notes and messages for other players. By the time we got back from breakfast, the message board was filled with condolences and well wishes from other teams and players. There were even some teams who sent us flowers. My players were truly touched by the kindness and understanding shown towards them by their competitors.

The game was scheduled for late afternoon, so following breakfast we headed back to the hotel for our team meeting and mental preparation for the game. It is always difficult to fill time on a game day, and it was especially challenging this day. Each player had plenty of time to be left with her own thoughts and the opportunity to try to sort things out before game time.

It was a relief to finally arrive at the field to begin our pregame warm-ups. We tried to keep everything as normal as possible, but we obviously had to adjust batting practice since John was not there to pitch. The atmosphere seemed a little strained, but I believed everyone was doing the best they could to get focused and ready to play. To think about facing the defending national champions and then the #1-ranked team on two consecutive days of competition was a daunting task, even under the best of circumstances.

I spoke privately to Dani Keiffer just before game time. I was trying to reassure her, but in fact I think the tables were turned, as the conversation, instead, reassured me. I marveled at Dani's composure and resolve. If it was up to her, I thought, maybe we could actually win the game.

The very first inning presented our first big challenge. Their leadoff hitter, Molly Parrott, looped a single over the head of our second baseman, and then promptly stole second. The Central team was a team based on speed, and their lineup was full of quick little slappers who could create havoc once they got on base. Following a pop-up, Parrott moved to third on a two-out ground out. Another ground ball on a Keiffer drop ball got us out of the jam.

The second inning was not any easier as their first hitter reached first base on an error. A sacrifice bunt moved her to second, and she immediately stole third. A hard ground ball back to Keiffer allowed her to throw the runner out at the plate. For the second day in a row, catcher Tami Anglin ended the inning when she threw a runner out at second who was trying to steal.

When the magical third inning rolled around, the score was tied 0 - 0. Freshman right fielder Jen Shay led off the inning with a weak blooper over the pitcher's head that dropped halfway between the pitching rubber and second base for an infield single. Erin Zupko hit a ground ball to the third baseman that moved Shay to second base. This brought All-American Carla Kampschmidt to the plate. Central's head coach, George Wares, opted to intentionally walk Carla and pitch to our next batter, Chantelle Andrews. Chantelle was our #2 batter, who specialized in bunting and finding a way to move runners. Carla had a hot bat and could hit for power, so I could easily see why he decided to pitch to Chantelle.

When Chantelle walked to the plate, you could see a look of defiance in her eyes. She was determined to show them that it was a bad decision for them to put her in a clutch situation. She succeeded. Chantelle hit a bomb over the center fielder's head to easily drive in both Shay and Kampschmidt. Although Central escaped the inning with no further scoring, the damage had been done.

Central was frustrated when they wasted a two out triple in the bottom of the third. Neither team was able to mount much of a scoring threat throughout the rest of the game, so the final score ended up 2 - 0.

Dani had pitched another gem, giving up only four hits, striking out two, and walking no one. When Dani was interviewed after the game, she said she could hear John's voice throughout the game reminding her of the two things that he always said to her during the course of the game. She could hear him saying, "Push off, Keiff, push off," and "Keep'er down, Dani, keep'er down."

All we had to do now was to wait and see which team would come through the losers' bracket to determine who our opponent would be for the national championship game. It was clear that we had the crowd on our side. Some of the teams had already been eliminated, and any of the eliminated teams or fans who had previously been neutral were now cheering for the Muskies. I think everyone at the tournament admired what we were trying to do, and respected the difficulty of the circumstances.

In the losers' bracket, Central battled to face Wheaton, Massachusetts, for a chance to play us again. They defeated Wheaton handily by a 5 - 1 score in the 12:00 game on Sunday, so we would match up a second time with Central at 2:30 for the national championship.

It was great to be sitting in the winners' bracket, knowing that someone would have to beat you twice to eliminate you. However, that mentality can also create problems in getting your team to play with the same desperation and intensity that the losers' bracket team brings to the field. There is something about the "one and done" mentality that can raise a team's level of play, and I certainly did not want Central to outshine us in effort. I made sure that my team understood all of those things before we left the practice field.

The atmosphere when we were warming up was tense. Mixed with the emotional drain of losing our friend and coach, John Wells, was the emotion of knowing that we were about to take the final step in fulfilling the dream of winning a national championship. I tried to time our warm-ups so that we finished about the same time the losers' bracket game was finished.

Although we ended up with about ten minutes of down-time on our hands, I was at least grateful that the winner appeared fairly certain about midway through the game, and I could start to prepare mentally for Central.

There was a little extra time needed to groom the field, and as I stood watching the grounds crew, I tried to absorb the whole picture. Gelein Field is a beautiful facility located at Carson Park. Eau Claire had hosted the national championships one other time, so they were familiar with the amount of effort and attention to detail that it takes to put on a quality tournament. They had done a superb job.

My favorite thing about this field was the scoreboard. It was one of the old-fashioned kinds like you see at Boston. It has a person perched on a ledge behind the board who slides the numbers into the appropriate slats inning by inning. The outfield fence was a temporary fence that converted a slow-pitch field into a fast-pitch field. The fence was a bit intimidating, as it was a six-foot-high plywood blue monster that definitely discouraged the outfielders from crashing into it.

It had looked like we might get a thunderstorm throughout the morning. Although it was still a bit overcast, it seemed doubtful that we would get rained out. I was hoping that we would play as scheduled so that their pitching staff did not get the extra rest. The national committee approached me to see if we would want a moment of silence for John before the national anthem. I declined the offer because I thought it would be too emotional for my players and make it even more difficult for them to play the game. All that was left was to hear them call, "PLAY BALL!"

The players put the bucket that John usually sat on in its normal spot in the dugout and crowned it with his ball cap. If John could not be with us in body, he at least would be with us in spirit. We were the home team, so Keiffer drew her smiley face and fired the first pitch.

The first couple of innings had plenty of excitement. In our first at bat, Andrews drew a one-out walk, followed by a single to center by Julie Ryan. All-American Mandy Carnes moved those two runners to second and third with a ground out, but the following batter struck out to end the threat.

Central had a huge scoring opportunity in the top of the second as their first two batters both singled to right field. They laid down a sacrifice bunt to move those two runners to second and third. The next batter smashed a hot grounder to third that Megan Monsman was able to snag and fire home to get the runner at the plate. The runner at second had moved to third and the batter-runner had gone to first. Central had tried to create a defensive dilemma for us by jockeying their players at first and third, but the lead runner was called out for leaving third base after the ball was in the pitching circle. Fortunately, Dani did what she had been coached to do in that situation, and held the ball without making any kind of attempt to play on the jockeying runners while the ball was in the circle. It was gratifying to see their strategy backfire as it helped us get out of a potentially big inning.

The score was still 0 - 0 going into the bottom of the fourth. Mandy Carnes reached first base on an error by their second baseman. On the next pitch, Central's catcher tried to pick Mandy off first base, but her errant throw went into right field and Mandy moved to second. Second baseman Shelly Delucas grounded out to first base to move Carnes to third. Megan Monsman then hit a screaming line drive that was snagged by their second baseman for the second out. With a runner at third and two outs, it looked like our scoring chances were again in question. Our #7 batter, Shelly Manson, then stepped to the plate and belted April Miller's first pitch over the center field fence.

The bench had not completed their celebration when our #8 batter, Jen Shay, drove the first pitch she saw to almost exactly the same spot. Suddenly, it was 3 - 0. For Jen to hit that homerun was a story in itself. She was a freshman who had also played volleyball during the fall, so she had missed all of our fall practices. By the time she joined us in winter practices, there was not much time to assess her skills or make up for lost time. As a result, we left her at home and did not even travel her on our spring trip to Florida. For the first part of the season, she played on our junior varsity team and saw little varsity action. Many athletes would have quit or been disgruntled under these circumstances, but Jen was living proof of what determination and perseverance can do. As she continued to prove herself, she gradually increased her playing time. Before the end of the season, she was starting in right field for the varsity. She went from being a junior varsity player at the beginning of the season to a hero in the national championship game, proving what perseverance can accomplish.

Central still had plenty of fight in them. They began their half of the inning with a single to center field. After grounding into a fielder's choice to get an out at second base, a double to left center put runners on second and third with one out. A sacrifice fly to right pushed their first run across to make the score 3 - 1.

Keiffer was pitching a great game. She was clearly fatigued, but sometimes when she was fresh, she tended to overthrow and lose the movement off of her pitches. When she was a little tired, she sometimes pitched better because her ball moved more if she didn't try to throw too hard. Freshman Angie Burnside had been our backup pitcher throughout the season when needed, but this was not the time or place to be thinking about making that kind of substitution.

Muskingum answered in the fifth when Chantelle Andrews hit a one-out single just past the infield grass to center field. Julie Ryan hit a chopper in front of the plate that couldn't be scooped up in time to get an out, to put runners on first and second. Carnes then hit a double to left center field to score Andrews and put our lead back up to three runs.

178

In the final two innings, Keiffer allowed only one base runner. Every inning I would look out to the old scoreboard in center field and watch another zero go up for Central. In my head I was holding a backward countdown of outs as the game wound down – "6-5-4-3-2-1." The final out will be forever etched in my mind. A hard one-hop ground ball was hit to third baseman Megan Monsman, which she fielded cleanly. She then threw a chest high bullet to Carla Kampschmidt to end the game.

Carla threw her arms in the air as Megan raced across the field. Keiffer had jumped in the air and was being mobbed by her teammates. It was pandemonium as the players jumped around crazily in the pitching circle, drinking in every moment of the greatest elation they would ever feel in sport. Sandra Sanford and I walked arm-in-arm from the dugout area toward the celebration. I watched, I hugged, I cried, and I drank in every moment, knowing that I would want to remember it for the rest of my life.

It almost seemed anticlimactic when the championship trophy was awarded to us because it temporarily silenced the mayhem and brought sanity to the wild celebration. After each player accepted her individual award and took a turn holding the national championship trophy, each found her private way to celebrate. I saw Monsman scooping up a handful of infield dirt, safely sealing it in a zip lock bag. I saw players signing autographs for probably the first time in their lives. I saw others standing quietly on the sideline reflecting on what we had just accomplished.

President Anne Steele had made the trip to Eau Claire to support us during the tragic death of John, and to support us vocally and with her presence at the game. She generously offered to take all the players and the parents out for a wonderful meal later in the evening so that we could celebrate together and enjoy each other's company.

There were a number of radio broadcasters and newspaper journalists on hand who wanted to interview me. Probably the most commonly asked question was, "How did it feel to win a national championship?" The question was difficult to answer because I was feeling such a wide gamut of emotions. I was elated with the accomplishment, but I was deeply saddened that John was not there to be a part

179

of it. After everything he had given to our program, he never saw it come to fruition.

Dani Keiffer was also a popular target for interviews. She was the top pitcher in the tournament, giving up only one earned run and two runs total in twenty-eight innings of work. She had struck out only three batters in four games, proving that you don't have to be a strikeout pitcher to win ball games. She kept the ball down the whole tournament, and scattered the twenty-six hits that she gave up so that they did not do much damage. The national championship win had enabled us to break the consecutive game win streak with thirty-four straight wins. It also gave Dani her thirtieth win of the season with a final record of 30 - 3.

Dani dodged most of the attention that applauded how well she had pitched. Mostly, she tried to give John credit for everything that he had done for her and for the program. She thanked John for helping her keep a positive attitude throughout a career where she was a three-year bench sitter, and recognized that most of her confidence resulted from his constant positive reinforcement. The drop ball that he had taught her had helped her defeat three of the best teams in the nation.

The celebration that night was one that we never wanted to end. President Steele pulled out all the stops to properly entertain the team and their families who had won the first national championship in the history of Muskingum College. We enjoyed good food, good company, and replayed all the highlights of the game multiple times. But all good things must come to an end, so we headed back to the hotel to pack up luggage and prepare to go to the airport the next morning for our flight home.

As we were walking down the hotel sidewalk rolling our luggage towards the bus, a man who had also just checked out called out for one of the players to stop because he needed to talk to her. Each of us was wearing a Muskingum College softball tee shirt as we proudly wanted to be identified on our trip home. He asked her how much she wanted for her tee shirt, and then before she had time to answer, he held out a one hundred dollar bill and said, "I'll give you a hundred bucks for it." She politely said that the shirt was not for sale. I chuckled to myself as I thought about the tee-shirt exchange when our players could not give their tee shirts away. A national championship certainly made our stock go up.

Everyone was a seasoned flier on the way home, so the kidding had ceased and most of us were in our own little world on the return flight. It was about 8:00 P.M. when our flight touched down in Columbus and by the time we got luggage and equipment transferred to our team bus, it was past 9:00 P.M. That put our arrival time in New Concord at about 10:30 P.M.

I could see the players beginning to get anxious about our arrival. As we exited the interstate, you could see them looking out the bus windows in hopes that a welcoming party might be waiting on them. As we turned onto Main Street, there were a few parents parked in the IGA parking lot, and they waved wildly as we passed by. The players seemed to be pleased that at least someone had taken the time to greet them.

However, when we got on the campus and turned the corner by our Rec Center where the bus would unload, it was a crazy scene. There were 250–300 people madly cheering and waving with homemade signs and posters in hand. New Concord is a sleepy little village of about twenty-five hundred people, so unless there is a Friday night football game, you do not ever see crowds of people out late. There were looks of pride as each player stepped off the bus and got a big cheer when her foot hit the bottom step. I came off the bus last, carrying the national championship trophy. I hoisted it above my head as I walked down the bus steps while the crowd roared their approval. For that night, New Concord was a very special place to be for both the players and the residents.

～

The first thing on my to-do list the next morning was to go see Jane. Except for a quick phone conversation, I had not been able to speak personally with her. I did not anticipate the fact that I would have to make another stop on my way to her house. When I left for the national tournament, my beloved dog, Diamond, was sick from old age, and was not in good shape. I had hired a dogsitter while I was gone who took good care of her, but she was on her last leg by the time I got home and fighting for her life. Diamond was a boxer who had been given to me by a player when the dog showed up at her parents' house, abandoned as a puppy. She was a great dog and a loyal companion, but I knew it was time. After twelve years of having her as my roommate and friend, I took her to the vet and had her put to sleep.

My grieving for Diamond could only last as long as my drive to Jane's house, as my attention turned to John and Jane and working through the grief of that situation. It was uncomfortable when I got to Jane's house for only a moment. As good friends who had known each other for a long time, there was not much that needed to be said.

The roller coaster of emotions continued with the team as they went back and forth between a campus celebration and the viewing hours for John. The players stayed on campus until the next day so that we could attend John's funeral as a team. The large attendance at the funeral was indeed a tribute to John and the way he had lived his life. It seemed like everyone knew John, and when you combined his work associates, his softball buddies, his friends, and his family, it was almost more people than the church could hold.

John was one of the most unselfish people that I have ever known. He willingly gave of his time to the softball community, but he also gave of his time when you were in a bind and needed a water pump fixed, or your air-conditioning went out, or any countless number of problems that he seemed to know how to fix. His life was cut short, but he still fit a lot of living into his sixty-two years of life.

In winning a national championship, I had achieved a goal that I had pursued for my entire career. When someone said to me that I had waited a long time for this, I corrected them by saying that I had only waited twenty-seven years. When you figure there are nearly four hundred NCAA Division III schools pursuing a championship, you could wait a long time if you had to wait your turn.

One of the things that I want for my players is for them to experience the pinnacle of success. It is a long, hard climb, but the view from the top is spectacular. No one will ever be able take that feeling of accomplishment away from them, and they will proudly carry the knowledge that in the year 2001, they had performed better than anyone else in the nation.

Chapter 11

Guyana

Nothing splendid has ever been achieved by those who dared believe that something inside them was superior to circumstances. Happiness is not so much in having as sharing. We make a living by what we get, but we make a life by what we give.

Norman MacEwan

I loved my summer experiences, but I didn't want to repeat them. There were too many things to see and do to duplicate a trip that I had already made. However, I changed my mind about that philosophy after my first trip to South America. There were things about the village of Kwakwani, Guyana, that created an irresistible urge to return.

I first visited Guyana with my brother Dave, a long-time minister for the Church of Christ, a Bible-based, fundamental, non-denominational church. Although he has a home congregation in America, Dave's passion is international mission work. When he was younger, he spent seven years in Italy working to establish some congregations of his church, and in 1994, he traveled with a group of Christians from Columbus, Ohio, to South America to do some preaching there. While Dave started with a focus around the populated Georgetown area of Guyana, he took his sense of adventure and began to explore what other surrounding areas might provide fertile work for the church.

Through a little exploration, he discovered the village of Kwakwani, a relatively remote village located deep in the rainforest and much more appealing than was the city to his love of the outdoors. He made a trip to the village to investigate the possibilities of future work and quickly decided that this was a place in which he needed to invest.

To some, the thought of mission work might mean simply preaching God's word and trying to teach people what the Bible says. But to Dave, and many others, the term is far more encompassing than that. Mission work entails embracing people and their way of life while doing what you can to improve their standard of living or help them in areas where they need help. It doesn't matter whether it involves education, medicine, recreation, sanitation, nutrition, or whatever. If it is of value, then it is important to see what can be done to help.

Dave approached me in the fall of 1996 to plant the seed that this would be a worthwhile trip for me to make with him the following summer along with the others he had gathered from his home congregation of the Lubeck Church of Christ in West Virginia. The main focus of his work was for the church, and although he wanted me to help teach Bible school at night, he sold me on the idea of offering sport clinics to the children in the village. In particular, I could introduce softball to a country that had likely never seen the game played, and certainly had no softball skills except those that might carry over from playing cricket. The children there often started working at a fairly young age, and he felt that they had been deprived of the opportunity to recreate.

I decided that this was an opportunity that I could not turn down. Not only would I be able to expand an area of my professional life by introducing softball to an area that had previously had no exposure to the sport, but I could also have an opportunity to share the Gospel and to feel like I had a hand in helping people who were not as fortunate as I was. Of course, in hindsight, this was kind of a selfish reason for choosing to go – thinking that I was going to help them. In the end I got far more from them than they got from me, but the only way to learn that kind of profound lesson is to go. So I did.

In preparing for my first trip to Guyana to introduce softball, I solicited donations from my OAC fellow institutions who had old softball equipment that they no longer needed or used. The volume of equipment that was donated was amazing, as I collected well over a hundred bats, approximately fifty gloves, plenty of balls, and six full sets of catching equipment. I collected much more than I had anticipated, so the biggest issue became finding a way to get the equipment down there without it costing more than the equipment was worth.

Fortunately, my brother Dave had connections with some folks who had a shipping line that went from Miami to Georgetown. He was able to arrange an economical way to pack things up and get them there at a minimal cost. We squeezed what we could in the luggage that everyone carried, but with weight limits and other items that we needed to get there as well, we had to be creative to get the equipment down there so we could put it to good use.

Dave had a good understanding of what should be prioritized for transporting on this trip. We clearly had to bring teaching supplies for Bible school, but various types of medicine were also high on the list. I had contacted the local Colgate-Palmolive Company, and they generously donated a huge amount of hygiene-related supplies, such as soap, toothpaste, and shampoo. The best part about their donation was that there was a Colgate-Palmolive factory in Georgetown, so they arranged for us to pick up all the supplies there to avoid shipping costs.

The reality of my first trip set in when I went to the health clinic to get all the necessary immunizations needed to travel to this type of environment. The fear of malaria or yellow fever lingered in my head as I played out scenarios of what the trip would be like.

I divided my time before departure between preparing to teach Bible school and preparing to teach softball, fully knowing that I would be teaching those who had no background in either of these areas, but not understanding what the implications of that would be. I read as much as I could about Guyana, thinking that I could arm myself with knowledge and it would make the trip easier, but sometimes the more I read, the more apprehensive I became about how much I did not know.

There were family members who would be making this trip along with me and Dave, including my sister Diane, my niece Nikki (Dave's daughter) and her husband Frank, as well as several church members who would go to help out with the church work. I was extremely excited to have the opportunity to introduce softball as a sport, and I greatly looked forward to another experiential learning adventure.

The flight down went through Miami. From Miami, we traveled on BeeWee (British West Indies) airline, did a little island hopping through Barbados and Trinidad, and eventually landed in Georgetown, the capital and largest city in Guyana. When our flight finally touched down, it felt unusual to disembark just off the runway and then walk into the terminal.

The first thing I noticed as I made it to the steps and started my way down to stand on Guyanese soil was the oppressive heat. I had been in hot environments, but this heat was different; it was high humidity mixed with high temperatures that made breathing difficult and sweating a requirement. It was strange, however, to look around and notice the fact that the only ones seemingly bothered by the heat were the Americans. Everyone else looked dry and comfortable, looking at us with a gaze that seemed like it was saying, "Good luck – you're going to need it."

My first impression of the airport was one of disbelief. The airport was not air-conditioned and was hot and dirty. There was only one toilet for the men and one for the women. The condition of the toilet made our worst service station restroom in the states look like heaven, with a commode that would not flush, no toilet paper, a faucet that would not turn on, and filth all around. Needless to say, the need to go to the restroom suddenly did not seem as urgent as it once did.

Standing in line to go to the baggage area was another interesting experience. In later trips, it did not seem so traumatic, but on the first trip, it seemed like the uniformed guards were looking for a reason to accost and detain one of us. There were no smiles as each agent put his hand out for your passport, and without speaking darted his eyes from your picture to your face multiple times. They seemed to be in a state of anger when they slammed the stamp down on each passport and waved you through. I am sure it was my own paranoia that created the fear, but the thought of inadvertently violating a law in this unfamiliar country and somehow being detained alone and afraid, was a silent film that kept playing over and over in my head.

We eventually got our luggage and loaded it into vans (they call them buses) to make a drive that same night to Linden, the next largest city in Guyana, where we had reservations to stay at a hotel. The drive was about an hour, and even though I was so tired I could hardly function, I was wide awake once the drive to Linden began. It was late at night, and I was shocked at how unnerving it was to be driving on the left side of the road. As much as my head recognized the difference in driving laws, I was in a state of panic every time headlights approached from the wrong side as I anticipated head-on collisions. The driver knew only two speeds – fast and faster. It seemed we were in a constant state of passing vehicles, dodging cattle that were in the road, and honking our horn at anything that looked like it might slow us down.

It was a relief when we pulled into Jac's, the local hotel in Linden. It provided very modest accommodations, but it gave us what we needed. We had a bed to sleep in, running water for showers, and a hot breakfast provided on the balcony the next morning to give us a good start to our day. The view from the balcony made me sad, as it overlooked a dirty and disorganized market, and let you see passersby that ranged from women carrying large baskets on their heads, to tiny unsupervised children, to a man who had nothing to wear but a gunny sack with a rope tied around his waist.

There was a certain smell to Linden that would eventually become familiar to me. It was a smell not easily described but unique enough that it could be mistaken for nowhere else. It seemed to be a combination of the river water that crossed the town and the open sewage alongside unclean and unsanitary streets, combined with roaming animals and high heat and humidity. Whatever it was, it became a smell that enabled me to know that I was in Linden, and that made me appreciate the fresher environment of Kwakwani.

By mid-afternoon, we were on the trail that connected Linden to Kwakwani, and I was looking forward to getting to know the village and her people. We arrived in Kwakwani on a Saturday. By the time we had moved our belongings into an empty house and tried to organize some things, it was already late and we were all extremely tired. We were grateful just to get a full night's sleep and begin our work the next day.

Sunday morning, of course, was spent in church services. However, as soon as services were done and we had eaten some lunch, the work began to prepare for the next two weeks. For me, that meant trying to get the athletic area cleaned up so that it was suitable for sports. There was a huge flat grass area by the school that was primarily used for soccer and cricket, and as was true with many of the public areas in Kwakwani, there was a lot of trash and debris that needed to be cleaned up. I, along with a couple of helpers, spent most of the afternoon picking up trash and trying to clean up enough of the animal droppings to give us adequate space to play sports without worrying about what we might be stepping on or stepping in. Eventually, I saw how most of the children went barefoot and were far less worried about their feet than I was, but I felt an obligation to provide as safe an environment as possible.

By the time all the clean-up and organizational work was done, the day was nearly done. Monday would be my first test of working with the children. We had advertised around the village that the sport clinic would start at 9 o'clock on Monday morning. When I arrived at the field, I was expecting to see a whole group of children anxiously awaiting their introduction to softball. Instead, what greeted me were a couple of boys who were kicking around a soccer ball, and a couple of girls who sat shyly in the rundown bleachers of the soccer field, watching. I was disappointed that we only had a few children show up as I went up to the storage area that we had found above the bleachers where we could safely store the equipment. There were some others from our group with me who were going to help out, but I thought to myself that I could probably handle half a dozen Guyanese children alone.

My brother had warned me about what he called "Guyanese time." He said that the Guyanese were perpetually late. They put little emphasis on being on time, and pretty much figured things would start when they got there. I thought he meant for mundane things, like working or going to school. I didn't think he meant fun things, like playing sports.

By the time all the equipment bags were dragged down and the bases had been measured out, the crowd, as well as the excitement, was starting to grow. Gradually, kids meandered down the dirt path that led to the field, along with a few bicycles carrying at least two passengers. By 9:30, we probably had fifty participants and another twenty-five curious onlookers. It was clear from the first day that the girls were not interested or welcome to join the boys for sports. Fortunately, we had brought what we needed to set up for volleyball, so a couple members of our group took over trying to teach the girls volleyball, while I set out to tackle softball.

Over the course of time that I traveled to Kwakwani, I tried to remedy the gender stereotypes. I made some progress, but it was hard to promote something that violated principles that were ingrained in their culture.

I wanted to stick with the basics on the first day, so I figured if we could do a lot of instruction and drills with just throwing and catching, it would be a good start. It was so different than the teaching experiences that I was used to in the States. There, learning sometimes occurred because we as teachers almost force-fed the students. Here, the children were hanging on every word that was said, anxious for both the instruction and the opportunity to participate.

I showed them what a softball looked like. I explained that today we would not be learning the whole game, but rather we would learn some skills that would help them play the game. I explained that you wore a softball glove so that the ball would not hurt your hand when you caught it and so it would be easier to catch. When I dumped the bag of gloves on the ground, there was temporary pandemonium as all the children scrambled to get one that they liked. Then it was almost total silence as I saw their looks of dismay, and they were mumbling things like, "This is too big, it doesn't fit," or "I am right-handed, and this is for your left hand." Clearly, I had a great deal of teaching to do.

It was a huge challenge to get them organized into drills. They were not used to being taught in this kind of structured environment. They were so excited to play and learn that it was difficult to keep them organized and progressing at a pace that they could handle. However, it was also gratifying to see the progress at the end of day one, as many of them were picking up nicely on how to throw and catch and how to use a glove properly.

It didn't take long for the word to spread, because by day two, the participation had nearly doubled. To complicate things, we had arranged for the children who were too young to play softball to have their Bible school in the morning while sports were being conducted. Although there were over one hundred younger ones with my sister at the preschool building, it seemed like at least another hundred were at the athletic field hanging out. We finally had to arrange for some children's games like Drop the Hanky or Duck Duck Goose to be taught in order to keep them busy and out of the way as we continued with softball.

By the third day, there were children waiting for us outside the house where we were staying, anxious to walk with us to the field and help us with equipment. I felt like the "Pied Piper of Kwakwani" as the children merrily skipped, jogged, and danced their way following me to the athletic field. The morning usually started with herding off the cows and goats from the field, and cleaning off any droppings that were on the infield or in the base paths. As we performed this morning ritual, I reminded myself daily that maybe I should complain less about our field at home not being dragged properly before a practice or the grass not being mowed low enough for a game, and appreciate what I had a little more. The kids were in a grass field in the middle of the jungle in their bare feet with probably one set of clothes to their name, and they were having the time of their lives.

We slowly moved through a skills progression that included throwing and catching, fielding ground balls, fielding fly balls, batting, and base running. The boys had become accustomed to a woman telling them what to do, and by mid-week pretty much all of them simply called me "Coach." The "oa" sound in coach was pronounced more like the "o" sound in cold, but in any language, I considered it a compliment.

The day I taught the rules was quite a challenge. I had made diagrams on posterboards and had the basics of the rules all laid out for them. We went through them one by one, and I answered questions; I thought we were just about at a point where we could play a modified game. When the game got underway, there was some confusion about what a force out was, so I stopped play and explained again that if a runner was forced to run because the runner behind him was approaching that base, then all the defense had to do was to beat the lead runner to the next base with the ball, touch the base, and the runner would be out. They did not have to touch the runner. It was clear that they still did not get it when on the next occasion of a force out, the baseman got the ball, proudly held the ball in his bare hand, and declared the runner out. I guess I needed some lessons on how to explain the basics more clearly.

By the end of our stay, the village children were proficient enough to play a competitive game. We divided into several teams and had a little tournament on the final Saturday. The number of spectators exceeded the number of participants, and any way you counted, it was clearly a success. The children brought me many gifts to thank me for what I had done, ranging from doilies that their mothers had crocheted for me, to small wood carvings that they had made themselves. I could hardly believe my own words when I told them that I would leave the equipment for them to practice, and that I would be back the next year.

The opportunity to introduce softball was one of the most fulfilling athletic experiences I had ever encountered in my sport life. In much the same way, teaching Bible school was one of the most gratifying spiritual experiences of my life. Many of the children who were at sports would come back in the evening for Bible school. My experience with Bible school in the States was that you almost have to drag kids there, and the older they get, the harder it is to get them to attend. In Guyana we had the opposite problem. We had so many children who wanted to attend that we eventually had to put a guard at the gate of the school to keep children out when we had no more room. Children of high school age were trying to get into the under-age classes, just so they would not miss out on things.

The children had to sit on the concrete floor when they were in the common area for singing or group activities, but it did not deter them. When we divided them up into smaller groups for classes, they were the most teachable students that I had ever experienced. Even though their parents were not there to discipline them or oversee them, they were extremely well-behaved and had an attention span that far exceeded the students that I have taught in the States.

One of my most memorable times came when I was teaching the ten-year-old children the story of the crucifixion of Jesus. With each part of the story, I had poster-sized pictures that I would hold up so that the children would better understand. Sitting in the front row were two beautiful girls who were holding hands and paying rapt attention. Both had tears running down their cheeks. I finally had to stop the story to see if everything was all right with them. They said, "Why were they so mean to him? He didn't do anything to them." It was their first time hearing the story of Jesus and his death, and they were moved to tears. It reminded me of why I had traveled that far to help spread the message.

For four consecutive summers, I traveled to Kwakwani with my brother Dave, my sister Diane, and a mix of other relatives and Christian friends. Each year that I went, relationships with the villagers evolved to increasingly deeper levels, and I gained a broadened understanding of life in the rainforest. Every trip, different events happened to give each summer trip a sense of uniqueness.

The village of Kwakwani is as deep into the rainforest as you can go by road. Once you get to Kwakwani, the transportation switches to river travel. I use the term "road" loosely, as most of the Guyanese refer to the road that connects Kwakwani to the city of Linden as the "trail." I think their terminology is more apt, as I have spent as much as seven hours trying to traverse the seventy-mile-long trail in a van. It is a dirt pathway cut through the jungle that on a good, dry day can be traveled by anything ranging from a car, to a van, to a heavy truck. On a bad day, if a tractor does not happen along to pull you out of the mud each time you get stuck, it is highly likely that the seventy-mile ride on the trail will become an overnight trip.

Travel conditions during the monsoon season are a little unpredictable, but generally things had dried out by mid-July when we made our trips. However, there were years when the flood waters had not receded and the rains continued to come at that time of year. If you tried to travel the trail when it was wet and muddy, you could plan on being stuck multiple times and pushing the vehicle in calf-deep mud. The type of soil in this area makes the mud so soupy that you can hardly stand up, and it is almost impossible to find traction.

At the same time that you were engaged in pushing your vehicle out of the mud, you were praying that if you did get the vehicle out, it wouldn't break down until you got to Kwakwani. Then you continued your prayer that if you did make it to Kwakwani, your arrival would be in time to catch the ferry that only runs a few times a day to carry vehicles across the river to the village.

The trail conditions are enough to discourage even the most seasoned traveler from making the trip to Kwakwani. In some ways, the trail mentally prepares you for the living conditions in Kwakwani, and as a result things didn't seem as bad in the village since you had already faced the multiple trials required to get there.

The village itself is sizeable, consisting of approximately five thousand people. It seemed like about four thousand of those were children, all of whom were seeking attention and were anxious to learn. The village sits on the Berbice River and a large number of people live right on the river in an area called The Waterfront. The rest of the villagers live a little farther from the water in an area called Berbice Park.

Although you would see an occasional vehicle in Kwakwani, most of the transportation was by foot or by bicycle. As long as you didn't mind walking, a three-mile walk would get you to about anywhere you could go in the village. The roads or paths that traverse the village are primarily traveled by cows, goats, or other livestock that freely roam. Because the animals are not confined, sanitary conditions are lacking as cow patties and other droppings make pedestrian travel a little precarious.

Guyana is an underdeveloped country and a trip around the village reinforces an acknowledgment of the level of poverty found there. Many of the houses are one-room dwellings made of rough-hewn lumber and a rusty tin roof, and they sit up on stilts to escape the perpetual flooding. It is not unusual to find a dozen or more people living in one dwelling. About the only time the inhabitants are all inside is to sleep, with cooking, bathing, laundry, and other household chores done outside. I am not sure that they even all sleep inside as most of the houses have hammocks slung underneath for sleeping and providing a reprieve from the heat. A more affluent villager might have a modest concrete block dwelling with a common living area, a kitchen, and bedrooms.

Clean drinking water is a chronic problem for the village. Although they had a small water-processing filtration system, it was very ineffective and only worked between power outages. Many of the villagers have large water storage tanks sitting on stilts above their house so that they can collect the clean water when it is running, and then let gravity bring it into the house through a tubing system when needed. Many of the health problems in Guyana stem from bad drinking water and unclean bathing conditions in the Berbice River, which carries water-born diseases.

The most challenging thing we had to adjust to was the oppressive heat. High heat and humidity combine daily to create an environment where plants flourish and people melt. Sometimes when we checked the thermometer that we brought, putting it in the sun, the gauge would go as high as it could to 120 degrees in a matter of minutes. Physical labor in the heat of the day was almost impossible, so it was common practice to get out of the sun in the afternoon and resume activity after the heat of the day had passed. Fortunately it cooled down to the upper seventies or lower eighties at night, so sleeping was not too difficult.

I would not want to get sick in Kwakwani, as the hospital consists of a block building with two large wards, one for men and one for women. When we were there, the conditions were not very sanitary, the personnel were not well trained, and the services were limited. If you were an overnight patient at the hospital, you either had to have a friend or family member who would carry in your meals, or you went hungry. Providing food for patients was beyond the scope of this hospital.

The school system was even worse. The nursery school and the primary school were old, wooden, rundown buildings with limited supplies and cramped space. They made some gradual improvements in the schools over the course of time that I traveled there, but the conditions were still not good. I was most familiar with the high school, as the village graciously allowed us to use that building to conduct our evening Bible school. As long as we were willing to go in and clean it up, they said that we were welcome to use it. The high school was a concrete building that looked much better from the outside than it did from the inside. The exterior walls only went halfway to the roof. The rest of the "wall" consisted of wire screen that connected from the top of the block to the roof. Much of the screen was torn or rusted, so it was not unusual to have birds or other unwanted critters roaming around on the inside of the building.

One night in the middle of my Bible school lesson, a bird flew into where I was teaching the children. One little boy raised his hand and asked me, "Miss, do you want me to get it?"

The bird was a huge distraction, so I quickly said, "Yes, please do." I wasn't sure what he meant exactly, but I interpreted his question to mean that he would find a way to chase the bird out of the classroom and thus restore order. Instead, he pulled a slingshot out of his pocket, and in one shot, he dropped the bird straight to the floor. He then walked over, picked it up, and took it outside. It's too bad that we were not studying the story of David and Goliath that night.

I spent another evening teaching a Bible lesson with a large tarantula clinging to the wall just above my head. All of the children must have been well taught by their parents to leave this type of spider alone, as none of them would go anywhere near it. I had to wait until the end of the Bible school that night to clear the room of children and find someone to help me get rid of the tarantula.

The high school building was extremely dark, with only a few working light bulbs and plenty of exposed electrical wiring hanging from the ceiling that looked like an electrocution waiting to happen. There were a few ceiling fans to help circulate the air, but the few of them that worked generally only had one or two blades that remained. The concrete floor was dirty, and the desks consisted of small, rickety wooden tables with a wooden bench that had no back on it. The blackboards were elevated, and to write on them you had to climb up on a platform that would remind you of the platforms found on American highway billboards.

The worst part about the building was probably the smell. We were there in the middle of summer, so the building had not been used since the end of the school year. It smelled like urine. The reason for this became apparent when we went back to the restroom area. The concrete stalls served as walls for relieving yourself, and dried urine and urine stains made it almost impossible to bear the smell and the sight of the community bathroom. It took a brave effort to clean it up, but doing so made a big difference because we could use the building without being overwhelmed by the smell or the sight.

It became clear that one of the biggest deficiencies in the school system was simply a lack of teaching supplies. The library had no books. The children who attended Bible school were amazed by the most basic supplies. Some of them had never seen a crayon, and water colors astonished them. It was a luxury for them to have their own paper and pencil to use. For them to be able to make a simple craft with art supplies was a new experience. Even the older children (teenagers ranging from thirteen to nineteen years of age) were so thrilled with the opportunity to make a simple craft that you almost had to fight with them to keep them away after the rooms became so crowded that you could not wedge another student into the class.

We also took down supplies for the older people. We took a large number of used eyeglasses, as the need for glasses was desperate for the aging people in the village. We set aside an afternoon to conduct an eyeglasses clinic and did the best we could to provide people with glasses so they could see to read or sew. We also made an effort to supply the school libraries with books. We collected thousands of books in the States and managed to get them to Georgetown via the shipping line connection. It was not unusual for me to fill one whole cargo bay with boxes of books on our softball bus when we took our spring trip to a tournament in Orlando. A man would drive up from Miami to Orlando hauling a trailer to transport the books, then take them to Miami so that they could be shipped and waiting for us in Georgetown. I knew it would be hard to motivate children to learn to read when they had nothing *to* read.

The village of Kwakwani had a market area where local vendors could sell their produce from a small wooden shack. If you timed it right in the early mornings, you could get fresh baked bread, but my favorite thing to purchase there was fresh fruit, especially the bananas and the pineapples. It took some adjusting to learn their currency system, as one American dollar equaled approximately 150 Guyanese dollars. I could not get used to paying $70.00 for a bottle of Coke.

There were not too many sources of income in Kwakwani. There was still some gold mining that went on, and a few of the villagers made a living from selling their fruits or vegetables. There were also some who profited by working at lumber camps outside the village. Cutting and sawing lumber in that kind of heat was backbreaking labor, and the living conditions in the lumber camps were primitive and unsanitary. Probably the single biggest employer for the village was the bauxite mine. Guyana is rich in bauxite, the raw material used to make aluminum. The Reynolds Aluminum Company, for quite a while, owned and ran the mine. There were several Americans who moved there as executives of the mine and built nice houses up on a hill over-looking the village. The Guyanese government had since reclaimed ownership of the mine, and some of these houses now stood empty and reminded the villagers of what things were like in earlier times.

It was in one of these empty houses that we stayed during our summer trips. The houses were, for the most part, void of any furniture. It was a large empty living space, and once it was cleaned up, it was perfectly tolerable for a couple weeks of living. We slept on air mattresses in the living room area. On good days, there was cold running water available so that you could shower. Boiling our drinking water was an everyday chore, and we struggled to keep up with a major supply and demand problem. We would all have been sick if we had allowed ourselves to drink the same water that the villagers drank. The house did have electricity, but you never knew from day to day whether the power from the village would be available.

Because the house was on stilts, it created an inviting living space underneath the house. We had a couple of cows in residence, as well as a rooster that was our most reliable alarm clock. Below the house, a capybara lived in the creek, and just off the back porch was an ant hill that was bigger than my bed. Beside the house, in a tree, was the biggest termite nest that I have ever seen.

The biggest challenges inside the house were the roaches and bats. My first night in the shower flushed out jungle-sized roaches that were nearly as long as my ink pen. There were many bats living in the ceiling; you never wanted things to be too quiet at night because it allowed you to hear them scratching on the ceiling tiles. We learned the hard way that you should leave some lights on at night. The lights kept the bats from coming around, but if you chose to sleep in darkness, you could be sure that you would spend the night battling bats swooping down at your head as you tried to sleep.

There was one part of the village where the poorest of the poor lived and where conditions for living were worse than they were in the rest of the village. The area was called Jonestown, and I have since learned that about every village in Guyana has a section like this that is labeled Jonestown. Although the Guyanese, for the most part, have been very receptive and welcoming to the Americans, the memories of Jim Jones and the nearly one thousand people who committed suicide as a result of the brainwashing of his cult lingers on.

The more I was around the Guyanese people, the more I was struck by their ability to trust. The Guyanese are so cordial that it seems easy to make friends and build relationships quickly. They have a youthful quality about them that allows them to accept people quickly, never doubting that you have their best intentions at heart. I worry that it would be easy for someone to take advantage of the loving nature of the Guyanese and lead them down a perilous path that they may not recognize until it is too late.

There were many challenges to living in Kwakwani, but it was the positives that drew me back year after year. As someone who loves nature, I felt like I was in paradise. The pristine beauty of the rainforest could not be duplicated. Even walking around the village, you saw incredibly beautiful flowers and vegetation. When you ventured deeper into the jungle, you were surrounded by flora and fauna that was unmatched by anyplace else I had ever been.

The word "Guyana" means land of many waters. The countless rivers that crisscrossed the landscape provided not only a scenic transportation system, but also provided a food source for many Guyanese who depended on fishing for either food or for their livelihood. When we traveled to a nearby village, I looked forward to each trip that we made by boat, just so I could see what wildlife we might encounter. On any one trip, you might see anything ranging from a family of monkeys playing in the trees to cayman slithering off a log. If you were really lucky, you might catch a glimpse of a manatee, and for the more adventurous, if you watched the river banks closely, you would probably see an anaconda.

The boats were long wooden structures that sat very low in the water and invariably had a couple of empty containers that passengers would use for bailing water when the boat started to leak. There never seemed to be a limit to the number of people that could be transported in one boat, and they certainly had no rules about life jackets or safety concerns. I could never figure out if the Guyanese were joking or not when they warned their American passengers about dangling fingers or toes in the water as you traveled. The river was full of piranha, and the natives insisted that it would be a good way to lose an appendage. In the event that it wasn't a joke, I always kept my hands and feet inside the boat.

My favorite time was at night. You could look up at a sky that displayed stars with brilliance that I have never seen at home. Every night, the sunset created another artistic canvas that a mere photograph could not seem to capture. The best thing about night, however, was the cacophony of sound. To just sit in silence and listen to everything from the sounds of frogs, to the howling of the monkeys, to the unknown sounds that could be anything your imagination wanted them to be, was a living surround-sound system that nearly overwhelmed your senses.

But the one factor that created the irresistible urge for a traveler to return to Kwakwani was the beauty of its people. The first few days of my first trip there, I was a little uncomfortable trying to integrate with a people whose culture and lifestyle was so different than mine. Guyana is the only English-speaking country in South America, so the language barrier was not a problem. They spoke with a dialect that was difficult to understand, but once you got accustomed to listening, communication was possible. However, I wasn't sure how well I would be received in many other areas. I was an American in a foreign country, a white person among blacks, a "rich" person among poor, and a woman teaching athletics to a mostly male audience that was not accustomed to a woman being in that role.

It was my own reservations that allowed my apprehensions to linger as long as they did. Never had I been around a people more welcoming, more appreciative, or more loving than the people in Kwakwani. Any thoughts that I had about them resenting me, or not accepting what I had to offer, disappeared as quickly as I was able to let go of them. Never had I been in an environment where people were more open to learn, to make friends, and to share, than I was when I was in Kwakwani, Guyana.

In succeeding years when we traveled down, my mom had fashioned some handmade puppets that we could use for Bible school. The children in Guyana had never seen puppets, and they were enthralled when it was time for the nightly puppet show. It was amazing to see 250–300 kids sitting cross-legged and shoulder-to-shoulder on the concrete floor, so engrossed in the puppet show that at least for the moment, they had no other cares in the world. It was intriguing to watch them try to sneak in after Bible school had ended to see if the puppets were really alive.

The adults were as warm as the children. They could not find enough ways to thank us for teaching their children and for spending time in the village. Gifts ranged from baked goods, to handmade cards, to hand-crafted hats and baskets. One adult who will always stand out in my mind was the first man that I met while I was in Kwakwani.

My sister and I were supposed to check with the security guard at the school to make sure the building would be unlocked for Bible school in the evenings. We were a little apprehensive when we walked up to him, as we were new to the village and did not yet feel comfortable trying to carry on a conversation. Kenneth Mason had only one arm, as he had lost his right arm in a mining accident. Being partially disabled, he was fortunate to have a job, but he had been hired to work twelve hours a day (6:00 A.M. to 6:00 P.M.) to sit at the school gate and make sure it was secure. I doubt if he got paid more than a dollar or two of U.S. money per day for the work, but it was better than nothing.

We struck up an immediate friendship, finding him to be very friendly and open, as well as being very spiritually minded. We talked to him on a daily basis and often brought him food left over from our evening meals. He would attend the adult worship services every evening, then would be back at work at 6 o'clock every morning.

He invited Diane and me to his house the night before we were to leave Guyana to see where he lived and to visit. We walked on old wooden planks through a wet field to get to a wooden shack that was his residence. His bed was metal springs covered with cardboard that he used as a mattress. His food was hanging in sacks from the ceiling to keep the rats out of it. He had a small creek outside his house with a wooden plank that extended to both banks of the creek. He would sit on the board to bathe, wash clothes, brush his teeth, wash dishes, or take care of other needs. He was concerned that we would be walking back close to dusk and warned us of poisonous snakes that lay in the field that we would have to cross. He told us stories of killing some of these snakes when they had gotten into his house in the same tone that we would have used to tell someone about swatting a pesky housefly.

I have stayed in touch with Kenneth ever since the first summer that I met him. He has since moved from Kwakwani back to Lethem, Brazil, which is his hometown. My last contact with him was about six months ago when I sent him some clothing and food supplies that he had requested. I have not heard back from him since, and usually he is quick to respond with his thanks. He is probably nearly seventy years old by now and has been in poor health for a while, so I wonder if he is even still alive. Every time I start to complain about my work or an issue with my living conditions, I think of Kenneth.

The Guyanese population is made up of a mix of several nationalities. Guyana was a British colony, and slaves were imported to work the sugar industry and remained after slavery was abolished. The Guyanese are a mixture of South Asian, African, and Amerindian peoples. Although there was at one time a good deal of political friction among these groups, for the most part they now enjoy a peaceful coexistence. The Guyanese Amerindians look much like the North American Indian in appearance with dark hair and complexion, and often a muscular, stocky build.

Hururu is an Amerindian village located about an hour downriver from Kwakwani. We got permission to hold a Bible school for their children using the school house in the village. Each afternoon a small group of us would go up river to the village, conduct a small Bible school, and, because river travel was dangerous at night, wait until the next morning to come back in time for the sport clinic.

If I thought that Kwakwani was primitive, then there are no words to describe Hururu. The village was tiny, with a dirt path through the middle of the village being its only road. There was no running water or electricity, and the houses were generally small wooden shacks with a thatched or tin roof. All cooking and baking was done out-side over an open fire or improvised oven. Most of the children under three or four years old ran around naked. Besides seeing a few houses where boat building was in progress, I did not see any signs of how these people might have made a living beyond just living off the land.

We brought a generator with us to the village so that we would have some light after Bible school was over. We were going to sleep in the upstairs of the school house, so we needed to have enough light to try to cook some dinner and rig up some way to sleep. The first night I was there, we could not get the generator started. It eventually did start, but we were in the dark for several hours before the repairs were completed. We cooked our meal on a small backpacking type of stove, and in order to sleep, we shoved school desks together to give us a platform big enough to lay a mattress on. We threw mosquito nets over top of us to keep the mosquitoes at bay, but I wasn't sure if we had a plan for any bigger critters that might venture in for a visit.

The sounds at night as you were trying to sleep were incredible. I guess they would not have been as eerie if we had been able to identify them, but unknown sounds encourage your imagination to run wild. The most mysterious sound was what sounded like lions roaring, but knowing that lions do not live in Guyana, I was able to dismiss that as a possibility. It required a conversation with one of the Amerindians the next morning to learn that what we had been hearing were the monkeys, possibly howler monkeys. I never dreamed that monkeys roared, but in fact they do sound a lot like lions and were certainly noisy enough to keep me awake most of the night. The first night in Hururu was indeed a memorable one.

There was another strange encounter with one of the Amerindians from Hururu when he came to Kwakwani one morning looking for Dave and Bob Long, another Christian minister who was part of the group. He had not yet found them, but because I was pretty visible as I was working with all of the children, he found me first. He was with his twelve-year-old son, and they had come by boat seeking help. He was clearly distraught, and I quickly told him where to find my brother.

Apparently his wife had just given birth to their twelfth child, and she had had a lot of trouble in the process. With Hururu being so primitive, at best she would have had a midwife to assist her. Her husband said that in spite of their best efforts, she had died in child-birth, he had sought Dave and Bob out to come to Hururu to conduct the funeral.

Dave and Bob willingly made the boat trip back down the river to assist the man and his family. When they arrived, there was already a large gathering of friends and relatives at the house of the deceased. Because they had no way to keep the body and did not embalm it, they simply stored the body in a cool cave-like area until time for the funeral and burial.

When the Amerindians went to retrieve the body, much to their amazement, they detected breathing and movement in the woman. With the lack of sophisticated medicine, they had no way of deter-mining if someone was officially dead. Apparently in her case, they could detect no signs of life at the time of the crisis, so they assumed she was dead and took her body to be stored until they could properly bury her. You can only imagine the range of emotions that occurred when the news spread that she was still alive.

Dave and Bob did the best they could to get her to Georgetown, which was the closest place to seek any kind of competent medical help. That meant getting the woman down the river to Kwakwani, traveling the trail to Linden, and arranging a trip from Linden to Georgetown. In all, it took nearly two more days before medical per-sonnel were able to assist her. At the time of our departure from Guyana, she was still alive, but we heard after getting back to the States that she had passed away. Who knows what the outcome might have been had she been properly diagnosed at the time of the problem?

The incident certainly gave me renewed appreciation for the level of medical care that we have in this country. I began thinking that maybe we should not complain when we have to wait a short time for treatment in an emergency room or when we have to wait in an air-conditioned reception area for an appointment with our doctor. For the most part, medical care in these small villages is not convenient, competent, or in many cases, even available.

My friendship with Ann Gordon, a prominent resident in Kwakwani, is a relationship that I enjoyed and that I will always treasure. Ann did not fit the mold of most of the women in Kwakwani. She was a single, independent, strong-minded woman who seemed to be ahead of her time with her goals and aspirations. She was probably in her early to mid-thirties when I first met her, and she immediately put me at ease with her quick wit and determined mind-set.

The mining company had established a television station in Kwakwani, and Ann worked as the sole operator of the station. The station was fairly antiquated, and because she pretty much had control over what was broadcast, that alone gave her a good deal of clout in the village. She was one of the few citizens who recognized the need and value of recreation for the village. Fighting lack of equipment and facilities and a *laissez-faire* mentality towards sport, she had worked endlessly to try to establish some recreational leagues in the village for the children. She was an advocate for all sports, but her passion was volleyball.

After I met Ann the first year, she introduced me to the village volleyball team, a group of young women who had taught themselves the game and even occasionally traveled down river to a few local tournaments held in surrounding villages. I was pleasantly surprised at the skill level they possessed when I was invited to attend one of their practices. They had never been formally taught, but through trial and error and reading, they had a decent grasp of the game.

Even though volleyball was not necessarily a sport that I was trying to teach or emphasize on my trips there, I made a special effort to help Ann's team. I was able to get a supply of old volleyballs from our volleyball coach at Muskingum, as well as a set of used uniforms that were no longer in use. Eventually, I was able to get a new net for them as well. Each year that I was there, I taught them a few new drills and helped them some with their strategy. Eventually, they were champions of the volleyball challenge that was held annually along the Berbice River, and even though it occurred several years ago, it still remains a great source of pride for those who were involved.

I have tremendous respect for Ann. In some ways, she brings back memories of when I was younger and fighting for Title IX rights. She fights an uphill battle daily in Kwakwani to get support for recreational opportunities for the children. She has worked hard to get a basketball league established, as the village has one concrete court with two baskets that is a center of activity in the village. I tried to help her out as much as I could with equipment for various sports, and I continue to admire her efforts and tenacity in a village where there is simply no money to provide recreational opportunities for the children.

Each year that I traveled to Kwakwani, I gained better insight into what would work, what was needed, and how to go about meeting some of their needs. I was thrilled when the Converse Shoe Company agreed to provide enough shirts to put about a dozen different teams in uniform. When we eventually got to the tournament at the end of our stay, I was able to give each team a shirt with their team colors, compliments of Converse. The looks on the faces of those children when they received their shirts are still embedded in my mind. Not only was it a great source of pride, but it was probably the only new piece of clothing that they would receive all year.

I still have memories of the children coming to the house where we were staying and trying to sell things in order to raise enough money to buy a school uniform so that they would be allowed to go to school the next year. One boy brought the skin from a jaguar that his uncle had shot, hoping to make a sale. Another boy brought a macaw in a cage, not understanding that we could not transport something like that with us back to the States. It made you seem almost helpless when you were not able to help each child.

You never knew day-to-day what you might encounter that was out of the ordinary. There was one afternoon when my brother got back to the village after coming down the river, and approached the house with a gunny sack that was tied at the top. I knew it wasn't a good sign when the sack started to squirm a bit. He had been riding with a snake hunter who saw an anaconda along the river and wanted to bring it back, but did not want to kill it on the spot because he needed to preserve the skin. He simply clubbed it enough to enable him to handle it and brought it home alive in the boat. I was not too excited about the idea of holding a live anaconda, but I forced myself to do it as a test of my will and self-discipline.

But my favorite memories are the children and the joy that participating in sports brought to them. It was refreshing to be in an environment where the opportunity to compete was far more important than winning. It was wonderful to see players so excited about their homeruns that they unashamedly turned cartwheels to cover the distance from third to home. It didn't matter that the catcher's gear was raggedy; it was real equipment, and they got to wear it. For a brief time in their lives, when they got up in the morning there was something to do besides taking care of their younger siblings or doing chores assigned by their parents.

After making four consecutive trips to the rainforest village, I took a little time off and invested my time in some different summer ventures. But as a few years went by and I could see my own career moving swiftly, my mind continued to venture back to Kwakwani and the lessons that it had taught me. The thought was in my mind that I should make more of an effort to share the experiential learning environment with our students at Muskingum. If it had been good for me, surely it would be good for them. Maybe instead of making a summer trip alone, I should bring some students with me and immerse them in a new learning environment. It seemed a little selfish to drink up the lessons alone that Guyana had to offer instead of taking with me some students who could begin to explore the boundaries of their own comfort zones.

Chapter 12

Student Trip to Guyana

Everyone can be great because anyone can serve. . . . You only need a heart full of grace – a soul generated by love.

Dr. Martin Luther King

Each of my trips to Guyana gave me a refreshed feeling about the true joy of sport, which motivated me to organize a group of athletes from Muskingum to go with me on a summer study abroad program. I had traveled to Guyana each summer from 1997 through 2000. After taking several summers off from the rainforest, I decided in the fall of 2007 that I wanted to share this Guyana experience with Muskingum students, and I began to solicit interested athletes who would be good candidates for the trip.

I had been advised by other faculty who had organized study-abroad programs that it could be a frustrating venture. Airfare was unpredictable, and it was a challenge to come up with a reasonable yet affordable budget for the trip. Many students who expressed interest early would likely bow out without paying their deposit, and things would be in a constant state of flux. It might be impossible to get students to follow through with their plans so that the trip actually became a reality. Regardless of the warnings and the pessimism, I was not deterred in my determination to bring this trip to fruition. I knew how much my trips to Guyana had enriched my life, and I wanted my students to get the chance to experience the personal growth that I knew would result from the trip.

Even though he was not an employee of Muskingum, the college agreed to allow my brother, Dave, to be a second advisor on the trip. Arranging travel and staying on top of accommodations and the itinerary is very difficult when planning travel to an underdeveloped country. Things can be unpredictable, and arrangements that you make can disappear as if they never existed. Dave had, by now, made at least twenty-five trips to Guyana, so he was the perfect one to handle arrangements and run interference while we were there.

I decided that we would focus on sport clinics in the sports of basketball, soccer, and volleyball. I would have loved to continue with softball, but we found that the jungle humidity had caused the gloves and other equipment to deteriorate, and I would have to start all over with equipment. The three sports that I chose would be relatively easy to equip, and I knew that they had the space in the village for us to have a useable facility.

Interest was high as I presented the idea to athletes and physical education majors. Nothing was sugar-coated, and the students who signed on knew that they would be in for a physically challenging trip with rough accommodations. The one rule that they all had to agree to abide by was, "No whining!"

I was amazed at how anxious our students were to involve themselves in such a venture. I screened students who expressed interest, and for all of those who were accepted as potential travelers, a $250.00 deposit was needed to hold their spot. The paid deposits came in quickly, and much to my surprise, the first fourteen students who paid never wavered from their initial commitment. Those first fourteen were the same fourteen that later boarded the plane in Columbus, Ohio, on the day of departure.

We met regularly throughout the spring semester in order to learn more about the country, prepare lesson plans for our sport clinics, and to take care of all the necessary things like passports, immunizations, and specific travel arrangements. There was a good deal of apprehension as well as excitement when we gathered at 5:00 A.M. at the Columbus airport on departure day.

Except for an unexpected two-hour delay in Trinidad, the flight down went relatively smoothly. Once we landed and got our luggage, the students had the same wide-eyed look that I must have had when they experienced their first ride from the Georgetown airport to Linden. The arrival in Linden was memorable. The night we arrived happened to be Independence Day in Guyana, a day that was set aside to celebrate the day that slaves were freed. When we pulled into Jac's

Hotel, there were huge speakers blaring in the streets with Caribbean music louder than any music I have ever heard. People were dancing and drinking with no intent of stopping until the daylight hours. The walls of our rooms literally shook from the loud music, but we were so tired that we slept pretty soundly until morning. It takes some pretty loud music to impress a college student, but the decibel level from this night was a topic of conversation for days.

When we got up the next morning, we started the day with a traditional breakfast at Jac's, followed by a little exploration as we waited for our trip down the trail later in the day. It was interesting to watch the students encounter their first cultural exchange in a city like Linden. It was a little unnerving to make our way through small streets and a wrought iron gate to get to the area where we needed to exchange our U.S. currency for Guyanese money. Then to actually wander about and spend a little of that money on fresh pineapple or a wide brimmed hat to protect us from the unrelenting sun was a shopping trip that was a little different than the weekly stop at a shopping mall back home. The surroundings in Linden would be pretty developed compared to what would be coming up in Kwakwani, but the students would need to find that out for themselves.

We were on "Guyanese time," so I figured we would be late leaving for Kwakwani. We were a couple of hours behind schedule, but overall, the day was still young. Several of the Linden residents had warned us that the trail was in bad shape. The monsoon season had hung on longer than normal, and the extensive rains had flooded out some portions of the trail, while other parts were simply muddy. Although I think a few of the students may have thought that Dave and I were exaggerating our concerns about the trail a bit, they were soon to find out that those concerns were probably understated.

The trail was a mess. We made it as far as a pull-off spot that travelers often used for picnics, and we ate some chicken that we had purchased in Linden for lunch. The travel became progressively more difficult after lunch. It did not take long for the trail to be so muddy, and the potholes so deep, that the van got stuck. It was mostly the strong-backed guys that did the pushing, but we were stuck in soupy mud that was almost impossible to stand up in. Somehow, we managed to get the van through the first crisis, but within a few miles, we were standing in ankle-deep mud with the van immersed in mud above its hubcaps. The guys were covered from head to foot in mud being sprayed out by the spinning tires. In spite of wedging limbs and sticks and anything we could find that might give traction under the tires, it was to no avail. I was already entertaining thoughts of what it would be like to spend the night on the trail, when a tractor happened down the trail from the other direction and was able to pull us out with a logging chain.

There were several other close calls as we continued, until we finally hit a point where the trail was impassable. A detour had been cut through the jungle that hugged both sides of the trail. As I looked at the detour, I could not envision the van making it through the narrow rough-cut path, but there was no other choice. It was a nail-biting ride as we slowly made our way through the bush and heard branches and vines scraping the sides and roof while we felt the tires sliding underneath us. It was getting dark, so I knew if something went wrong at this point, we would definitely be stuck until morning. Fortunately, we made it through the detour and reached Kwakwani in the black of night.

The flood waters had not receded in Kwakwani, so the Berbice River was well above its banks when we signaled the ferry that we needed to cross. Our first experience in Kwakwani was shining our flashlights in the flood waters while standing on deck of the ferry, trying to spot the eyes of cayman as they swam about.

We arrived on a Saturday night. With the next day being Sunday, my first priority was to attend church. I was very proud of our students, as pretty much all of them opted to attend services and bravely step out to meet some of the people in Kwakwani. By the time we walked down the hill to the church building, many of us were already covered in sweat. The overhead fans in the open-air building did little to keep it cool, and probably by the second song, there were pools of sweat dripping from the chins of some of the Muskies. I overheard one of the Guyanese church members innocently ask, when they saw water dripping from our faces, why the Americans were crying.

Our first introduction to the real heat occurred later in the day. We needed to use the time that we had on Sunday afternoon to prepare the areas for our sport clinics that would start on Monday. As we traveled from the basketball court, to the soccer field, to the improvised volleyball area, it didn't take more than thirty minutes to be drenched in sweat and in need of water. We worked hard to hang the nets that we had brought onto the soccer goals, to put chain nets on the basketball baskets, to find a way to suspend the volleyball net, and then to clean up all three areas. We worked to get balls pumped up and equipment organized, and went through the village with one last effort to advertise the clinic using our bullhorn. The children were excited as they saw the "American athletes" descend on their village, and I knew that my students were in for a memorable experience once things got underway.

Dave and I decided later in the day to take the students to the "bush pool," a local swimming hole that the locals assured us was safe from cayman and piranha. As we started towards the path that we had always walked to get there, we realized that the flood water still had much of the path underwater, and at times we would have to walk through knee-deep water to get to the swimming hole. Although it would not bother me to do this in a more familiar setting, it was a bit unnerving to be walking through swamp-like conditions when you weren't exactly sure what creatures might be sharing the water with your feet. However, it was so hot that it seemed like the risk/reward was worth the hike.

We eventually made it to the bush pool without incident, and it was a wonderfully refreshing way to spend the rest of the afternoon. The students regularly visited the swimming hole, and it especially came in handy on all the days that the power was off and we had no water for showers.

Monday was the first day for the sport clinics, and my students jumped in with a mix of excitement and apprehension. There was a bit of a language barrier until they got their ears accustomed to the accent that almost made it seem that the children were speaking a foreign language. It was brutally hot that first day, so we were not only fighting the nerves of trying to teach children of a different culture in a very challenging setting, but we were also fighting the heat.

My athletes were divided into three teaching groups, with three to four athletes in charge of each of the three sports – basketball, soccer, and volleyball. We had arranged to do clinics for the ten- to twelve-year-old children the first half of the mornings, a clinic for the thirteen- to fifteen-year-old group in the second half of the morning, and a session for those sixteen and older in the later afternoon in each sport. On paper the idea worked fine, but, in reality, there were many children who tried to come to both sessions or who came even though they were too young. We had envisioned the older group to be children aged approximately sixteen to eighteen, but there were even adults who came to the clinics after they got done with their work day.

The participants were more than willing to go through drill progressions, but because most of them had never done anything more than simply try to play the sport, it took some acclimatizing to get them to execute a drill and work on skill improvement. It was equally challenging for my students as they were working to discover the correct pacing of drills, the most efficient way to organize the drills, and the all-encompassing challenge of discipline and listening skills that every teacher faces.

By noon on the first day when we took our lunch break, it looked like my students were exhausted. The heat had physically worn them down, and the children had mentally worn them down. They barely mustered up the energy to eat, and I wasn't totally convinced that a couple of them would make it to the second session of the day. To make things tougher, we also committed some time that afternoon to work on building some bleachers that we had decided to construct and donate to the village so they would have seating at the basketball court. Instead of being able to rest and stay out of the sun on that first afternoon before the later session began, we were back in the heat working on the bleachers. I knew from experience that the first day would be the toughest, and if we could make it through to evening, things would get progressively better. I was confident that my students would evolve from wondering if they would survive at the beginning of our stay, to wishing they would not have to leave at the end of their stay.

It was interesting to watch the students deal with situations that would be far more challenging than anything they would encounter as a teacher or coach in the States. They surprised themselves with how much they were able to teach in spite of horrible facilities and very limited equipment. There were daily distractions, such as a monkey tied to a rope on the sideline that created crazy disruptions. The heat was oppressive, and the students finally concluded that no matter what adjectives that you used to describe how hot it was once we got back home, it would be impossible to exaggerate. All of them were coming to the understanding that if you were well-prepared with the material that you wanted to present, and you had students who wanted to learn, there was nothing else that mattered much.

In any learning situation, the more you can experience, the more you can derive from the situation. My hope was to immerse these students in not only sport experiences, but to let them integrate with the villagers and children, and to leave feeling like they had truly experienced a different way of living (Figure 7). We spent one

Figure 7. The Muskingum College student athletes who accompanied Coach Newberry to Guyana in the summer of 2008 – exhibiting newly acquired corn-row coiffures and familiarity with the machete, an indispensible tool in and around the tropical rainforest.

afternoon at the house of a basket maker in the village and gained an appreciation for how hard it might be to earn a living by hand-making baskets. One night after dark, we loaded into our wooden boat and floated quietly with the current down the Berbice River simply to listen to the jungle sounds. The night float trip became a time of solitude and reflection that encompassed each of us in the sounds of the jungle mixed with the sounds of our own thoughts. One afternoon was spent in role reversal, as the children taught us how to play cricket and we became the students. One of the evenings provided an opportunity for a soccer game where the villagers challenged the Americans. The spectator turnout was amazing, and it created such a feeling of camaraderie between the villagers and the students that it became one of the highlights of our trip.

Even the meals became an immersion in Guyanese culture. Lunch was pretty predictable as the students had been paired up, and a pair of students each day was required to fix lunch for the group using ingredients that they either brought from home in their luggage or that they purchased in the village. However, we had hired a couple of Guyanese women from the village who came to the house and prepared dinner for us each evening. Even the picky eaters and the fast food junkies came to appreciate the wonderful cooking and Guyanese specialties.

Throughout our stay, I had carried a video camera with me to record some of our activities, and, more specifically, to record the children at the various clinics as they learned and interacted with the American athletes. With Dave's help on our last day, we were able to set up a video presentation that brought all the children together and enabled them to see themselves in action for the first time on camera. It was a wonderful event, with giggling, finger pointing, applause and all the drama of a major cinema production. Although we had some culminating games at each sport venue, this had been a great way to wind down our stay and give the village children one final capstone experience.

By the end of our trip, the children felt comfortable stopping by the house to visit in the evening. It was a pleasure to watch the Guyanese children teach our athletes native games and songs, and to see how much fun both groups had enjoying each other's company. It was times like this that cell phones and televisions seemed totally unnecessary and light years away.

The morning of our departure was bittersweet. A number of the children came to the house where we were staying and just hung around outside, hoping to milk just a few more minutes with their American friends. Although our athletes were ready to head home, they were also reluctant to leave and let go of a place that had seemed so foreign just a few days ago, but now held memories that would stay with them for a lifetime. When we finally got to the ferry crossing and headed for the other side of the Berbice River, it officially left behind a small chapter in each of our students' history that would forever be intertwined with Kwakwani, Guyana.

After we returned from Guyana, all the students submitted a journal and a paper sharing their reflections about the trip. I think the reflections of Jacob, one of the soccer players, summarized best what the trip meant to the athletes who were involved. Jacob wrote the following:

> *It is crazy to think how one place you visit for two weeks can change your life. This trip was definitely a once in a lifetime experience that has changed my life forever. It really makes you step back and look at your life and look at theirs. They don't have much; in fact they don't really have anything. And you look at us and we have everything. We have cars, nice houses, money, and we don't have to worry about how many pineapples we have to sell to have enough money to buy something.*
>
> *But look at them and then look at us. They are all so happy and are actually living life. We are just thinking about the next way we can make more money or get ahead. They are so innocent and oblivious to how things are in the United States . . . Being down there really makes you take a step back and realize what you really do have. I honestly believe that everyone should make a trip down there, and maybe our country would be different. Everyone would truly appreciate what they have and not be so concerned with what they don't*

have. Maybe we wouldn't be so materialistic, always wanting to have something else or have something more. . . .

Going into the experience, I knew they didn't have a lot, but I wasn't expecting to fall in love with the people down there or their way of living. They are truly living life and not just going through the motions like a lot of people do . . . I didn't know how much a place would change me, but it has honestly made me appreciate everything I have . . . I was the one who always took everything for granted, and now I have learned not to do that.

When we returned from Guyana, it was an adjustment to get back into the fast-paced life in the States. It seemed that everyone and everything in Guyana were so laid back that time slowed down and things that seem so important when you are home suddenly are of little significance. We viewed the Guyanese as a very poor people, but once we spent time with them and saw their hospitality, sense of humor, faith, and day-to-day approach to life, it was difficult to view them as poor. It was almost embarrassing to come back to the States and see the materialistic and money-driven lifestyle that we experience here. It made us wonder what actually constitutes poverty and what constitutes affluence.

The trips to Guyana gave me a better understanding of one of the quotes that I saw engraved on the grounds of the Betty Ford Center that said, "The best things in life aren't things."

As I knew they would, the athletes fell in love with the Guyanese children. The first few days, the athletes sort of held the children at arm's length, not sure how to react or how close to allow themselves to get. As the days progressed, the smiles, appreciation, and receptivity of the children made it impossible to remain neutral. I saw athletes picking up and hugging the crying children, I saw them hold the children's hands as they walked them home after sports, I saw them experience the gratification of actually giving their knowledge and expertise to children who were starved for this kind of adult interaction, and I saw them cry on the day we had to leave.

Maybe the only thing better than having a wonderful summer learning experience is being able to share that experience with those who appreciated it as much as I did. I witnessed some of our students who truly had a life-changing experience. I cried as I read through some of their journals and gained insight into the impact that the experience had on them. They will be better teachers, coaches, and human beings as a result of the time they spent there. My hope is that they will not let themselves forget the things they saw and experienced, but as they encounter difficulties in their career, they will draw upon this experience to gain the strength needed to get through.

My intentions were that I would continue this venture and take several study abroad groups to Kwakwani in succeeding years. However, the year after I got back, my third diagnosis of breast cancer halted those plans. Because of health issues, it is highly unlikely that I will be able return to Kwakwani, but I will be forever grateful to the village and her people for their willingness to share a part of their lives with me.

Chapter 13

The Final Message

If you are not doing something with your life, then it doesn't matter how long you live. If you are doing something with your life, then it doesn't matter how short your life may be.

John C. Maxwell

I am now, late in the summer of 2010, entering my thirty-seventh year of coaching, and based on my health, in all likelihood it will be my last year. There are questions in my mind as to whether I can even make it through this year, but as long as I am able to function, I just put my fate in God's hands and keep coaching day by day.

During the course of time that I have coached, I would like to think that I have learned a good deal about what will work and what does not work. However, I will be the first to admit that I have seen coaching styles and philosophies on opposite ends of the continuum that are able to produce winners. To have any chance of being successful, a coach must coach with a technique that is consistent with her personality; to try to be one person on the field and a different person during the rest of your life is a sure step towards failure.

I can only share what has worked for me. I am not implying that other methods won't work, or that the way I do things is absolutely the way things should be done. If you know yourself, you are true to yourself, you care about your players, and you remain updated and passionate about the game, regardless of specific philosophies, there is a good chance that you will emerge as a successful coach. I have had many people share their observation with me that players have changed so much over the years, and now they are difficult, if not impossible, to coach. I have certainly seen differences emerge over my many years of coaching, but the core of the athlete still seems the same; players will respond to your discipline and expectations if you communicate clearly what the goals are and how you plan to go about reaching them, and if you treat the players fairly in the process.

I have often been asked, "What do you look for in a player when you are recruiting her?" I consistently answer that question with, "First I want a good kid, meaning that I would like to have someone with a good attitude who has a decent sense of morals and values. Secondly, I want a good student. You don't need to be a 4.0 student, but you need to be someone who values getting your education and that I don't have to constantly monitor to see if you are attending class. Thirdly, I want a good athlete." If I can get a player that has all three of these ingredients – a good kid, who is a good student and a good athlete, there is a pretty reasonable chance for success for both me as a coach and for the athlete. My job would be easy if this described everyone in my program.

However, sometimes what I think I recruited is not always what the person turns out to be. Sometimes recruiting is like a job interview where a candidate only allows me to see what she thinks she wants me to see. The athlete gives one impression, but when I actually coach her, she turns out to be quite different than I thought she might be. Or it might be that I know I am not getting the whole package that I wanted to start with, but I am willing to take the chance and make the athlete a project so that the finished product will be the athlete that I envisioned and needed.

Rarely do I get athletes who do not require some shaping in order for them to be what I want and need them to be. The shaping process is what makes individuals better people and what helps build character and maturity. As a coach, I am sure that we all want to win, but our nobler and more important goal is to mold our athletes into better people by helping them become better decision-makers and encouraging them to become more responsible, trustworthy, and hard-working citizens. I seldom see coaches grow tired of the Xs and Os as they age, nor do I see their passion wane for competition and winning. However, I do see them grow weary from investing the energy that is required to shape young lives.

As soon as a coach grows tired of shaping, it is time to get out of the profession because it means the most important part of our job will not get done to the best of our ability. We can give the appearance that we are still fully invested in coaching by our enthusiasm during practice, by our new strategies and techniques, and by our halftime speeches. But outside the lines, when practice is over, do we still have the energy to shape? When we are tired of shaping, it becomes easier to ignore a poor choice or misdeed by an athlete than to confront it. It becomes easier not to have a rule than to enforce it. It becomes convenient to excuse an athlete's poor judgment off the field or out of season by simply saying that it is none of our business.

By shaping, I am not advocating that we pry into our players' private lives and dictate what their social and personal lives should look like. I am, however, saying that we should be proactive when we see poor choices being made and bad images being created. By advising, educating, and reinforcing what a good decision should look like, we help to maintain discipline and help to prevent the disaster. Rather than standing idly by as we see a problem unfold and simply making ourselves available to pick up the pieces of the aftermath, we should be racing to the top of the cliff to head off a misguided athlete who is headed for sure destruction.

One of the first indicators of coaches who have grown tired of shaping is their willingness to compromise. I believe that the greatest sin of coaching is compromise. By compromise, I don't mean changing coaching strategies to stay current or getting players' input before establishing a team rule. I am talking about the kind of compromise that occurs when you start to alter or diminish the values that you and your team stand for in order to appease disgruntled players or parents, or compromising what you know are morals or truths that you must stand for in order to appear to be more "trendy" or to be a "player's coach," or to be more appealing to a recruit who loves the game but resents the discipline.

I have watched rules about alcohol on various teams become so watered down that just about anything goes. Even when a coach believes that a "no drinking during the season" policy is the right thing to do, compromises have been made to keep players happy. In spite of the fact that most of them are underage anyway, you see rules like the "twenty-four-hour rule," where drinking within twenty-four hours of a contest is the only thing prohibited. Or you see the "responsible drinking rule," where drinking is okay as long as you don't do it in a way that embarrasses the program. We find a way to appease the coach's conscience that at least we have a rule without offending the players' desire to do their own thing.

I have watched rules about language and swearing and cursing become so irrelevant that now the coach herself is sometimes accused of not caring if she doesn't swear violently at her team after a loss or after a poor half-time showing. Four-letter words almost seem like the second language of sport. I not only prohibit swearing, I define exactly what I mean by swearing. For example, the use of substitute words, the most recent trend being "frickin'" is unacceptable to me. I am not ashamed to require my athletes to have enough self-discipline that they can learn to control their tongue and think before they speak.

I have watched coaches compromise the dress code for a team. There is nothing wrong with keeping up with current fashions, but when it evolves to where a team portrays a slovenly image either on or off the court, I would hope that we could step in rather than succumb to the whims of our players. The trash talking, rebellious attitude that you often see in athletes is a direct result of gradual compromise until we have lost sight of some of the pure truths that sport should teach and represent.

I am not naïve enough to believe that all of my players meet all of my expectations all of the time. Just like any team, there are challenges in getting players to mature to the point where they follow the rules because it is the right thing to do for the team, rather than because it was a rule and they feared getting caught. However, I don't believe that the answer to that challenge is to compromise rules or disband rules. The answer is to maintain a reasonable set of expectations and help your players evolve to the point that they understand the need for the rule and expect compliance both from themselves and from their teammates.

It is much easier to compromise than it is to take a stand. One of my more difficult coaching dilemmas occurred during our softball season in 1993. We had won the OAC regular season and tournament, and as a result, we had qualified for the NCAA regional tournament. We had a great team, and to make it even more special, we were selected as the host site for the regional tournament, so we had home-field advantage.

By the time the regional tournament rolled around, final exams were over and school was out for the summer. Because my players had to stay for the tournament, the administration agreed to keep a dorm open for them to make their stay more convenient. One of my players (I will call her Mindy even though that was not her real name) approached me and asked if she could stay with a friend who lived in Cambridge, Ohio, instead of staying in the dorm. Cambridge is a small town located only about seven or eight miles from campus, and she pled her case by saying that she would rest much better there and be in a better mind-set to play.

Mindy was not the most mature player, and at times was a little irresponsible and carefree. On the other hand, she was a great player who was a key figure in our lineup, and if I could do something that she thought would help her play better, then I should at least consider it. After much thought, I decided that I would let her stay off campus. In return, she had to promise me that she would abide by all team rules, that she would attend and not be late for any team function, and that she would conduct herself in a responsible manner. She had been a pretty solid citizen throughout the season, and I felt this would be a good opportunity for her to prove herself further and take another step towards maturity. Although the team knew nothing about the promises that Mindy made to me, I informed them that I was permitting her to stay in Cambridge, and everyone was fine with the decision.

Things went well during the regional tournament up until the championship game. We had gone through undefeated, including a comfortable 8 - 0 win over Allegheny, Pennsylvania. However, Allegheny had come out of the losers' bracket and defeated us in the first game of the championship. Because it was double elimination, they had to beat us twice, so the final game was scheduled for Sunday afternoon to determine who would represent our region at the Division III World Series.

I never enjoy playing on Sunday because it interferes with worship and church services. Because school was not in session, the cafeterias were not opened, and I needed to feed the team breakfast. We decided that we would go to a restaurant in Cambridge that had a breakfast buffet, and we should be in good shape getting back to campus with plenty of time to warm up. I told the team that I would not be at breakfast so that I could attend church, and I put one of the captains in charge of the team in my absence.

The next morning I decided that I would go ahead and try to make it to breakfast, which would cause me to miss Bible class, but I could still make it to church for the worship service. When I arrived at breakfast unexpectedly, the team was glad to see me, and everyone was there on time and ready to eat except for Mindy. When I inquired about her, the team captains said she had called to tell them she would eat breakfast at home and just meet the team at the field, giving everyone the perception that she had permission to do so. I didn't say anything, but inside I was seething as I thought about our agreement and the way that I had been manipulated, as well as her selfish attitude in regards to the team. Because she thought I would not be at breakfast, it was the perfect opportunity for her to sleep in and violate a team rule without getting caught.

We didn't have much depth on this team. Mindy was our best hitter and batted clean up. She was also an outstanding third baseman. I first wrote out the lineup card with her in her usual spot, thinking that if I did not compromise on discipline, it might cost us the game. To move her off third base meant that I had to move our starting catcher to third base as she was the only other person I ever practiced there, and in turn that meant putting an inexperienced catcher behind the plate. Not only did it take our biggest bat out of the lineup, but it created a domino effect with our lineup.

I rationalized that no one else on the team even knew anything was wrong. They thought she had my permission to miss breakfast, so this could remain a well-kept secret between Mindy and me. I could deal with it later. Had it been any other player or any other game, I would have had no problem sitting the player out for the game, but this was perhaps our most key player in the biggest game of the season. In my heart, I wanted to play her because I knew we needed her game presence to have a good shot at winning, but in my head, I knew that compromising the rules was not an acceptable option.

I knew when a player has broken a team rule and has been manipulative in the process, the best reinforcement is immediate discipline that teaches her consequences for her actions. Just before I had to turn the lineup card in, I did what I felt I had to do and removed Mindy from the lineup and made the resulting necessary changes. I called Mindy and the rest of the team in to explain the situation and the adjustments that we would have to make as a result.

Two of the seniors approached me in tears, begging me to let her play. They said I could discipline her later, but right now the seniors wanted their best shot at moving on to the National Championship. It was gut-wrenching to tell them no, but I knew that ignoring what she had done just because this was a big game was a compromise that might help us win, but in the big picture, it would send the wrong message to her and to the team.

Our catcher played a respectable game at third base, committing only one error. Our new catcher had a couple of bases stolen on her. Twice in the game, Mindy's spot came up in the batting order with the bases loaded, and we did not score a run either time. We lost the game 4 - 2. I don't know if Mindy's presence would have changed the outcome or not, but I do know that I did the right thing.

It took several years for the seniors on that team to forgive me, but I believe that they eventually understood. Their blame was misplaced when they were blaming me for a decision that might have kept them from a chance at a national championship. Their blame should have been directed at the player who made the decision that forced me to react. It was one of the most difficult game decisions that I have ever had to make, but as I stated earlier, "Compromise is the greatest sin of coaching."

Mindy has grown into a wonderful teacher and responsible adult. She remains very loyal to our program and takes great pride in being able to say that she was a Muskingum softball player. She represents our program well and remains active as a recruiter, regularly recommending good players from her area. I received a letter from her a couple of years ago, and part of the letter read as follows.

I just wanted to thank you for all the confidence, knowledge, and especially the desire and feeling of winning that I experienced in four years as a Lady Muskie under you. I'm now seeing the trouble and chaos I created for you and I would like to apologize for it. I find myself confronted with similar situations as you were (and are) and only hope that I can handle them with the same dignity and professionalism as you did (and do). I feel as if I owe you a bottle of Tylenol for all the headaches I caused you!! I find myself saying the same thing to myself that I'm sure you did when I did something stupid, "You'll understand one day when the tables are turned."

Also, I'd like to apologize again for missing breakfast. Benching me taught me a big lesson (I'm sure as well as others) about the importance of respect and responsibility. I can joke about it now, but I do know how stupid and thoughtless it was then.

Again, a big thank you and good luck.

I am confident that the decision that I made to bench Mindy was the right decision for the betterment of Mindy. Whether it was fair for a team to suffer the consequences of their teammate's poor decision is a question that is a little more difficult to answer, but it seems like that was the question that Mindy should have asked herself before creating a situation that tortured me as I decided the punishment.

Regardless, the whole issue of being fair is of paramount importance in successful coaching. The challenge is that coaching decisions, whether they involve positions, playing time, strategies, or whatever, are seldom judged with objectivity. There is so much vested interest and energy from athletes, parents, and spectators, that each party views a decision differently because they are viewing it through their eyes only. For example, some want playing time to be based strictly on raw talent, others want it based on attitude and effort, some on seniority, some on reputation, and on and on the preferences go.

In an attempt to get my athletes to understand how I make some of my decisions, I usually give my team one lecture each season describing Coach Newberry, the banker. I compare my position to the president of a bank, and I compare my players to my customers.

Each year, my customers come in with their credit rating; for freshmen, it is based on their high school performance, statistics, and credentials; for upperclassmen, it is based on their collegiate credentials from past seasons. Every customer has an opportunity to do business at my bank. The dividends that eventually get paid represent playing time the players are given in a game.

I would rather do business with an established customer, so if I have upperclassmen who have a good credit rating and whose deposits exceed their withdrawals, I will look at them first. There are many ways to make deposits. In the sport of softball, deposits include things like key RBIs, sound fielding plays or decisions, good base running, quality at-bats, solid pitching performances, etc. In basketball, it includes things like fundamentally sound defense, good shot selection, making clutch shots, minimizing turnovers, hustling up and down in transition, rebounding, etc.

There are also many ways to make withdrawals in softball. These include poor base running decisions, strike outs or other poor at-bats, errors, inability to perform in clutch situations, etc. In basketball, withdrawals are equated to turnovers, poor defensive hustle, bad shot-selection, poor decision-making, etc. The players who consistently operate in the black are generally the starters, and those that operate in the red are generally bench players. The hardest to judge are usually the freshmen, as you have not done enough business with them yet to know if they will be a good customer.

There are some types of deposits and withdrawals that remain consistent sport to sport. Regardless of the sport, it is always an asset to show good leadership, to hustle, to have a positive attitude, or to encourage your teammates. Likewise, it is always a detriment to complain, to display poor social behavior, to be irresponsible, to blame others, to cheat on drills, or to be selfish or negative.

All of these things go into deciding what and how much business you want to do with a customer. Being fair is not just about assessing how many of these qualities each player possesses. Fairness also involves your ability to have a difficult conversation with customers to tell them what is pulling their credit rating down, so they have a chance to fix it. As president of my bank, if I only complain to my vice president about unworthy customers, but never tell the customer what the problem is, not much will change. The ability to have a difficult conversation in a tactful yet truthful manner is an art that coaches must develop in order to be successful. Playing head games with a player or beating around the bush because we are too uncomfortable to speak the truth will not accomplish much, and will usually lead to frustrated and disgruntled players.

When I have a junior or senior who has built up a lot of credit in my bank, I generally will do business with them even after they have made a few withdrawals because they have proven themselves to be good enough customers that I feel eventually they will be back in the black. I am more reluctant to take them out if they make a couple of mistakes or to bench them if they have a bad game, simply because they have made so many deposits in the past that their line of credit remains good for a while.

On the other hand, if I insert a freshman or unproven player who has no money in her account into a game, and she immediately makes a couple of mistakes, I will probably take her out pretty quickly. I am not ready to do business with her yet, and she will have to wait for another opportunity to make a transaction. She needs to build up some credit before I will tolerate many withdrawals. A freshman can start to make deposits in practices through work ethic, listening skills, hustle, and other positive practice habits, but these deposits are only worth pennies. The big credit build-up comes when they can come through in a game and prove that they are worthy customers.

I have started many freshmen in my career, but they have to be able to get it done at game time. When freshmen come into my office to ask me why I let a senior starter play through her mistakes, but I took them out quickly after a couple of mistakes, I usually just have to remind them about their bank account, and they understand. Before I will do extended business with them, they need to prove they are a good customer, and before they start making withdrawals, they need to have made some deposits.

In those rebuilding years, when you really don't have a lot of proven customers waiting to do business with you, you sometimes have to be willing to loan out some unearned playing time. I hate loaning playing time to players who have not built up any credit with me, but sometimes it is necessary. Occasionally it turns out to be a great business decision, even though it was made out of necessity, but more often than not, the bank takes a few hits before it can operate on stable ground again.

There are so many things that must be considered when you choose a team or make up a line up, and, depending on who you talk to, the decisions will not appear to be fair to everyone. Those who value attitude above talent will have one opinion, those who value experience over new talent will have another, those who value role players over stars will have another, and on the list goes. I simply try to run a sound business, where I reward loyal customers and sound customers, but where I also give new customers a chance to open their account and make a deposit towards a championship.

I don't want to make it sound like my coaching is all about what I can get from my players. What I want *from* them is only a means to the end of what I want *for* them. *What I want from them* is hard work, loyalty, execution under pressure, a willingness to sacrifice for the team, tough-mindedness, acceptance of their role, and a whole myriad of other things that require them to dig unpleasantly deep into their personal lives. *What I want for them* is the opportunity for them to experience the pinnacle of success.

I want them to wear a championship ring, knowing that it represents the fact that they worked harder and were more deserving than all of their competitors. I want them to know what it feels like to become a leader and to develop a sense of responsibility. I want them to develop an understanding that good things don't come easy, and those looking for shortcuts will usually be left behind in the long run. I want them to be confident and independent women who have a strong sense of community and who will never hesitate to stand up for what they know is right. I want them to be proud, yet humble women with a sense of values that will not be compromised. I want them to be patient women, yet to have a sense of urgency in important matters that does not allow procrastination to become part of their lifestyle.

Oftentimes, I am not totally sure if the players who graduate from my program have departed possessing everything that I wanted for them. In most cases, I believe that they leave as better people than they were when they entered, and although some of them remain a work in progress, all of them show remarkable growth. As a coach, there is not much you can do about the way a player is when she comes into your program. However, we are responsible for how a player is when she exits our program, and it is our failure as much as it is hers when a player leaves the program and is not the type of individual that we want her to be.

It is often not until after players graduate that they develop an appreciation of the positive changes that occurred in their lives as a result of athletics. While they are still athletes, especially in their first and second year, they may resent what you demand *from* them and have no idea about what you want *for* them. However, as they grow and start to see the bigger picture, that maturity leads them to higher levels of loyalty, sacrifice, and performance within the program. No goal becomes too high and no demand becomes too great. It is when the majority of your players are on that plateau that you have a chance to win a championship.

I usually use as a measuring stick the letters that I receive from my players after their career has ended to see if I am accomplishing what I wanted to accomplish for them. One of the greatest paychecks of coaching is receiving acknowledgment from a former player that you did, in fact, make a difference in her life. I make it a point to never throw those paychecks away. I keep them so that I can read one and cash it in anytime I am running low on motivation.

I think a few excerpts from those letters reinforce what the coaching profession is all about.

- From a student assistant:
  Though I served a minor role on the team, your words echo to me in daily life now. When I find myself lacking focus, I hear, "Be here now." When I face adversity, I hear, "Control the controllables." And when I need to meet a deadline I hear, "Have a sense of urgency."

- From a basketball/softball player:
  I can never thank you enough for what you did for me during my college years. The love and passion that you shared

with each of us was, and still is, overwhelming. I have become a better student, teacher, and most of all, parent to my children, because of the life lessons that I learned from you 20 years ago. Throughout my life, I have had people, and my kids ask me, "Who influenced your life more than anyone else?" The answer is simple and always will be as I answer, "Coach Newberry."

- From a basketball/softball player:

I am so grateful to have played for such a wonderful coach, but more so, a wonderful person . . . You never wanted to set an example for your players, the team, or Muskingum, that was anything less than professional. I never heard a cuss word cross your lips. You were tough but never demeaning. You displayed the professionalism and behavior you expected from your players. You never asked of us anything you couldn't or wouldn't do yourself. We were always very clear about your expectations. . . .

I'm not sure any of us who played for you realized how we grew as people until our careers were over. I am able to handle pressures of big responsibilities in my career. I am able to handle and balance my personal and professional lives; I am responsible to others, dependable, a good team player and not afraid to lead because I was a Muskingum athlete that played for Donna Newberry. More importantly, I appreciate life, keep things in perspective, love with my entire heart, and soul, laugh and smile more, and try every day to be the best person I can because I was blessed to have Donna Newberry in my life.

- From a softball player who sat the bench throughout most of her career:

I thought I knew the game arriving as a freshman, but boy was I wrong. In four years, I learned more strategies and techniques that were needed to win than what I had learned in my previous ten years of playing. I never got to play as much as I would have liked, but looking back I am grateful for the memories and knowledge that I have as a result of playing under you.

It is hard to pinpoint one way you made a difference for me because you made a difference in me not only as a player, but as a young lady. I never knew another woman like you who carried herself with a confidence that wasn't cocky, but genuine; a woman that commanded and earned respect based on her knowledge and actions; someone who held true to her faith, and showed the love of Christ in her actions, words, and commitment to teaching. You constantly challenged us on the field and in the classroom to be better. I am a different and better person for being in your program.

- From an All-American softball player:

You have managed to create a successful softball program that not only fosters softball but life lessons as well. I have learned more about softball and life from you than from any other single person. The impact that you have had and still have on my life is something I will be forever thankful for.

You have taught me how sweet victory can truly be. Through you, I have come to know that winning the game is not always the victory, but rather accomplishing a feat that you did not think could be accomplished. You have shown me how to win and lose with class. You have educated me to run not only to the line, but through the line; because in life one must go above and beyond in order to meet desired goals. The fact that you demanded nothing less than perfection always kept me yearning for more. I now expect better of myself because you have demonstrated to me that settling is not going to get me to where I want to be – with the big dogs. You have embedded in me that my best can always be better. The bottom line is, Coach, I am a better person because of you and all of the lifelong lessons you have instilled in me. I look up to you more than you will ever know or realize.

- From an assistant coach:

Over the past months I have had time to reflect on my time at Muskingum College. Now looking back, those two years developed me more as an adult than I could have ever imagined. There were many factors that went into this transition, but none as important as you, Coach Newberry. . . .

When I am in the office trying to make coaching decisions, there is one phrase that comes to mind and I think about you: "Practice what you preach." I really do try to live by that and make sure my athletes understand that. I can't expect more out of them than I expect out of myself. You are the true example of this and how it is supposed to work by keeping it consistent. There was never a time when you let your guard down or did something that was hypocritical of your teachings. You were always professional, prepared, and in control. That is something most coaches can never say that they have been consistent with during their career. . . .

A lot of times I am put in situations and my first thought is, how would Coach Newberry handle this? I know I am not you, but I admire you to the fullest. I will never be able to thank you enough for all you have done for me. I miss you and the team more than I ever thought I would. I thought I would just turn another page in my life and move on, but it's not like that. With the program you have built, there is something that becomes a part of you. You have built so much respect that those players would run through a brick wall for you. You take a lot of those things for granted while being a part of the program, then you just move on without taking a moment to make sure you take it all in. Now being out of the program, I realize that I had an opportunity of a life time. Most coaches go through their whole career and never have a mentor like you. You are the best coach I have ever seen or been lucky enough to coach with, and I thank you for all of that.

Coaching is a fulfilling profession that demands a full investment from any of us who are fortunate enough to have made it our livelihood. As I reflect on all the amazing opportunities that I have had as a coach, I am overwhelmed because I know that my career could not have been successful without all the wonderful athletes that I was privileged to coach.

It is impossible to name every athlete who has left an indelible impression on me. Regardless of the influence that a coach asserts on players, there is a reciprocal gratification that goes from player to coach. It is not even necessarily the great players who are the ones that always stand out, but rather it is sometimes the players who have shown great resiliency or loyalty as they have gone through the program.

My mind first goes back to the team-van accident. I will always remain inspired by players like Laurie, Julie, and Deb, who were so severely injured, yet who fought back from injuries and became an example to me and the rest of the team about how to overcome adversity and to remain strong. I am deeply appreciative to Kate. Although she was not injured in the accident, she became a rock for all of those who struggled, including me, and displayed wisdom beyond her years in her interactions with her teammates. She led us both on and off the court during a time when we were simply struggling to survive.

I am grateful to Lindsay Bramhall, who is the most passionate athlete that I believe I have ever coached. Her love for softball and competition exceeds that of any other player that I have known. She serves as a constant example to me to be grateful that I have been able to be involved in sport for nearly forty years. I am so thankful that she is now a head coach and is able to stay involved in the sport that she loves.

I admire so many of my former basketball players, especially those who were on the brink of helping us build a powerhouse. People like Jana Montague, Kim Schimmel, Tracy Weaver, Dee Ann Mell, Michelle Harkness, Diane Lancashire, Sheri Conrad, Kathy Lee, and a multitude of others gave so much to the program in both work ethic and performance that a coach could not have asked for more. They set the tone for all the players who came after them.

I deeply appreciate people like Tara Thompson and Arica Robbins, who were role players but remained in the program for four years as intense competitors and contributors to our success. I think of Jen Klutts, who hardly pitched any games above the junior varsity level. She never complained, she was one of our hardest workers, and when she finally got a chance to pitch a big game in her senior year, she helped us win another conference championship by coming through in her "moment in the sun."

I appreciate players like Kim Tackett and Nicole Blubaugh, who were not only outstanding players for us, but who had to work extremely hard to find a way to go to school. They lived a life where things were not handed to them, yet they remained grateful for everything that they had and always worked to better themselves.

The entire national championship team holds a special place in my heart as they were able to achieve something that no other team in Muskingum's history had been able to achieve. That team was the epitome of unselfish play, determination, and confidence.

I have had numerous former players come back and coach with me after graduation. It was gratifying to build a relationship on a different level with players like Jen Segner, Kathy Lee, Erin Zupko, Erika Hoyt, and Kari Hoying.

The list of players who have impacted me could continue on. I hope that any of my former players who remain involved in coaching will be better coaches as a result of playing in my program. I hope that they will treasure the opportunity to pass on their knowledge of sport, but more, importantly, I hope they will never lose sight of the need to help their players grow and develop into young women.

Kari Hoying has been entrusted to carry on the tradition of the program (Figure 8). Kari came to me as a recruit seven years ago.

Figure 8. Coach Newberry and Kari Hoying at the National Fastpitch Coaches Association Annual Meeting Banquet, 2008.

Although I had been recruiting her throughout the year, she was very reluctant to go too far away from home, and she had a substantial offer on the table from a Division I school for softball. It was a very difficult decision for her, and Kari waited until the last day possible to finally commit to Muskingum as a player. I am so glad that she decided on Muskingum.

Kari excelled here as a player and was an All-American catcher. She experienced winning four conference championships, four trips to the post season, and three trips to the World Series. She played four years under me and is now beginning her third year of coaching with me. Kari will be her own person when she becomes the head coach here, but I know that she shares enough of my philosophies, morals, and values that the program will be in good hands. I am grateful to Muskingum for enabling me to keep her on the staff as a full-time assistant so that the transition will be smooth when I step down as the head coach.

I have no regrets about the career path that I chose or the way that my life has unfolded. I could wish for more time to continue coaching, but the important thing for all of us is not the quantity of time that we have, but the quality of what we do in the time we have been granted. It has been a blessing to have been around young people who loved the game, who valued the experience, and who allowed me to become a small part of their lives.

It is with gratitude and humility that I have written this book. I trust that anyone who reads it will be motivated to reflect on his or her own career and examine ways to increase the significance of his or her own life. The influence we have on others may often go unnoticed, but we can be sure that there is always someone watching, imitating, and being impacted by our daily decisions, actions, and example.

May God bless all of you who have enriched my life by being a part of it.

Epilogue

Here is the final test to find whether your mission on earth is finished. If you're alive, it isn't.

Richard Bach

August, 2010.

God has indeed blessed me in that I have been granted a long enough life that I was able to complete the writing of this book. When I began writing, I questioned whether it was a worthy way to spend a good piece of my remaining time. I questioned whether I would live long enough to even be able to finish writing the book. It turns out that both of those concerns were unfounded.

Even if it benefits no one but me, the book has been well worth the time I spent to write it. On those beautiful summer days when I felt like doing nothing more than sitting on the porch of my log cabin with my dog, a Boxer named Red, who was a gift from my softball team, I was at least able to engage my mind and gather my thoughts as I reflected on the path my life has taken. As I marveled at the decisions and twists of fate that have brought me to where I am now, as I pondered on how I could have done things better, and as I analyzed the impact that family, players, and friends have had on me and the impact that I, in turn, have had on them, it stimulated my memory and helped me appreciate the life that I had lived, rather than dwelling on the shortness of a life that would not be extended as long as I had hoped.

My health has deteriorated over the summer as the chemo treatments have not been successful in putting the cancer in remission. Although it has slowed down the progression of the disease in some of my body, the cancer has continued to progress in other parts. For the most part, the pain that I experience can only be masked with painkillers. The chemo treatments take their toll with frequent nausea and vomiting, energy drain, and an overall feeling of helplessness that makes you wonder whether the treatment is worse than the disease itself. My most recent symptom has been neuropathy as a side effect of chemo, which has caused total loss of feeling in my lower legs. It has made walking difficult, but currently I am trying to be grateful that it has not affected my hands as well.

I was always someone who took pride in never needing to take pills, and I was forever mindful of a healthy diet, proper exercise, and an overall healthy lifestyle. However, cancer has proven that it is no respecter of people, and I am trying to be strong enough, with God's help, not to question "Why me?", and not to feel sorry for myself. I know that there are thousands of people before me who have endured cancer and thousands more who are currently fighting the battle, so I am not alone in the fight and in my suffering. With God by my side, it is a matter of taking it day by day.

I am grateful that I have a loving family standing by me through these difficult times. My eighty-year-old mother is sacrificing her own life and peaceful time at home to come to my house and stay with me so that I can live, as much as the disease will allow, a quality life. With her help, I can at least stay at home and continue to work, and teach, and coach as I am able. Without her cooking, cleaning, laundry service, and a myriad of other duties that she performs for me, there is no way that I could continue to maintain my household. There are days where I hardly have the energy to get out of bed, so doing all the other chores would be impossible. I am pretty sure that I inherited my mental toughness and strength of will from my mom.

My sisters have also sacrificed their time by using vacation days, sick days, and personal days to come and stay with me to give my mom a break, or to make sure that I had what I needed. My brother has made countless trips to my house to do a variety of chores and to help me hold things together here. I have always been very independent, and have tried to not have to rely on others to help me maintain my own lifestyle. My disease has humbled me, and my family has shown me the true meaning of love, as I have learned to submit to their willingness to sacrifice by tucking my pride away and replacing it with appreciation and gratitude.

It is fruitless to worry about what the future holds. It is truly a "one day at a time" journey for me right now. With the help of Kari Hoying, my assistant coach, I hope to continue coaching this year. There are times when she will have to do more than her fair share of work when I hit days that I cannot function. I hope that I will be wise enough to recognize the moment I become a burden to the softball program, rather than an asset, so that I can remove myself from those responsibilities. In the meantime, I hope that my experience as a coach and my ability to be a mentor will counterbalance what I am unable to do physically.

Any of us who are in the coaching profession have truly been blessed with an opportunity to be a positive influence in the lives of the athletes who play for us. There will always be athletes who, no matter how hard we try, have conflicts with us that seem to build a wall that prohibits us from interacting with them in a positive and useful way. We cannot become discouraged when that happens to the point that we stop trying. There will be many more athletes, however, who learn from our example, who take our advice, and who become better people as a result of being on our team. It is those athletes who need to continue to motivate and encourage us to be better coaches and to help us recognize the positive influence that we can have on young lives.

As I have gone through my career, winning, and everything that winning represents, has been very important. However, as I reflect back and look forward, I think the purpose and fulfillment in my life is best summarized in the following Bible verse:

Micah 6:8 – He has told you, oh man, what is good; and what does the Lord require of you but to do justice, to love kindness, and to walk humbly with your God?

Biography

Donna Jean Newberry was born on November 14, 1951, in Parkersburg, West Virginia. She graduated from South Parkersburg High School in 1969, Glendale State College in 1973, and Ohio University in 1974. Beginning in 1974, at twenty-two years of age, she served as a head coach in the Athletics department and as a member of the faculty at Muskingum College (now University}. During her career, she coached softball, basketball, field hockey, and volleyball.

She was the head coach in softball for thirty-six years and won more games (907) in her career than had any NCAA Division III coach in the nation. Her teams won eighteen OAC Championships, made eighteen appearances in NCAA post-season play, and made eight trips to the Division III Women's College World Series. In 2001, Muskingum won the Division III national championship in softball.

Her basketball career spanned twenty-six years and compiled 403 wins, five conference or tournament championships, three trips to the national quarter-finals, and a national runner-up finish in 1991. In total, she was recognized as OAC Coach of the Year fourteen times and NCAA Regional Coach of the Year seven times. She became the only coach in NCAA history to receive the award of National Coach of the Year in two different sports.

She served on the NCAA national committee for both basketball and softball, including being the national chair for softball in 2009. She was also a member of the NCAA softball rules committee when the NCAA manual was being written. She was active throughout her career as an instructor at various sport clinics and as a motivational speaker for businesses and civic organizations. In 2008, she was inducted into the National Fastpitch Coaches Association Hall of Fame.

Donna Newberry died at the age of 58 on November 10, 2010.

Table A. Selected Records and Recognition for Coach Donna Newberry – Basketball

Career wins total	403	
Career wins ranking, NCAA Division III	31st all time	
Career wins ranking, OAC	2nd all time	
WBCA/Converse Coach of the Year, NCAA Division III	1 time	1991
Coach of the Year, OAC	3 times	1989, 1993, 1996
Tournament appearances, NCAA Division III	6 times	1985, 1989, 1991, 1992, 1993, 1996
Conference champions		
OAC regular season	2 times	1989, 1993
OAC conference tournament	3 times	1985, 1989, 1991
Players named All-American	5	

Table B. Selected Records and Recognition for Coach Donna Newberry – Softball

Career wins total	907	
Career wins ranking, NCAA Division III	1st all time	
Career wins ranking, NCAA all divisions	26th all time	
Career wins ranking, OAC	1st all time	
NFCA Coaching Staff of the Year, NCAA Division III	1 time	2001
Coach of the Year, OAC	10 times	1988, 1989, 1990, 1992, 1993, 1997, 1999, 2000, 2003, 2004
National ranking, NCAA Division III, top 25 teams	11 times	1999, 2000, 2001, 2002, 2003, 2004, 2005, 2006, 2007, 2008, 2009
Tournament appearances NCAA post-season appearances	18 times	1986, 1988, 1989, 1990, 1992, 1993, 1995, 1998, 1999, 2000, 2001, 2002, 2003, 2004, 2005, 2006, 2007, 2008
NCAA Women's College World Series	8 times	1992, 1998, 2001, 2003, 2004, 2005, 2006, 2008
OAC conference tournament	26 times	1985, 1986, 1987, 1988, 1989, 1990, 1991, 1992, 1993, 1994, 1995, 1996, 1997, 1998, 1999, 2000, 2001, 2002, 2003, 2004, 2005, 2006, 2007, 2008, 2009, 2010
National champions, NCAA women's softball	1 time	2001
Conference champions, OAC	18 times	1986, 1988, 1989, 1990, 1992, 1993, 1995, 1998, 1999, 2000, 2001, 2002, 2003, 2004, 2005, 2006, 2007, 2008
Players named All-American	14	
NFCA Hall of Fame inductee		2008

Index

* PG = Photo Gallery

243